SPIDER-MAN
AND
PHILOSOPHY

SPIDER-MAN
AND
PHILOSOPHY

THE WEB OF INQUIRY

Edited by
Jonathan J. Sanford

WILEY

John Wiley & Sons, Inc.

For general information about our other products and services, please contact our Customer Care Department within the United States at (800) 762-2974, outside the United States at (317) 572-3993 or fax (317) 572-4002.

Wiley also publishes its books in a variety of electronic formats and by print-on-demand. Some content that appears in standard print versions of this book may not be available in other formats. For more information about Wiley products, visit us at www.wiley.com.

ISBN 978-0-470-57560-4 (paper); ISBN 978-1-118-21541-8 (ebk);
ISBN 978-1-118-21575-3 (ebk); ISBN 978-1-118-21535-7 (ebk)

Printed in the United States of America

10 9 8 7 6 5 4 3 2 1

To my MJ, Rebecca, and to all of our wall-crawlers, Isaac, Joseph, Benjamin, Elijah, Jonathan, Mary, and David.

CONTENTS

ACKNOWLEDGMENTS

Special thanks go to the Philosophy and Pop Culture series editor, William Irwin, who set me to work on this project and provided invaluable support throughout the process. Thanks go as well to Constance Santisteban at Wiley for her help each step of the way, and to Richard DeLorenzo for getting the book into top shape and over the finish line. I'm especially grateful to all of the contributors who offer us here their great creative talents at no small cost of time and effort. Finally, I wish to thank my friends and colleagues who pulled off the delicate balance of teasing and encouragement when they learned I was working on this book. That's right, I wasn't kidding.

INTRODUCTION

Have you heard this one yet? A carpenter, Spider-Man, and a philosopher walk into a bar. The bartender asks, "What'll it be?" "A screwdriver," says the carpenter with a sigh. "A Bloody Mary Jane," says Spider-Man with a smirk. "Did I just hear you ask about "being"?" says the philosopher, dead serious.

No, of course, you haven't. I just made it up—and it's pretty lousy. You'd probably have to know a few philosophers to get the last punch line. You see, we philosophers are known for taking things seriously, sometimes too seriously. Such as Spider-Man. "A book about Spider-Man and philosophy? Seriously? No, no; wait. Seriously!?" Yes, seriously.

And why the heck not? Spider-Man, after all, climbs buildings, swings from strings, and wears bright form-fitting clothes. Why shouldn't we subject him to analysis?

But seriously, I'm sure I wasn't the only Generation X kid to sit through *The Electric Company* just to catch the latest cartoon of my favorite superhero or the only adult who could hardly wait to see Spidey in action on the silver screen. In fact, Spider-Man's been around far longer than I, and probably you, have. Since Stan Lee and Marvel introduced him in *Amazing Fantasy* #15 in 1962, we can't seem to get enough of Spider-Man. He's been in series after series of amazing and spectacular comic versions of Spider-Man, in cartoon versions, in a brief dramatic television series, and in cinematic variations, and he's even made it to Broadway. Over the years, Spider-Man seems to have acquired two additional superpowers: ubiquity and perpetual youth.

What accounts for Spider-Man's massive appeal? I don't know that there is any one answer to that question. Certainly, our fascination with coming-of-age stories motivates a good part of that appeal—and Peter Parker's coming of age is certainly a lot like ours while also spectacularly different. Peter is a bit of geek, struggles to fit in with his peers, and has experienced serious heartache already in life. In other words, he's the classic underdog, and who doesn't have a soft spot for underdogs? Like a lot of us, Peter learns to combat the evils in his life with abilities he didn't realize he had.

Yet the reasons for the appeal go deeper. Peter is self-reflective. He's a seeker. He's trying to figure this world out and find his place in it. He has a strong moral compass, but he sometimes struggles to follow its lead. Yet in the end, he triumphs. In these ways, too, he's like us. Like us, but with abilities we can only dream to have.

All of the ways Spider-Man appeals to us, and all of the ways he gives evidence of a philosophical disposition notwithstanding, this is not really a book about Spider-Man or why he fascinates us. This is a book about the sorts of questions Spider-Man inspires and the sorts of answers to significant questions this fictional character provides us with; it's a book about philosophy. Philosophy is, if Plato (428–348 BCE) can be trusted, a frenzied passion for the truth, the love of wisdom, the pursuit of answers to fundamental questions, a way of life.

The authors of the chapters in this book are all philosophers, most are college professors, and all are teachers of one sort or another. We thought we'd snag a few more students into our webs while writing about our favorite wall-crawler. Sneaky of us, isn't it?

There are all sorts of philosophical questions prompted by thinking about Spider-Man. What is it to live a good life? What do we owe to our family, to our friends, to our neighbors? Do our particular talents come with obligations? How do I know what I think I know? Am I the same person throughout the vast changes of my lifetime? Are there ethical limits to attempts to enhance my abilities? What role should friendship play in my life? With whom can I, or should I, be friends? How publicly should I live my life? How seriously should I take my life? Is there, ultimately, any meaning to life?

These and more are the questions taken up in this book. If you've been around the philosophical block once or twice, you'll notice there aren't too many questions of a strictly metaphysical sort—no attempts to categorize modes of being or to think about absolutely first causes and principles or to ponder how we might tell the difference between the real world and illusion. This isn't because the authors aren't interested in those questions—far from it. No, if you're looking for someone to blame for the dearth of metaphysical analyses, blame Spider-Man. The philosophical nerves he tends to touch are more immediate and palpable—the ones that get us thinking about the question that the most famous philosopher of all, Socrates, put ever before us: how are you going to live your life?

Get serious! Have fun! Enjoy! You can blame us if you soon find yourself snagged in a web of inquiry.

PART ONE

THE SPECTACULAR
LIFE OF SPIDER-MAN?

DOES PETER PARKER HAVE A GOOD LIFE?

Neil Mussett

Spider-Man is a geek. Don't get me wrong—I call him that with affection. I myself am quite a geek: computer programmer by day, secret philosopher by night. I'm just saying that if Batman weren't a superhero, he'd spend his days on yachts with supermodels; Superman would work as a pro-bono lawyer; and Wonder Woman would start an animal preserve in Kenya. (Can you tell I'm more of a D.C. guy?) Peter Parker would work at a lab in a university, design Web pages, or teach high school science. We care about Spider-Man because he's just like us but with special powers. Peter Parker has all sorts of problems: he's an orphan. He was raised by his older, old-fashioned aunt and uncle. He grew up poor and stays poor in many of the story lines. Even when he does find love, he doesn't seem to be any good at it. He's interesting because he doesn't have it together. Even his superpowers cause problems for him—he has to lie to the people he loves to protect them, and that keeps him from getting close. Other superheroes have their secrets, but for some reason, Peter always feels the consequences more than they do.

The question is, then, would you like to be Spider-Man? Does Peter Parker have a good life? What is a good life, anyway? It seems like a simple enough question. Some answers seem *too* simple: If I play *The Sims* video game, I learn that the good life consists of color-coordinated furniture, successful parties, career advancement, and regular trips to the bathroom. Other answers sound good (or at least complicated) but don't stick with you: when I see an author on this week's talk show promoting his *Secret to Happiness*, I can't help wondering what happened to last week's secret on the same show.

If philosophy is good for anything, it has to be for the Big Question, the Meaning of Life. There have been a lot of philosophers since Thales of Miletus (ca. 624 BCE) first put in his big plug for water—designating it to be the first principle of everything, by which he seems to have meant that all things really are at bottom water or at least came to be from water. In this paper, I'm going to discuss only five: a Roman slave, a begging friar, a novelist, a psychiatrist, and an academic. Two atheists, and three followers of three different religions. Three of these were imprisoned, two were tortured. Two spent time in concentration camps. One lived under an assumed name to protect the innocent, and we don't even know the name of another. One never wrote a book, and one wrote more than forty-five. Three have appeared in comic books. Each of these philosophers has given us a complete, and completely different, way to understand ourselves and our lives and a way to find a place for pain and pleasure, other people, morality, and God in the good life.

Paul Kurtz—A Life of Pleasure and Care for Others

I'll start with the contemporary philosopher Paul Kurtz, partly because he lives near me in Buffalo, New York, but also because I suspect that his answer to the Great Question will most resemble yours. You may not have heard of him, but he's the author or the editor of more than forty-five books and more than eight hundred published articles. He has popularized the term *secular humanism* to describe an approach to life that focuses on joyful, creative living, a rejection of all religious claims, and a rational consequence-based ethics.

The good life, Kurtz tells us, has two components: First, the good life is the happy life. What is happiness? Historically, philosophers have described happiness either as pleasure (the hedonists) or as self-actualization (the eudaemonists). Kurtz argues that both are essential to the good life:

> If an individual is to achieve a state of happiness, he needs to develop a number of excellences. I will only list these, without explication: the capacity for autonomous choice and freedom, creativity, intelligence, self-discipline, self-respect, high motivation, good will, an affirmative outlook, good health, the capacity to enjoy pleasure, and aesthetic appreciation.[1]

Does this describe Spider-Man? Peter has certainly determined his own destiny. We know that he's smart; he actually invents his own web shooters in the comic book. In general, he keeps his cool, but we have seen Spider-Man lose control at times. In *Spider-Man 3*, we see him go to some strange lengths to embarrass Mary Jane at a jazz club after she breaks up with him. He is young, however, and at the time he was under the influence of an evil spider suit from another planet, so we can forgive him.

Does he enjoy pleasure? His parents are dead. His uncle is dead, and it's his fault. His aunt is poor, alone, and constantly in danger. In the comic, Peter accidentally kills his first love, Gwen Stacy, when he pulls too hard on his web while saving her from a fall. It does not seem that Peter has enjoyed the "multiplicities of sexuality," which Kurtz sees as "so essential to happiness."[2] He never seems to have any money. He's a brilliant scientist, but he doesn't have the reputation he deserves.

J. Jonas uses the newspaper to turn the public against Spider-Man, so Peter can't even enjoy popular acclaim. I submit to you that it is part of the very essence of Spider-Man that he has a pointedly painful life.

For Kurtz, happiness is important, but we can't live the truly good life alone. Kurtz insists that each of us needs to develop in ourselves the ethical principles of integrity, trustworthiness, benevolence, and fairness. We also need to "develop love and friendship for their own sakes, as goods in themselves."[3] Finally, we need to "consider all members of the human family to be equal in dignity and value."[4] Not only does Peter Parker place himself in danger to save innocent lives, he's also a good friend, a loving nephew, and a kind boyfriend. They don't call him "friendly" for nothing.

It wouldn't be a discussion of Kurtz's philosophy without mentioning religion. Kurtz believes strongly that God is a postulation without sufficient evidence.[5] Does Pete believe in God? It's hard to say. God and religion aren't central to Spider-Man's story, but some have argued that Peter may be a mild Protestant Christian.[6]

I think for Kurtz, the jury is out on Peter Parker's life. On the plus side, he has realized his extraordinary talents and displayed goodwill toward man. On the minus side, his difficult life and obsession with monogamy have robbed Peter of some of the best parts of living. Kurtz might say that Peter is happy; he does have an "active life of enterprise and endeavor," but Kurtz also believes that life should be fun, and fun seems hard to come by for Peter.[7]

Ayn Rand—Life and Integrity

Although Paul Kurtz and Ayn Rand (1908–1982) are both atheists, they give incompatible answers to the Big Question. Kurtz wants you to realize that you can be altruistic without religion; Rand wants you to stop being altruistic. Kurtz asks you to develop a "deep appreciation for the needs of other human beings,"[8] Rand asks you to "learn to treat as the mark of a cannibal any man's *demand* for your help."[9]

You may know her through the video game *Bioshock*, which was inspired by her writings. You may have seen the 1999 movie *The Passion of Ayn Rand*, based on her life. You may also know her as the star of the comic book *Action Philosophers* #2 (2005). Steve Ditko, the original artist for *The Amazing Spider-Man*, had what one author calls a "cultish devotion" to her philosophy of Objectivism.[10]

Alisa Zinov'yevna Rosenbaum was born in St. Petersburg, Russia, in 1905, and her family suffered at the hands of the Communist Revolution of 1917. After completing a degree in history, she moved to Hollywood to become a screenwriter. Fearing for her family's safety in Russia, she changed her name to Ayn Rand when she began to write anti-Soviet stories. She's most famous for her 1957 novel *Atlas Shrugged*, about a future in which the producers, the artists, and the entrepreneurs of the world go on strike. (I just checked Amazon.com, and it's still number one in political philosophy.)

In a lifeless world, she said, there are no choices and no alternatives. With life comes the most fundamental alternative: existence or nonexistence. Matter is indestructible, life is not. A living organism can succeed or fail to sustain itself. If it fails, it dies. Life creates *value*, that which a living organism acts to attain. Things are *good* or *evil* to the extent that they sustain or destroy life. Happiness is achieving one's values, and "pain is an agent of death."[11]

Man has the unique power of *rationality*. Just as nonrational animals use whatever faculties they possess to survive, man's rational nature demands a rational means of survival. He has no *instinct* of self-preservation, no "automatic code of survival."[12] The lower animals have no choice but to act for their own good; man must choose his own actions by thought. "What are the values his survival requires?" she asked. "That is the question to be answered by the science of *ethics*."[13] Rand's model for an ethical act was the *trade*. In a trade, each man must "give value for value."[14] The opposite of the trade would be force, violence, or theft, which would be unethical because it requires the sacrifice of one rational agent for the benefit of another.[15]

I'm afraid Ayn Rand wouldn't have had good things to say about Spider-Man. Think about it: Peter Parker has super-human strength, scientific genius, and the ability to climb walls and see the near future. How does he use it? At first, he uses it to make money as a pro-wrestler (in the comic, he has quite a successful career). When he decides not to intervene in a robbery that has nothing to do with him, his uncle is murdered. This event moves him to dedicate his life to saving a public that hates him. He hides his identity and lives in squalor, all for the sake of his uncle's advice about power and responsibility. In other words, Peter becomes Rand's "prostitute whose standard is the greatest good for the greatest number."[16]

In many ways, Spider-Man is an allegory, a fairy tale, of what Rand called the "morality of sacrifice," which she believed was the opposite of true ethics.[17] For the morality of sacrifice, the good is always the *good of others*. The morality of sacrifice praises any act motivated by the welfare of another person and criticizes any act motivated by one's own welfare. Rand summarized the morality of sacrifice this way: "If *you* wish it, it's evil; if others wish it, it's good; if the motive of your action is *your* welfare, don't do it; if the motive is the welfare of others, then anything goes."[18] According to Rand, this self-destructive theory demands that we *love* those whom we do not value and tells us that "To love a man for his virtues is paltry and human . . . to love him for his flaws is divine."[19] This is the sort of love Spider-Man has for his public, and it's the reason why Rand would have said that he is not living the good life.

Epictetus—Self-Control, Duty, and Knowledge of the World

Ayn Rand believed that (traditional) morality is destructive to happiness, but there was a philosopher who believed that morality is *sufficient* for happiness. Unlike Rand, who lived under an assumed name, we don't even know the name of this philosopher. All we know of him is that he was a slave in Rome, so we call him "Acquired" (*epiktetos* in Greek). He was born about 55 AD, and if our five philosophers were to fight, I would put my money on him. Origen gave us a snapshot of a man who is tough as nails:

> [T]ake Epictetus, who, when his master was twisting his leg, said, smiling and unmoved, "You will break my leg;" and when it was broken, he added, "Did I not tell you that you would break it?"[20]

While he was still a slave, Epictetus attended the lectures of a Stoic philosopher, Musonius Rufus. He became a philosopher himself, and when he was given his freedom sometime before the year 89, he taught philosophy in Rome and lived to be almost a hundred years old.[21]

Epictetus lived the life of a slave and an exile, but he considered his own life to be good. His answer to the Big Question was simple: to have a good life, you must (1) master your desires; (2) perform your duties; and (3) think correctly about yourself and the world. Most people neglect the first two and focus only on the third.

Epictetus would say that Kurtz and Rand have a huge underlying problem: they base happiness on chance. Most of life is out of our control. The pleasures they describe may sound attractive, but what if you were born a slave? What if your parents die and your uncle is killed? What if there is more pain in your life than pleasure? Is your life bad? Epictetus puts happiness in the one place that's immune to life's disasters:

your own power of choice. We can lead happy lives under any circumstances, as long as we master our desires and depend only on those things that are in our control:

> I must die. Must I then die lamenting? I must be put in chains. Must I then also lament? I must go into exile. Does any man then hinder me from going with smiles and cheerfulness and contentment?[22]

Epictetus addresses something that is essential to Spider-Man and every other superhero: attachment. What is Spider-Man's greatest weakness? His attachment to Aunt May and MJ. Even if Spider-Man were immortal, his friends aren't. Nothing he has is his very own; it is given to him for the moment, not forever or inseparably, but for a season. Peter should remind himself of this whenever he saves his loved ones from danger or even takes pleasure in their company. Epictetus asks us this provocative question:

> What harm is there in whispering to yourself as you kiss your child, "To-morrow you will die," and to your friend in like manner, "To-morrow you or I shall go away, and we shall see one another no more?"[23]

Would Epictetus have given Spider-Man a passing grade in his school for Stoics? Peter is a hero and a scholar, so he gets full credit for duties and learning. Has Peter mastered himself? Peter is no coward—he doesn't run from pain or mortal danger. Yet self-mastery is more than courage in battle; it's freedom from the pains of this world. In the movies, he spends years pining for MJ, basing his happiness on something he can't obtain. He spends his life torn between the call of duty and a need for personal comforts. He doesn't prepare himself for loss and pain, so when they happen to him, he loses his peace. Spider-Man has a long way to go before he can be counted among "The Wise." As much as he cares for Aunt May, he needs to learn that his obsession with her safety keeps him from living the truly good life.

Viktor Frankl—Meaning and Sacrifice

Perhaps it's just the opposite. Perhaps genuine care for others is what the good life is all about. Viktor Frankl (1905–1997) lived a life just as hard as Epictetus's but came up with a different answer. Frankl was a Jewish psychologist who suffered in several concentration camps, including Auschwitz, Dachau, and one camp without a name. While he was in Auschwitz, he decided that the best way to keep himself going was to write a book on the psychology of death camps. He did survive, and what started as a book became an entirely new school of psychology that seeks to relieve emotional distress through meaning.

For Frankl, the good life is the life of meaning. "Meaning" is primarily a matter of responsibility—there is some good I *need* to do.[24] In a meaningful life, I have a sense of my own irreplacability—nobody else can carry out my particular duty for me. In that sense, there's no one "meaning of life." Rather, each person's life has an entirely unique meaning that needs to be discovered.[25] Meaning shapes and organizes everything else within my life. It's the reason I get out of bed in the morning. Meaning also changes the nature of suffering. Frankl claimed that "There is nothing in the world . . . that would so effectively help one to survive even the worst of conditions as the knowledge that there is a meaning to one's life."[26] He was fond of quoting Friedrich Nietzsche (1844–1900), who wrote, "He who has a why to live can bear almost any how."[27] If suffering is associated with meaning, with love, it becomes sacrifice. Sacrifice, rather than being something to avoid, is actually an essential part of the good life. Frankl is very clear that the very worst life is the life of *boredom*, which can only lead to an obsessive pursuit of temporary highs.[28]

To decide whether Spider-Man has a good life, it's not enough to admire his heroic actions—Peter must see the purpose himself. Although it's obvious to us that nobody else can do what he does, he may not see the point of it all. The pain in Peter's life is real. Not only did Peter suffer from his childhood as a poor, unpopular orphan, he suffers in the present from his own actions and lifestyle. He suffers when he gets hurt, and he suffers in his personal life.

Frankl, on the other hand, would have asked *Peter* to decide whether his life is good. He would have sat Peter down and asked him, "Why don't you kill yourself?" This rather shocking question would not be meant to *encourage* Peter to jump off a bridge. Instead, it would force Peter to find the things that keep him going, despite the suffering. Frankl said that it's ironic that most people think the job of the psychologist is to relieve stress. The best way to help people in crisis is often to *increase* the amount of tension in their lives by helping them focus on their responsibilities. He used a metaphor from architecture—to strengthen a weak arch in a building, you *add* weight. Frankl could have added to Uncle Ben's advice: with great responsibility comes the knowledge of your own purpose.

The closest thing we have to Peter's answer to this question may be the encounter he has with the evil psychologist Dr. Judas Traveller, in *Amazing Spider-Man* #402 (1995). During the infamous *Clone Saga* (1994–1996), Traveller meets Spider-Man at an all-time low point in his life: Aunt May is dead, his baby with MJ may have genetic defects, and Peter has been imprisoned. Traveller offers Peter a chance to have the peaceful life he always wanted but at the cost of innocent lives. He refuses and attacks Traveller. In doing so, Peter shows us that he'd rather live a life of great sacrifice and pain than betray his love of humanity.

Thomas Aquinas—God and Virtue

There's one superhero we haven't talked about so far. You may not have heard of him, but there are specialty stores where you can still get his books, pictures of him, and even his emblem on a chain. Like Harry Osborn, he was born to a rich and powerful family. They wanted to use their influence to get him a cushy job, but he wanted to join a rag-tag band of men who wandered the world helping those in need. His family was so opposed to his plans that they had him kidnapped and locked in a castle tower for almost two years. His mother had a change of heart and had his sisters rescue him with some ropes and a basket. He has some nicknames, the Angelic Doctor and the Dumb Ox, but most know him simply as Thomas.

Yes, I am talking about St. Thomas Aquinas (c. 1225–1274). I put him last—a dead giveaway that he's my favorite. Thomas Aquinas wrote on most major branches of classical philosophy. Believing that faith and reason are entirely compatible, he also wrote on a wide variety of subjects, including angels and even economics. If you're brave, get a hold of the medieval equivalent of a comic book, Dante's *Divine Comedy* (including the ultraviolent *Inferno*), which is an epic poem about a man who travels from Hell to Purgatory to Heaven. Dante was so inspired by Thomas's philosophy that he used it as the setting of his poem.

Like Kurtz, Thomas argued that all men want happiness, and that a perfectly good life would fulfill all of our desires, including that for the perfection of our bodies.[29] Also like Kurtz, Thomas believed that it's an essential part of our nature to care for others, and that all people are capable of living virtuous lives, whether or not they accept Christianity.[30] Like Rand, Thomas believed that true morality will always benefit the one who acts, and that pleasure in acting *increases* the moral worthiness of the action.[31] He held, with Rand, that we love what's good, what's deserving and praiseworthy and excellent.[32] Even the best person shouldn't love other people more than he loves himself.[33] Thomas agreed with Epictetus that happiness is ultimately a choice, and it cannot be taken away by the actions of others.[34] Finally, like Frankl, Thomas believed that in the good life, love is the ultimate motivation, and love allows us even to enjoy suffering for our friends.[35]

How could Thomas say all of this? I don't have enough room here to give even the roughest sketch of Thomas's ethics. It'll have to suffice to say that for Thomas, everything was good, our bodies, our minds, the world, and especially God. The only way you could even get anything bad would be if a thing was missing something it should have (people usually use blindness as an example or a car without brakes or a superhero without a costume). Every desire we have points to some good thing that can fulfill it. Our desire for happiness has no limit, and the more we experience of the world, the more we know that it can't perfectly satisfy us. Thomas said that everybody wants to be happy, but what they don't realize is that only God, Who is unlimited Goodness, can make them perfectly happy.[36]

Reading Kurtz or Rand, one would think that Aquinas hated this world, hated life, and hated the body, but it is quite the opposite. Thomas adopted Aristotle's (384–322 BCE) concept of a *virtue*. Yes, a virtue is a good habit, but it is more than that. A virtue changes you—it makes you enjoy doing good. A generous person actually *likes* giving. Doing an occasional nice thing here or there is fine, but if you do it enough, you get hooked, and it stops being work to do the right thing. That's how Thomas could link *morality* with *pleasure*. The truly virtuous person is filled with joy when doing good and, in a sense, can do whatever he or she wants.

Without any notion of God, people can still love one another, because every person is born with a sense of decency, a sense that moral actions are compatible, appropriate, and healthy. This is because of the Natural Law, called so because it comes from our nature as rational beings. We start with loving ourselves, but we can come to identify with others, see them as *other selves*, and love them as well. Through God's action, we can be given the virtue of charity, which allows us to love God in a completely selfless way, to love those around us as images of God, and to love ourselves and our bodies as God's creations.[37]

What would Thomas say about Spidey's life? I actually find it difficult to picture driving Thomas Aquinas to a movie theater, but if we could arrange it, I think he would have good things to say about Mr. Parker. He would praise Peter's moral and intellectual virtues: courage, creativity, good judgment, compassion, and restraint. Most of us don't have the opportunity to do good to all men, but Peter does, and his beneficence is very close to the highest virtue, charity.[38]

The life of a superhero does have its pleasures. Thomas would say that Spider-Man enjoys saving the world for three important reasons: First, the *effect*—the love he has for the people he saves allows him to enjoy their good as if it were his own. Second, the *end*—Peter knows (or at least hopes) that he'll receive good things for his efforts, such as gratitude and praise. Finally, the *principle*—he enjoys using his superpowers, exercising his virtues, and doing things out of love.

What about Peter's suffering? Thomas believed that in itself, sorrow or pain is not *evil* in a moral sense (disagreeing with Ayn Rand). There are actually several kinds of good pain: *remorse*, or sorrow for all of the harm we have done, is actually very good. Uncle Ben's advice is powerful because it's associated with a tragic mistake. The anger and loss Peter feels at the crimes of his opponents is also a kind of pain but a good pain. Suffering heightens Peter's awareness of risk and a desire to avoid repeating past mistakes, which is very helpful. Thomas agreed that suffering could be bad, but he insisted that no suffering, interior or exterior, could outweigh the badness of *failing to reject evil*.[39] If there's a balance to be struck, Peter has come out on the right side.

What Next?

Nothing is more depressing than talking to a philosopher who doesn't believe in anything. I have very strong beliefs about the Meaning of Life (a combination of Frankl and Thomas, with a little Detrich von Hildebrand thrown in for fun), but it's not my plan to argue for one particular winner in this chapter. There are two general approaches to answering this question, the academic (read everything you can and make a decision) and the concrete (find someone who has what you want and ask how he or she got it). Whichever way you choose, it's vital for *you* to pursue the answer.

NOTES

1. Paul Kurtz, *Living without Religion: Eupraxophy* (Amherst, NY: Prometheus Books, 1994), 41.

2. Paul Kurtz, *Embracing the Power of Humanism* (Lanham, MD: Rowman & Littlefield, 2000), 6.

3. Ibid.

4. Paul Kurtz, "Toward a New Enlightenment: A Response to the Postmodernist Critique of Humanism," *Free Inquiry* 13 (1992–1993): 33–37.

5. Kurtz, *Living without Religion*, 33.

6. See www.adherents.com/lit/comics/Spider-Man.html.

7. Paul Kurtz, "Where Is the Good Life? Making the Humanist Choice," *Free Inquiry* 18 (1998): 23–24.

8. Paul Kurtz, Vern L. Bullough, and Timothy J. Madigan, *Toward a New Enlightenment: The Philosophy of Paul Kurtz* (New Brunswick, NJ: Transaction Books, 1994), 21.

9. Ayn Rand, *Atlas Shrugged* (New York: Random House, 1957), 1059.

10. Andrew Hultkrans, "Steve Ditko's Hands," in Sean Howe, ed., *Give Our Regards to the Atomsmashers!* (New York: Pantheon Books, 2004), 209–223.

11. Rand, *Atlas Shrugged*, 940.

12. Ibid., 939.

13. Rand, *The Virtue of Selfishness*, 24.

14. Rand, *Atlas Shrugged*, 410.

15. Rand, *The Virtue of Selfishness*, 32.

16. Ibid., 1030.

17. Ibid., 959.

18. Rand, *Atlas Shrugged*, 1030.

19. Ibid.

20. *The Writings of Origen*, trans. Frederick Crombie (University of California: T & T Clark, 1872), 475.

21. John Lancaster Spalding, "Critical and Biographical Introduction," in *Discourses of Epictetus*, trans. George Long (New York: D. Appleton, 1904), iv.

22. Epictetus, *Discourses of Epictetus*, trans. George Long (New York: D. Appleton, 1904), 3.

23. Epictetus, *Epictetus the Discourses and Manual*, trans. P. E. Matheson (London: Oxford University Press, 2009), 97.

24. Viktor Frankl, *Man's Search for Meaning* (New York: Washington Square Press, 1984), 127.

25. Ibid., 131.

26. Ibid., 126.

27. Ibid.

28. Ibid., 128.

29. Thomas Aquinas, *Summa Theologica*, Ia IIae, q.1, aa.6–7; and Ia IIae, q.4, a.6.

30. Ibid., Ia IIae, q.91, a.2.

31. Ibid., IIa IIae, q.27, a.3; IIa IIae, q.123, a.12; IIa IIae, q.27, a.8; Ia IIae, q.59, a.2.

32. Ibid., Ia IIae, q.10, a.1.

33. Ibid., IIa IIae, q.26, a.4; Ia IIae, q.29, a.4.

34. Ibid., Ia IIae, q.3, a.2; Ia IIae, q.4, a.7.

35. Ibid., Ia IIae, q.32, a.6.

36. Ibid., Ia IIae, q.2, a.8.

37. Ibid., IIa IIae, qq.23–46.

38. Ibid., IIa IIae, q.31, a.3.

39. Ibid., Ia IIae, q.39.

WHAT PRICE ATONEMENT?

Peter Parker and the Infinite Debt

Taneli Kukkonen

Peter Parker can't catch a break! Whatever he does, however hard he tries, Peter struggles in vain to balance his obligations as a masked crime fighter with those he must face every day as a normal human being. Is Spider-Man supposed to chase down some costumed goon while Peter's Aunt May lies sick in bed? Then again, is Peter supposed to sit back and study when there's a crime taking place that only Spider-Man can prevent? And where, if anywhere, does love fit into the equation? Does Peter even have a right to date, let alone commit to, anybody? If he does take that step and give in to his heart, doesn't this impose on him duties fundamentally in conflict with the life led by Spider-Man?

To make matters worse, Peter never gets to explain himself fully to the people he inevitably lets down. Sometimes he has trouble justifying his decisions even to himself. Yet Peter persists, doggedly pursuing his impossible balancing act of a life, terminally fated to feel inadequate. Why? Two notions are central here: guilt and debt. On one hand, Peter feels guilt for Uncle Ben's death, and his costumed pursuit of criminals is a way of atoning for that sin. On the other, Peter also feels incredibly indebted to Aunt May and is thereby driven to be a good student, a doting nephew, and a fretful breadwinner. Because Uncle Ben is dead, Peter can never forsake his duties as Spider-Man; because Aunt May remains very much alive—despite five decades of funny-book senior life—he can never give himself completely to a life of crimefighting. Compare this with another parental avenger, Bruce Wayne, who really *is* the Batman, and for whom the role of Wayne has become merely a convenient facade. This is not the case with Peter, who feels genuinely torn. As Professor Miles Warren wonders, "Imagine learning what motivates such a man! Is it altruism—or deep-rooted schizophrenia? I'll bet he's even an enigma to himself!"[1] Guilt or gift? You decide, but consider this first.

Death and Taxes

It's curious that Peter feels obliged to avenge Uncle Ben's death over and over again. Consider the analogous case with Batman. Joe Chill, the hood who killed Thomas and Martha Wayne, is never caught, nor is Bruce Wayne in any way responsible for the killing. So it's understandable that he should displace his anger into a war against all criminals. Spider-Man, though, *does* have a reason to feel responsible for Uncle Ben's death, because he let the robber who would go on to kill Ben get away; then again, to balance things out, he *does* catch the murderer almost immediately. If what we're dealing with here is debt, why is this not enough to cancel it? Or, if not that, then shouldn't the hundreds of criminals and killers Spider-Man has put away count for something, at least? Apparently not; Peter feels just as guilty and indebted today as he did in his feature debut.

In the history of philosophy, this kind of ineradicable debt is most often associated with the debt that people owe to God. Indeed, the parallels between the two are remarkably close. Peter often ponders how much Uncle Ben and Aunt May have given him, how they are the two people to whom he owes everything. Ben and May have made Peter who he is, selflessly providing him with all he needs, in terms of both earthly goods and moral guidance. What does he do in his first act of newfound independence (plainly, Peter's emerging powers are a stand-in for emerging adolescent maturity)? Peter spectacularly lets down his protectors, failing to heed their moral teachings. Peter is thereby robbed of that cocoon of total love that had surrounded him earlier. Even his relations with Aunt May hereon take on an aspect of guilt, secrecy, and pain. There's a "Paradise Lost" feel to all of this, to be sure, and it is entirely self-inflicted. This is Peter's primordial act of transgression, a half-remembered experience of original sin, which puts him beyond the reach of heaven forevermore.

The operative notion here is "infinite debt." The question is whether repayment of such a debt is ever possible and on what terms. Anselm of Canterbury (1103–1109), one of the foremost thinkers of medieval times, built a whole theology of atonement around this question. The contents of this doctrine, which are encapsulated in his treatise on *Why God Became a Human Being*, can be summarized as follows. (1) As fallen creatures, we can direct our will either toward happiness or toward justice but no longer toward both: we primarily want either that which we mistakenly believe will make us happy or that which is in fact just in some universal sense. (2) In choosing their own happiness over justice, humankind and the fallen angels before it committed a sin against the majesty of God, to whom endless gratitude is justly owed. (3) This puts us infinitely in God's debt, for to repair one's behavior afterward is only to give God what was His due in the first place and therefore does nothing to make up for the original transgression. No amount of good deeds will ever absolve us of this debt.[2]

This last point is illustrated in "The Final Chapter," penciled and plotted by Steve Ditko.[3] Here, Spider-Man dares to dream of a time when he'll be free of his burden. The occasion presents itself to save the life of another loved one: "No matter what the odds—no matter what the cost—I'll get that serum to Aunt May! And maybe *then* I'll no longer be haunted by the memory—of Uncle Ben!" In a feat of superhuman strength, Peter fights against overwhelming odds to deliver the treasured serum to Aunt May. Still, in the next installment, "The Thrill of the Hunt," everything goes on much as it did before: Peter forsakes Betty Brant, for love interests may come and go, "but Spider-Man I've been—and always will be—for as long as I live!"[4] The demand for justice again trumps Peter's desire for personal happiness. Aiding Aunt May has done nothing to dispel the specter of Uncle Ben.

Perhaps this is for the best. As the Danish philosopher Søren Kierkegaard (1813–1855) noted in his *Works of Love*, it would be cold and unloving of someone who'd just performed some magnanimous feat for the sake of somebody else to then add, "See, now I have paid my debt."[5] According to both Anselm and Kierkegaard, it would be futile as well. There simply is no way one can repay a debt of love.

Anselm went on to argue that this was why the Incarnation was necessary. Only God could repay God and truly set us free, because only God made flesh could do *more* than was required of Him and thereby build a surplus of goodwill from the heavens, with which mankind in turn could be liberated from its debt. Yet if this is true (and if Uncle Ben in death can substitute for Christ, just as Uncle Ben in life substituted for the Father), then Peter seems screwed either way! For if justice is served measure for measure, then the only conceivable way for Peter to answer Uncle Ben's sacrifice would be to sacrifice his own life in the name of some greater good. In that case, however, he would extinguish the hopes that Ben and May had placed on him in life and would betray them in another fashion. Happiness and justice: can they ever be reconciled?

This dilemma, too, is mirrored in Christian philosophical theology. It would seem that if we accept Anselm's picture of how atonement works, then the self-sacrifice of Christ accomplishes nothing except for some additional bookkeeping. All we do is end up deeper in debt! For consider: a debt collector at least is an honest fellow, someone who tells you straightforwardly what the terms are for your annulling your debt to him. When you're in debt, you know where you stand and how you can work toward becoming self-standing once more. By contrast, when somebody professes to give you a completely free gift, no strings attached, that's when you should beware, for to receive a gift that you're never allowed to reciprocate is to be made to stand in your benefactor's debt forever. A gift, this is to say, is simply a more insidious form of tying somebody down to an economy of exchange, and the same goes double for forgiveness. According to the critics, God's giving us life in this way (just as with Ben's and May's giving Peter everything) places on us a tremendous responsibility, even as God's death—at least, according to the tenets of atonement theology—exacts on us the highest toll of all.[6]

Consequently, many modern thinkers have found Anselm's notion of debt cancellation distasteful and inconsistent with the notion of a divine love that is truly selfless. Kierkegaard voiced this doubt well:

> Ordinarily we say that a person who is loved runs into debt by being loved. Thus we say that children are in love's debt to their parents because they have loved them first, so that the children's love is only a part-payment on the debt or a repayment. And this is indeed true. But such talk is all too reminiscent of an actual bookkeeping arrangement: a debt is incurred and it must be paid off in installments.[7]

The portrayal of God as a stony-faced tyrant who would demand prostration and penitence rings false, just as false as the notion that the ghost of Uncle Ben would be some malevolent force hovering over Peter's head, wishing to guilt him into action. Surely that is not how he, or He, would want Peter to live.[8] What are the alternatives?

Ethics and the Infinite

One other possible reading of Spider-Man's origin is that Uncle Ben's death serves simply as Peter's awakening to what he already knew: that he should direct his gifts toward helping the entire world, not only toward helping himself and his loved ones. We are, after all, told that on apprehending Ben's killer, Peter has finally learned how "in this world, with great power there must also come—great responsibility!" How great, though? How about this: *unlimited responsibility*—that is, responsibility to come to the aid of anyone and everyone who crosses Peter's path, regardless of who they are and what their attitude to him is. Whether friend (Aunt May, Mary Jane), foe (the Green Goblin, J. Jonah Jameson), or indifferent (any number of New York City's residents), Peter is obliged to rush to the aid of whoever is calling. This is responsibility as *responsiveness*. What we have here is what Emmanuel Levinas (1906–1995) described as the transformation of our infinite debt toward God, or the absolute Other, into a debt owed to every other: it is the absolute demand made on us by the face of another human being to help and not to hurt.[9] (Perhaps it is those masks that make it easier for our superheroes and villains to slug it out!)

First and foremost, this is a transformation from ethical parochialism into ethical universalism (although, as we shall see, this needs to be adjusted to account for the singular—and indeed Levinas never neglected the importance of family, as his work *Totality and Infinity* shows). Notice how in Peter's origin story, the still-callous youth thinks to himself about

Aunt May and Uncle Ben: "They're the only ones who've ever been kind to me! I'll see to it that *they're* always happy, but the rest of the world can go hang for all I care!"[10] This isn't exactly an immoral attitude to assume toward the world, but it is far too limited. It's not what Ben would have wanted or what ethics demands. The whole point of ethics is that it places strictures on every human encounter we have.

Yet with this, we run headlong into Spider-Man's endless troubles with his obligations. If Peter always owes it to everybody to take calls for help seriously, then how is he to avoid or even resolve the many conflicts of interest this inevitably brings up? Peter owes a response to May, to Mary Jane, to his professors, to the man on the street, even to Jolly Jonah Jameson when the latter cries for help—and this is not even taking into consideration "the widow, the orphan, or the stranger" of whom Levinas spoke with such empathy; in other words, all of those who do not even have a voice with which to speak or to plead. However much Peter does, he will always fall short of what is required of him, just as we all do when faced with such a terrible, unbounded obligation.

Some philosophers have found this an altogether insufferable portrayal of human destiny. Georg Wilhelm Friedrich Hegel (1770–1831) called the kind of infinity we are dealing with here a bad infinity (*schlechte Unendlichkeit*), one that is characterized by everlasting lack, rather like the line that can be extended indefinitely, yet never finds completion anywhere. Against this bad infinite, Hegel set the true infinite, which signifies a fullness of being, of which God as described by Anselm forms the exemplar.[11] Such a superior kind of infinity is like the circle, ever complete in itself, and it is toward this sort of fulfillment that we should strive.

This picture of an actual or true infinite as one that exudes completeness, indeed overflowing plenitude, has a distinguished pedigree, going back to the Platonic tradition in antiquity.[12] The implication for ethics is that in order to find our rightful place in the chain of being, we need only realize fully our own nature, and the rest will follow of its own accord. Instead of neurotically trying to sound out the opinions and wishes of others, we need to develop our own inner compass, safe in the knowledge that in this way we will behave appropriately and in a beneficent manner in each individual circumstance. Some have suggested that this is the way we should read Nietzsche's (1844–1900) famous pronouncement of the death of God. Far from obliging us to sacrifice the self, God's death acts as our final release from sacrifice, debt, blood, and toil—it frees us to wander about happily, using our gifts as best we see fit.[13] This need not signal amoral or immoral behavior; rather, it could be seen as heralding the recovery of a superior set of values, one that emulates the ancient tradition of ethics as care of the self. Magnanimity, after all, simply means greatness of soul, and what is wrong with recognizing one's own greatness and even reveling in it a bit?[14]

Again, there's enough in Spider-Man's history to suggest that he'd find this line of thought tempting at least. In the anniversary tale, "Doom Service!" Uncle Ben gets to make a posthumous visitation and to say that Peter has "built up a fine sense of caring . . . of responsibility."[15] Ben adds that the only way Peter could disappoint his uncle now would be if he let these gifts go to waste. Guilt and blame are explicitly ruled out here. If Ben is again allowed to stand for God (and why not?), then it would seem that all Peter needs to do is learn to be himself, trust his finely honed instincts, and all will be well. Just go with it! Enjoy your spider-powers, spin those webs! Use the gifts you've been given! And chase some girls while you're at it!

Every Other Is Wholly Other

At the core of this approach is a very appealing idea. The best way to thank someone for a gift is to put it to good use. Still, there's something a bit too self-satisfied and cavalier about the way this understanding of ethics treats those who are supposed to be the beneficiaries of the fully realized hero's actions. It is as if all the world's merely a stage for an exuberant personality such as the one described by Nietzsche, an audience and a backdrop, rather than the actual center of the agent's attentions.

Take the case of alms, for example. If our reason for giving to the beggar is not that she stands in need of our help (let alone that we are *obliged* to do so), but only that giving expresses our magnanimous personality, then in what sense are we reaching out to the other person at all? Are we not, rather, engaging in a solipsistic exercise of back patting, doing something in order to be able to congratulate ourselves on how good we are? This is the second trap that awaits those who promote supposedly free and radically liberal gift giving. If there's no real obligation to the other, no imperative to listen to the needs of another person who's genuinely foreign to us, then there's nothing to prevent any given code of conduct from becoming just a slightly more sophisticated bit of navel gazing and narcissism.[16] One is reminded here of the criticism often ascribed to Augustine of Hippo (354–430), according to which all of the ancient Greek virtues merely amount to splendidly gilded vices, the problem being that they all issue from a fundamentally egocentric perspective.[17]

Let's go back to Levinas's original notion of us all being called to duty simply by virtue of being faced with one another. Who, then, is "the widow, the orphan, or the stranger" whose call Spider-Man must answer? Following up on a thread left by Levinas, Jacques Derrida (1930–2004) introduced in this connection a play on words that resonates in the French and has consequently become a bit of a favorite among commentators: "every other is wholly other [*tout autre est tout autre*]." This is to say that "God, as the wholly other, is to be found everywhere there is something of the wholly other. And since each of us, everyone else, each other is infinitely other in its absolute singularity . . . what can be said of Abraham's relation to God can be said about . . . my relation to my neighbor or my loved ones who are as inaccessible to me, as secret and transcendent as Yahweh."[18] The face of God, or Uncle Ben, if you prefer, is encountered equally in friend, neighbor, stranger, and foe: each of these presents us with a puzzle for understanding ("What is this person saying?") and a call for action ("How can I help?").

The landmark "Spider-Man No More!" neatly illustrates the point.[19] A kindly old policeman, randomly rescued by Peter in his civvies and peerlessly portrayed by Jazzy John Romita, just happens to have the exact same features as Peter Parker's revered Uncle Ben! In this way, he serves to remind Peter about the debt that he owes to the world as a whole. It's not by tending to his studies or by seeking a fulfilled love life that Peter Parker can find salvation, but only by heeding the call of anyone and everyone who needs his help.

> Now, at last—it's all crystal clear to me once more!
> I can never renounce my Spider-Man identity! I can
> never fail to use the powers which a mysterious destiny
> has seen fit to give me! No matter how unbearable the
> burden may be—no matter how great the personal
> sacrifice—I can never permit one innocent being to
> come to harm—because Spider-Man failed to act—and
> I swear that I never will!

So we have at least reached a conclusion: justice trumps happiness, it always must. The care of the self must yield to a care for the other, every other as wholly other.

Still, Peter's pronounced objective is manifestly impossible to achieve. Even if Peter does his very best, he'll still end up failing, and failing miserably. Thus, for instance, in the sweet latter-day tale "Whatever Happened to Crusher Hogan?" Spider-Man gets to help out an old wrestler whom he once defeated as a teenager, but this comes at the cost of being indisposed when Aunt May's boyfriend Nathan Lubensky gets badly beaten up.[20] "Isn't there any way I could have won?" Peter ponders. "Or was I destined to lose no matter what choice I made? Is that the price I must always pay for being . . . Spider-Man?" Well, in a word, yes. Such impossible choices between conflicting duties seem to come with the territory.

Derrida had an interesting answer as to why this is so. Taking his cue from a minor comment made by Kierkegaard, according to which "the moment of decision is madness," as well as the latter's musings concerning the inexplicable nature of any higher calling in *Fear and Trembling*, Derrida explained that the notion of infinite responsibility necessarily leaves us with a never-ending series of awful choices when it comes to determining which calls receive a response from us. This is not a matter of deliberation, because the choice has to be made in the moment, and any hearing is already a response (and therefore necessarily means turning a deaf ear to somebody else's cries, in that very moment). Nor is it a decision that we can readily explain to anyone else or even to ourselves, given that each of the other options would undoubtedly also have been the right one and simultaneously equally as wrong.

> I am responsible to any one (that is to say any other) only by failing in my responsibilities to all the others, to the ethical or political generality. And I can never justify this sacrifice, I must always hold my peace about it. Whether I want to or not, I can never justify the fact that I prefer or sacrifice any one (any other) to the other. I will always be secretive, held to secrecy in respect of this, for I have nothing to say about it.[21]

This could have been written by Peter Parker, who constantly ends up biting his lip when quizzed about why he was not here or there, when in fact he had to be in yet another place in order to deal with yet another pressing need. There really is nothing to say about such choices—at the moment that Spider-Man leaped one way, the only thing he heard was someone cry out in distress. This is the terrifying moment that lies beyond ethics, the suspension of the ethical about which Kierkegaard (on the reading of Derrida) spoke in *Fear and Trembling*—to assume one absolute duty is to neglect all other possible duties, at the same time that that action implies that those other duties were equally as real. It is the moment that the universal is overcome by the singular that the limits to our powers come across all too clearly—even with the speed, strength, and premonition of a spider, we can't reach out to all of those who reach out to us.[22]

Where does this leave us? On one hand, applying ourselves to single cases is all that we can do—as Aristotle (384–322 BCE) said, a doctor does not aim to cure humanity in general but this or that individual human being.[23] On the other hand, every time we choose to pursue a singular instance of duty, we affirm that every other instance was potentially ours as well. Thus, the ethical is only ever suspended, never actually discarded, for our universal duty remains all too clearly for us to see precisely in our painful awareness that we can't fulfill it.

Remaining in Debt

It's common among funny-book writers to describe superpowers as gifts. Yet if they're gifts, assuredly they're rather strange ones. Who gave them? Is it God? Or some strange cosmic force, the laws of causality—the will of heaven, as Chinese lore has it? Or perhaps it's merely cruel fate, the capricious *tukhê* of Greek tragedy? Perhaps none of this matters, as Plato (ca. 428–348 BCE) pointed out.[24] What's important is the fact of the gift itself and the way that it both structures and ruptures the recipient's life.

It's significant in this connection, I think, that guilt, debt, and responsibility all amount to the same thing: guilt—*schuld* in German. Likewise, it's notable that the gift is also always potentially a poison, *ein/eine Gift*—when somebody is handed a gift, that person instantaneously becomes tainted by association. A gift by definition is something one doesn't ask for but which nonetheless presents its recipient with a challenge and an obligation, an obligation to puzzle out its meaning.

Peter Parker's solution seems closest to that which Kierkegaard described in his *Works of Love* as "remaining in love's debt." Returning to the notion advanced earlier that annulling any debts of gratitude can never be the goal of the sincere lover, Kierkegaard went on to say that to the contrary, the lover resolves to take on the obligation of remaining infinitely in debt. Building on a passage in Paul's letter to the Romans (13:8), Kierkegaard submitted that the situation was rather like that of the fish that the fisherman had to plunk immediately into a bucket on catching it.

> Why must he put it in water? Because water is the fish's element, *and everything that is to be kept alive must be kept in its element;* but love's element is infinitude, inexhaustibility, immeasurability. Therefore, if you want to maintain your love, you must see to it that love, caught for freedom and life, continually remains in its element by means of the infinitude of the debt.[25]

If love were simply about returning favors, then it would die an instant death, because this would be a finite relation. Yet love's debt is felt in the gratitude we feel for the very fact that we get to love, and if this means for us unspeakable agonies and heartrending choices, as lovers we still would not wish for things to be otherwise. Every act that Peter performs in an attempt to further the cause of good inevitably leads to other duties going unheeded, which might be thought to be a recipe for despair. Paradoxically, however, each of these movements, as painful as it may be, leads Peter into a deeper engagement with his world, because each incomplete and furtive gesture reveals to Peter how much he would *want* to do for all of his loved ones—and for his enemies and strangers, too. We have thus come to an unexpected conclusion. Far from seeking atonement for his sins, Peter's heroics are a means of deepening his debt to the world. Such is the way of lovers, who often also make the fiercest fighters.

NOTES

1. "Enter: Dr. Octopus," *Amazing Spider-Man* #53 (1967).

2. *Why God Became a Human Being*, in Thomas Williams, trans., *Anselm: Basic Writings* (Indianapolis: Hackett, 2007).

3. *Amazing Spider-Man* #33 (1966).

4. *Amazing Spider-Man* #34 (1966).

5. H. and E. Hong, trans., *Works of Love* (Princeton, NJ: Princeton University Press 1995), 178.

6. See Jacques Derrida, "To Forgive: The Unforgivable and Imprescriptible," in J. Caputo, M. Dooley, and M. Scanlon, eds., *Questioning God* (Bloomington: Indiana University Press, 2001), 21–51. On the economical side of giving gifts, the classic work is Marcel Mauss, *The Gift: Forms and Functions of Exchange in Archaic Societies*, trans. I. Cunnison (London: Cohen and West, 1969); see also Alan Schrift, ed., *The Logic of the Gift* (London: Routledge, 1997).

7. Hong, *Works of Love*, 176.

8. Many thinkers throughout history have wanted to hold out the hope that forgiveness really does wipe the slate clean, offering a fresh start and a sense of renewed community. What the critics have liked about Anselm's debt-calculation model is that it pushes the economic presuppositions to the fore and thereby forces us to question whether there really is such a thing as a gift that comes with no strings attached.

9. A useful place to start with Levinas is *Ethics and Infinity*, trans. R. Cohen (Pittsburgh, PA: Duquesne University Press, 1985).

10. *Amazing Fantasy* #15 (1962).

11. See R. F. Brown et al., trans., *Lectures on the Philosophy of Religion* (Berkeley: University of California Press, 1988), 170–189. Hegel's bad infinite corresponds to Aristotle's potential infinite, for which see *Physics*, book 3, chaps. 4–8.

12. See Taneli Kukkonen, "Proclus on Plenitude," *Dionysius* 18 (2000): 103–128.

13. See, e.g., Thomas J. J. Altizer, "Eternal Recurrence and the Kingdom of God," in David B. Allison, ed., *The New Nietzsche* (New York: Dell, 1977), 232–246.

14. See Aristotle, *Nicomachean Ethics*, book 4, chap. 3; Gilles Deleuze, *Nietzsche and Philosophy*, trans. H. Tomlinson (Minneapolis: University of Minnesota Press, 1983); for a critique, see John Caputo, *Against Ethics* (Bloomington: Indiana University Press, 1993), 43–59.

15. *Amazing Spider-Man* #350 (1991).

16. There is a further complication, in that if the giving proceeds from a generous nature or disposition, as in the ancient ethical theories, then this cannot be a true

gift either, because there is no spontaneity here; see Jacques Derrida, *Given Time: 1. Counterfeit Money*, trans. P. Kamuf (Chicago: TheUniversity of Chicago Press, 1992), 161–162.

17. This is not the place to decide whether Augustine's criticism is fair; see Terence H. Irwin, "Splendid Vices: Augustine for and against Pagan Virtues," *Medieval Philosophy and Theology* 8 (1999): 105–127.

18. Jacques Derrida, *The Gift of Death*, trans. D. Wills (Chicago: The University of Chicago Press, 1995), 78.

19. *Amazing Spider-Man* #50 (1967).

20. *Amazing Spider-Man* #271 (1985).

21. Derrida, *The Gift of Death*, 70–71; see Mark C. Taylor, *Nots* (Chicago: The University of Chicago Press, 1993), 83–93.

22. Kierkegaard's "teleological suspension of the ethical" is a notoriously tricky subject: does it entail the ethical and universalist way of life being left behind or merely its transposition into a higher mode? For a primer, see the essays in Robert L. Perkins, ed., *Kierkegaard's Fear and Trembling: Critical Appraisals* (Drawer: University of Alabama Press, 1981).

23. Aristotle, *Metaphysics* 1.1, 981^a18–20.

24. Plato, *Epinomis*, 976e–977b.

25. Kierkegaard, *Works of Love*, 180; for a commentary that takes account of Levinas, see M. Jamie Ferraira, *Love's Grateful Striving* (Oxford: Oxford University Press, 2001), 117–136.

"MY NAME IS PETER PARKER"

Unmasking the Right and the Good

Mark D. White

In June 2006, Spider-Man made news—in both the Marvel Universe and the real world—when he unmasked on national television, revealing that Peter Parker had been everyone's favorite wall-crawler since he was fifteen.[1] Spidey had gone through countless changes over the years—in costume, marital status, and membership in the Avengers, to name a few—but this was the most shocking evolution in his character since he débuted in 1962.

Few superheroes guarded their secret identities as fiercely as had Spider-Man. So why did he decide to unmask after so many years? I'm going to argue that despite the extraordinary circumstances surrounding his revelation, Peter's unmasking was actually the result of a very familiar ethical problem: the choice between the *right* and the *good*. Although the distinction between the right and the good remains controversial among philosophers, it is nonetheless a convenient way to talk about ethical decision making according to the consequences of actions (the "good"), on one hand, and those made according to rules, obligations, or duties (the "right"), on the other. In Peter's case, he had to choose between keeping a promise and obeying the law, the "right" thing to do, and protecting the people he loves, the "good" thing to do.

To Unmask or Not to Unmask

If you were a superhero—maybe you are, of course, but play along anyway—would you have a secret identity? Most of us—uh, I mean *them*—do, but not all. Captain America and the Fantastic Four don't have them, but Daredevil and Spider-Man do, (and it often seems that Iron Man flips a coin when he wakes up in the morning to decide whether to go public that day). Why do some heroes operate in the open, while others don't?

The most common reason for hiding behind a mask is that a secret identity lets the hero protect his friends and family from his enemies. For instance, Matt Murdock tries to keep his dual life as Daredevil secret in order to protect his best friend Foggy Nelson, as well as his steady succession of girlfriends and wives (Matt's, not Foggy's!). He has every right to be concerned: once Wilson Fisk—the Kingpin, originally a foe of Spidey's who looms large later in this chapter—discovers who Daredevil really is, he executes a plan to destroy Murdock body and soul, which includes going after the people he loves. Later Fisk reveals Daredevil's identity to the world, which puts Matt and his loved ones in danger from the rest of his enemies.[2] On the other hand, Captain America has few close friends outside the Avengers or S.H.I.E.L.D., and Reed and Sue Richards keep their children under constant guard at the Baxter Building (which does get blown up a lot, come to think of it), so secret identities don't seem as important to them.

In contrast, Peter Parker has had two very important people in his life for years, his Aunt May and his wife, Mary Jane. (Sit down, Mephisto, I'm talking pre—"Brand New Day" here—more about that later.) Understandably, Peter does everything he can to protect them, and naturally the first step toward doing this is keeping his identity secret. Peter has already lost one beloved family member to irresponsibility—his Uncle Ben—and he can't bear to lose another. (Yes, Mephisto, I see you—sit *down*.) So he always takes any and all necessary measures to protect his secret identity—and thereby Aunt May and Mary Jane—no matter what the cost. That is, until Tony Stark convinces him otherwise.

The Irresistible Iron Man

Following a tragic event in the Marvel Universe that results in hundreds of deaths (including many schoolchildren), thanks to the irresponsibility of a gaggle of young superheroes, the United States passes the Superhuman Registration Act, which requires all superpowered humans to reveal their identities to the government and become federal employees with full salaries and benefits.[3] After initially opposing it, Tony Stark (aka Iron Man) becomes the figurehead for the registration effort, which is very unpopular among many of his colleagues (and comics fans), and which leads to a "Civil War" in which Iron Man's pro-registration forces fight against Captain America and the antiregistration heroes.[4]

Early in this story line, as Tony is preparing to speak to Congress against registration, he asks Peter to be his right-hand man in whatever follows: "I need your help. And your word, that you'll stick with me through what's coming, no matter what." Peter ponders (particularly pensively), then replies, "You've been good to us, especially to May, and MJ, and . . . and I owe you a lot. . . . I took a vow a long time ago to help people who needed me . . . and to be there for people who have always been there for me. . . . Whatever it takes, whatever it costs, in time or in blood—I'm there."[5] Yet little does Peter know what's coming (after all, he's never the futurist Tony is), nor that those costs will become all too real—especially the part about blood.

After Tony accepts that registration is inevitable, and he reveals his own identity when requested by the president of the United States, he asks Peter to do the same. Tony gets Peter's blanket assurance that he's onboard—"I stand with you, Tony. I told you that. I made a promise. I don't do that kind of thing lightly"—to which Tony says, "I know. . . . I want you at my side, Peter. But I need you as both Peter . . . and Spider-Man. Openly."[6] After discussing it with MJ and Aunt May—we'll get to that soon—Peter meets Tony at the press conference and reiterates his support: "You took us in when we had nowhere to go. You've been good to MJ, and to Aunt May. You stood by us. You've been like—like a father to me. I made a promise that I would stand by you, no matter what. I keep my promises, Tony. Do what you have to. I'll back you up. All the way."[7] After the infamous press conference where Peter reveals his double identity, he promptly loses his lunch in the restroom. Tony assures him, "You did the right thing, Peter. It wasn't the easy thing to do, but it was the right thing."[8]

All of this talk of doing the "right" thing, "no matter what" and regardless of "the costs . . . in time or in blood," even if it's not "the easy thing to do," suggests that these are deontological concepts. *Deontology* is the school of ethics that finds moral worth in acts themselves, rather than in their consequences. Keeping promises is a prime example of a deontological principle: promises should be kept, regardless of the consequences, because it's the right thing to do. "Because you promised" is presumed to be self-evident—for most people, no further argument or reason is needed.

Well, not for philosophers—we *always* need further argument! Why, exactly, is it "right" to keep promises, no matter what? Different deontologists will give different answers, but one simple explanation is that it's in the nature of a promise itself. A promise is a commitment to do something later, especially when there are reasons why a person might want to back out of it when the time comes. Peter might promise MJ to do the dishes after dinner, but he doesn't have to promise to eat his dessert. Furthermore, when the time comes to do the dishes, he might not want to, but his promise binds him to do them. A promise that is simply forgotten when something else comes up is not much of a promise at all; simply put, promises are meant to be kept.

Immanuel Kant (1724–1804), the most famous deontologist philosopher, put it a slightly different way. He held that when you propose a *maxim*, or plan of action, you have to be able to will that maxim to be universal law; in other words, it has to be possible that everyone could follow that same maxim. If you can't will that, you'd be claiming for yourself freedoms you denied to others, which goes against the moral equality of persons. So if Peter wants to break a promise, he should consider whether he'd want everyone to break promises when they found it convenient. The answer is obvious. No one would trust a promisor again, and promises would lose their meaning. So Peter has a duty to keep promises he makes, and that duty is binding, regardless of the circumstances he may find himself in at any given time.[9]

But on the Other Hand . . .

A common criticism of deontology is that by ignoring the consequences of actions, it commits people to doing very harmful things in the name of what's "right." In a very controversial essay, Kant himself wrote that if a murderer knocks on your door, intending to kill your friend who is hiding in your house, you *must not* lie when the murderer asks where your friend is.[10] Turning back to Spidey, we can see that keeping his promise to Tony may make Peter a fine, upstanding young man, but it may also result in very bad consequences, especially when it involves revealing his secret identity. Few philosophers are comfortable with an absolute commitment to deontological ideals, and some would rather base moral decisions directly on consequences. Appropriately named, *consequentialism* is the ethical theory that judges the morality of acts by their results: the better the consequences, the more ethical the action. As much as Peter wants to keep his promise to Tony, he also wants to keep his family safe.

As soon as Tony mentions registration and its implications (on a flight to Washington to testify to Congress), Peter's first thought is of the dire consequences for heroes' loved ones. "Are they nuts? How long do you think it would take any of the usual suspects to get their hands on that information?"[11] Later, Peter—much to Tony's chagrin—makes an impromptu speech to Congress, explaining that "the bad guys are bad guys most of the time. But the good guys . . . are only being good guys . . . part-time. They have lives, and families, and loved ones who would be at terrible risk to these very same bad guys if their identities were revealed."[12] Later, when dozens of heroes get together to discuss the possibility of registration, Sue Richards argues that secret identities are not really important, to which Peter responds, "Yeah, well . . . not until that day I come home and find my wife impaled on an octopus arm and the woman who raised me begging for her life."[13] Around the same time, Peter (in costume) unloads to journalist Sally Floyd, asking her, "Didn't it occur to anyone what this would do to my family? . . . We're husbands and wives . . . fathers, mothers, sons and daughters. . . . If I show my face to the world, all of the people who hate me will go after the things I hold most dear."[14]

Mind you, this is all in the context of heroes in general revealing their secret identities to the government—but it isn't long before Tony asks Peter to unmask publicly, making the issue much more personal and immediate. Peter's immediate reaction is refusal, based on consequences: "I can't . . . don't ask that of me. Anything else, but not that." Tony recognizes that Peter's promise may not be enough, so he, too, turns to consequentialist reasoning to make his case: "It's not me asking, Peter. If you don't unmask, you'll be just like the other powers who defy the law. Wanted criminals. Hunted. Jailed. Not just you, but MJ and your aunt, because they'd be considered accomplices. If you turn against the law, I can't have you with me. I won't be able to protect you . . . or your family."[15] Notice what Tony does here—he turns Peter's concern for his family into a reason in *support* of unmasking, implying that while they may be in danger from villains if Peter unmasks, they will be in just as much danger from the authorities if he doesn't (especially because Tony already knows who Peter is). Tony also subtly adds obedience to the law as another deontological reason to unmask—after all, we usually believe we should obey the law, even when we would rather not.

The Tangled Web
That Is Consequentialism

Before Peter makes his final decision, he has a long heart-to-heart with Aunt May and MJ.[16] Together, they work through the pros and cons of unmasking, including all of the possible consequences already mentioned and more, such as the possibility of having to help hunt down antiregistration heroes (such as Captain America, an idol to Peter and a longtime hero to May), or if he refuses to cooperate, perhaps being hunted down himself by Tony and being forced to go on the run with May and MJ, which would put them in a different kind of danger.

Despite its intuitive appeal, there are several practical difficulties with consequentialism that are illustrated well here. The first is the uncertainty of future events: if you're not sure what the consequences of various choices will be, it's hard to base an ethical decision on them. No one knows for sure what will happen if Peter does or doesn't unmask. What will Tony do in either case? What will the other heroes do? And what about Peter's enemies?[17] The second problem builds on the first: not only are the consequences unknown, they're also very complex. Finally, even if you can predict outcomes with some confidence, the positive and negative consequences of a significant decision are often incomparable or *incommensurable*. (Anyone who has faced a major life decision, such as taking a new job or accepting a marriage proposal, knows this!) After all, how does Peter compare exposing May and MJ to his enemies if he unmasks, on one hand, with running away with them as outlaws, on the other? These problems don't make a decisive argument against consequentialism, but they do make it harder to put it into practice in the real world—and they certainly don't make Peter's decision any easier![18]

As it turns out, Peter doesn't use consequentialist reasoning to make the decision—he simply listens to his aunt and her wisdom. She explains to him that when he originally revealed his dual identity to her, she was angry, but not at him:

> I was angry with the world. Because parts of that world called Spider-Man a monster. A criminal . . . and if I know one thing about my nephew—it's that he is not a criminal. There are hundreds of people alive right now because you were there at the right moment. You have nothing to be ashamed of. And much to be proud of. I'm proud of you, Peter. And now, maybe it's time for the whole world to be proud of you. To know you, as I know you.[19]

To Aunt May, Peter's being true to himself and to the world is a deontological value: "Some things are worth the risk, Peter. You're one of them."[20] So Aunt May also sets aside consequences, whatever they may be, for a principle—she emphasizes the right over the good (or the bad).

As we know, Peter unmasks to the world and then throws up in the restroom, while Tony assures him he did the right thing. When Tony tries to tell Peter he knows how he feels, Peter tells him, "No, Tony, you don't know what it's like. You don't know because you've never had a family to worry about. . . . Every day of my life since I was fifteen years old I've lived in absolute terror of just this moment."[21] Peter makes Tony promise him that he will take care of May and MJ if anything happens to him; even though Peter keeps his promise to Tony, he doesn't want his family to suffer for it.

Oops!

Soon afterward, the Civil War starts and Peter's life begins to unravel—the consequences of unmasking are very bad indeed. His enemies do come after him, Aunt May, and MJ, though no one is seriously hurt. (Well, May does give the Chameleon a wicked case of indigestion.)[22] Peter has to help Tony hunt down unregistered heroes, including Captain America, who tells Peter, "I respect you, Peter, and I know you. I know your heart. I know you hate what you're doing, but you think you don't have any other choice. You're wrong. You can still do the right thing."[23] Having to fight Cap, a person whom Peter has always associated with doing the "right" thing, no matter what, begins to shake Peter's confidence in what he's doing.

We see these doubts emerge when, after the fight, during which Cap loses his shield, Peter finds it and webs it to a wall, thinking to himself,

> When he finds it, I hope he understands. I hope he gets the message—that the shield represents the country, and the laws of the country decide who's right. Even the laws we don't like. Even the ones that suck. Cap thinks in terms of right and wrong, but this isn't a matter of right and wrong, moral or immoral. It's legal vs. illegal. At least, that's what I tell myself in the middle of the

night, when I wonder what the hell I'm doing here. I'm legal. I'm registered. I'm authorized. And as I feel this whole situation starting to unravel around me— I just hope to God that I'm also right.[24]

Peter begins to doubt his deontological convictions— obeying the law is usually right, but not always.[25] When Peter learns more about Tony's activities implementing registration— such as the negative zone prison for antiregistration heroes, as well as the windfall profits Tony makes from no-bid contracts to build it—his doubts are confirmed.[26] The death of Goliath at the hands of the clone of Thor ("Clor") that Tony and Hank Pym develop is the last straw. At the funeral for the fallen hero, Reed notices Peter, MJ, and May hunched together and asks Leonard Samson, "Is it just me or is Peter Parker acting very, very suspiciously?"[27]

Peter then decides to switch sides, which represents another decision in which the (newly discovered) right thing to do—breaking from Tony and joining Cap's antiregistration forces—takes precedence over the consequences, making an enemy of Tony Stark, becoming an outlaw, and forcing MJ and May to go on the run. As Peter tells them, "I've made a terrible, terrible mistake. There's going to be a price for both that mistake and any attempt I make to fix it. But I have to do what I think is right, and right now—God help me, I realize I've been on the wrong side, I—"[28] He is rudely interrupted when Iron Man bursts through a wall and carries Peter outside (through the other wall—drama queen!).

Of course, Tony doesn't take this desertion lightly. "I trusted you, Peter! I took you under my wing! Is this how you repay me?"[29] Ironically, he invokes Peter's concern for his family: "Don't be a fool! You really think you can just go back to your old life now that everyone knows who you are? This isn't just about you anymore! What about May? What about Mary Jane?"[30] To be fair, Tony does warn Peter of the consequences of being an outlaw, and the risks that it will expose his family to, but, as usual, Peter is not thinking about consequences. MJ and Aunt May agree, with May even telling him, "if we're all equally responsible for the decision, then we all have to equally share the consequences."[31] Yet even Tony the futurist could not have predicted what would come next.

Remember the Kingpin?

Peter may have chosen the right over the good, but good soon turns to bad—*very* bad—as the hypothetical costs "in blood" become all too real. From prison, the Kingpin learns of Peter's unmasking and immediately sends out an execution order aimed at Peter but including anyone close to him.[32] From that point in the story, we regularly see Aunt May and MJ camped out in their seedy motel-room hideout, depicted as seen through the sight of a rifle. At the end of *Amazing Spider-Man* #538 (February 2007), when Peter returns to the motel, that rifle fires. Alerted by his spider-sense a fraction of a second earlier, Peter pushes MJ to the ground, and looks up to see Aunt May with a gunshot wound to her chest.

While May lingers in a coma, Peter goes on a rampage, once again sporting his black costume to strike fear into the hearts of evildoers (or something to that effect).[33] Presumably having learned from his pal Daredevil how to beat information out of lowlifes, he eventually tracks the assassination attempt back to the Kingpin. Peter breaks into the prison and unleashes his rage on the Kingpin, stopping just short of killing him but promising to finish the job if May dies.[34]

This may make Peter feel a little better, but, of course, it does nothing to help Aunt May. So Peter pleads to his "special friends" to help May, and the first person he goes to, naturally, is a certain Armored Avenger whom he holds partly responsible for May's condition. "She's dying and it's your fault! I trusted you! I let you get close to me . . . you were like a father to me! I trusted you when you said I had to expose

my identity! That it was the only way! I kept it secret to protect May, and MJ, but you said they'd be safe! You said—and
now . . . now she's lying in a hospital bed . . . dying. . . . "[35]
Tony claims that he can't do anything to aid a fugitive from
the law, but after he returns to Avengers Tower and breaks
down in tears, he sends his loyal butler Jarvis to the hospital
with a $2 million check to pay for May's care.

Outside May's hospital window (to avoid attracting attention, given his celebrity fugitive status), Peter confirms the
reasons why he made the choices he did and the costs of those
choices. "I'm so sorry, Aunt May. . . . I should have found a
way to . . . to spare you this. . . . I never should have unmasked.
But . . . I was just trying to do the right thing. What the hell
kind of life am I leading, where whether I do the right thing
or wrong thing, it doesn't matter . . . because the people I love
still suffer?"[36] This is the often tragic nature of deontological
ethics: doing the right thing sometimes has negative consequences. Yet it also emphasizes the uncertainty of those consequences, which can reinforce the argument for deontology:
if you don't know which choice will lead to better results, perhaps you should just focus on doing what you think is right. As
Peter says, no matter whether he does the right thing or not,
bad things happen—so someone could argue that he ought to
do the right thing (as he does, at least according to what he
thinks was right).

So what happens to Aunt May? After consulting every
genius and magical being in the Marvel Universe—even Doctor
Doom—Peter is at the end of his web. Yet suddenly, in the very
controversial "One More Day" story line, the devil Mephisto
appears to Peter and MJ with a deal: he will save May's life in
exchange for changing history so that Peter and MJ were never
married, and restoring Peter's secret identity by wiping everyone's memory.[37] Peter and MJ accept the offer, literally making a deal with the devil.[38] So in the end, Peter gets a do-over,
as shown in the ongoing "Brand New Day" era, but with an

unimaginable cost: losing the great love of his life, at least for the time being.[39] Whether this serves the right, the good, both, or neither, remains to be seen.

Give Up? Never!

Peter's choice to do the right thing, regardless of the consequences, is best exemplified in this rant to a police officer who orders him to give himself up:

> Give up? Do you have any idea how easy that would be for me? Do you? Giving up would be a blessing! To throw my hands up! Turn myself over to you guys! Rot in some jail cell or the negative zone or whatever! The idea of "giving up" sits in my brain like a cancer, twenty-four/seven, just . . . just gnawing away at me! Maybe if I'd given up years ago, my aunt wouldn't have taken a bullet! My wife wouldn't be living in fear! Everyone I've ever loved has suffered because I wouldn't give up! Wouldn't give up helping cops or innocent people! Wouldn't give up the good fight! God in heaven . . . you talk to me about giving up?

Peter will never give up, no matter how bad things get for him, because he believes in doing the right thing—he was given great power, and he assumes the great responsibility that comes with it.[40] He knows that in order to honor deontological concepts such as promise, responsibility, and duty—the "right"—he has to put the consequences of his actions, the "good," out of his mind. Of course, determining the right thing to do isn't always easy, and as we saw, it can change as circumstances change. Yet Peter Parker wouldn't be Peter Parker if his life were easy, would it? And we wouldn't read his adventures, month in and month out, if he didn't face many of the same problems we do, including having to make tough choices between the right and the good.

NOTES

1. For the unmasking itself, see *Civil War* #2 (August 2006), reprinted in *Civil War* (2007), which includes *Civil War* #1–7 (2006–2007). For an example of the real-world reaction, see George Gene Gustines, "Spider-Man Unmasked," *New York Times*, June 15, 2006, http://query.nytimes.com/gst/fullpage.html?res=9502E2DB1031F936A2575 5C0A9609C8B63, and "Spider-Man Removes Mask at Last," BBC News, June 15, 2006, http://news.bbc.co.uk/2/hi/entertainment/5084326.stm.

2. See *Daredevil: Born Again* (1987), reprinting *Daredevil*, vol. 1, #227–233 (1986); and *Daredevil*, vol. 5: *Out* (2003), reprinting *Daredevil*, vol. 2, #32–40 (2002–2003).

3. See *The Road to Civil War* (2007) and *Civil War*.

4. For more about Tony's motivation in the registration controversy, see my essay "Did Iron Man Kill Captain America?" in Mark D. White, ed., *Iron Man and Philosophy: Facing the Stark Reality* (Hoboken, NJ: John Wiley & Sons, 2010), 64–79.

5. *Amazing Spider-Man* #529 (April 2006), reprinted in *The Road to Civil War*. When he mentions his debt to Tony, Peter is most likely referring to Tony's invitation to Peter, MJ, and Aunt May to live in Avengers Tower after May's house burns down; see *Amazing Spider-Man* #519 (June 2005), included in *Amazing Spider-Man*, vol. 10: *New Avengers* (2005).

6. *Amazing Spider-Man* #532 (July 2006), reprinted in *Civil War: Amazing Spider-Man* (2007), which includes *Amazing Spider-Man* #532–538 (2006–2007).

7. *Amazing Spider-Man* #532.

8. *Amazing Spider-Man* #533 (August 2006).

9. Immanuel Kant (1785), *Grounding for the Metaphysics of Morals*, trans. James W. Ellington, 3rd ed. (Indianapolis, IN: Hackett Publishing, 1993), 402–403.

10. Kant (1799), "On a Supposed Right to Lie because of Philanthropic Concerns," which is included in the edition of the *Grounding* cited earlier. Few of Kant's writings have stirred as much controversy among philosophers, for this is the most extreme case he made for refusing to lie, regardless of the costs. Most Kant scholars, including the present author, regard him as more moderate than this, based on the bulk of his work that emphasizes the role played by judgment in making hard choices in moral dilemmas.

11. *Amazing Spider-Man* #530 (May 2006), reprinted in *The Road to Civil War*.

12. Ibid.

13. *Civil War* #1 (July 2006), reprinted in *Civil War*.

14. *Civil War: Front Line* #1 (August 2006), reprinted in *Civil War: Front Line Book 1* (2007).

15. *Amazing Spider-Man* #532.

16. Ibid.

17. Later, Peter asks himself, "Why did I ever go public with my I.D. . . .? But . . . maybe it wouldn't have made any difference. Tony, the Avengers, they all knew who I was. Soon as I turned against them, the same thing would've happened" (*Friendly Neighborhood Spider-Man* #17, April 2007, reprinted in *Spider-Man: Back in Black*, 2008).

18. Ironically, during this discussion Peter invokes his promise to Aunt May, made when he was sixteen, to always protect her, which May dismisses: "Yes, you did. At sixteen. A child's promise that has nothing to do with how the world works" (*Amazing Spider-Man* #532).

19. Ibid. Although, a higher power puts that figures in the thousands—"counting team-ups"—when he plays "It's a Wonderful Life" with Peter in *Sensational Spider-Man* #40 (April 2007), reprinted in *Spider-Man, Peter Parker: Back in Black* (2008).

20. *Amazing Spider-Man* #532. In the same issue, before his big press conference, Aunt May invokes the classic line that her late husband, Ben, passed on to Peter, "with great power comes great responsibility," and adds that "responsibility means you don't run away when someone asks, 'who did that?'" Of course, taking responsibility for one's actions, regardless of the consequences, is another deontological principle, one that parents often teach their children.

21. *Amazing Spider-Man* #533.

22. *Sensational Spider-Man* #29–31 (October–December 2006), reprinted in *Civil War: Peter Parker, Spider-Man* (2007).

23. *Amazing Spider-Man* #534 (September 2006).

24. Ibid.

25. See the terrific exchange between Peter and Reed Richards (*Amazing Spider-Man* #535, October 2006), in which Reed tells a story of his uncle who stood up to the House Un-American Activities Committee in the 1950s. Reed thinks he was wrong because the law is the law—work to change it if you don't like it, but obey it until then. (Peter is skeptical.)

26. Ibid.; see also *Civil War: Front Line* #9 (December 2006), reprinted in *Civil War: Front Line Book 2* (2007).

27. *Civil War* #4 (October 2006).

28. *Amazing Spider-Man* #535. Later, he reiterates to MJ, "Tony's wrong. I was wrong. I have to do what I can to fix it. If that means fighting Tony—then that's what I have to do" (*Amazing Spider-Man* #536, November 2006). After he makes amends with Captain America, Peter thinks to himself, "It feels good to be on the right side again" (*Amazing Spider-Man* #537, [January 2007]).

29. *Amazing Spider-Man* #536.

30. *Civil War* #5 (November 2006).

31. *Amazing Spider-Man* #536.

32. *Amazing Spider-Man* #537.

33. Come on, you were all thinking it!

34. *Amazing Spider-Man* #539–542 (April–August 2007), reprinted in *Spider-Man: Back in Black*.

35. *Amazing Spider-Man* #544 (October 2007), reprinted in *Spider-Man: One More Day* (2008).

36. *Friendly Neighborhood Spider-Man* #20 (July 2007), reprinted in *Spider-Man: Back in Black*.

37. *Amazing Spider-Man* #545 (November 2007), reprinted in *Spider-Man: One More Day*. This was foreshadowed when MJ is waiting for Peter to come home after the climactic final battle of the Civil War, and she looks to heaven and says, "Just let him come home safe, God. I'll do anything, give up anything, if you'll just . . . let him come home. Please. I'll give up anything . . . anything . . . anything" (*Amazing Spider-Man* #538).

38. For more on this story line, see my chapter, "The Sound and the Fury behind 'One More Day,'" in this book.

39. "Brand New Day" started in *Amazing Spider-Man* #546 (February 2008) after "One More Day" ended.

40. Which is not to say he doesn't experience moments of weakness during which he almost gives up and turns himself in; see *Sensational Spider-Man Annual* #1 (May 2007), included in *Spider-Man, Peter Parker: Back in Black*.

PART TWO

RESPONSIBILITY-MAN

"WITH GREAT POWER COMES GREAT RESPONSIBILITY"

Spider-Man, Christian Ethics,
and the Problem of Evil

Adam Barkman

Nothing is more central to understanding both Peter Parker's transformation into Spider-Man and the subsequent internal struggles that result from his choice than the influence of Uncle Ben, who, paraphrasing Jesus's "to whom much has been given, much is required,"[1] famously tells Peter, "With great power comes great responsibility."[2]

We can appreciate the importance of this toward understanding Spider-Man if we consider the reason for the unpopularity of two *manga* adaptations of Spider-Man, in which this moral reason for his transformation, as well as other features of his moral depth and gravitas, are completely lacking. The main reason audiences were disappointed with the manga adaptations is that Spider-Man stripped of his Christian ethic is no longer Spider-Man at all.

I am not concerned about making the case that Spider-Man is a Christian. Rather, I want to explore the ethics that define Spider-Man, and those ethics are, broadly speaking, Christian in character. Two things need to be mentioned at the outset. First, I will try to set aside questions of particular versions of Christian ethics and approaches because, as far as I see it, the differences between Christian ethical systems can be made as small or as large as one likes, and Spider-Man's own Christian ethical leanings are never made explicit.[3] Second, Christian ethics aren't radically different from the ethics of other religions and philosophies that maintain the existence of a universal moral law (popularly called "the Natural Law"). Consequently, a lot of Spider-Man's ethical beliefs should be seen as universal—beliefs that all people, for instance, Jews (including Stan Lee himself), Platonists, Confucians, and others, could generally agree on.[4] As C. S. Lewis (1898–1963) wrote, "Only serious ignorance of Jewish and Pagan culture would lead anyone to the conclusion that [the body of Christian ethical injunctions] is a radically new thing."[5]

What makes Spider-Man's ethics specifically Christian are not only his core, universal beliefs but some of his additional beliefs and emphases, such as his belief in a God that is more than merely theistic in nature and his emphasis on mercy. To demonstrate this, we need to consider the Christian understanding of freedom and justice, both of which are intimately connected to what in philosophy is usually addressed as the problem of evil.

"I Have Called You Friends": The Christian Answer to Why People Were Created

God, so the Christian tradition maintains, is the totality of all perfections. He isn't merely powerful; he's the perfection of power. He isn't simply loving; he's the perfection of love. He doesn't just exist; he's the perfection of existence. He isn't only rational; he's the perfection of reason itself.

Nevertheless, there are many things that God can't do, and these many things can be summed up in a single principle: *God can't do the logically impossible.* That is, God can't act against his own nature; he can't change who he is. Because God is the one absolutely perfect being, he has no lack, which implies, among other things, that he can't change himself—he can't go from perfection to imperfection. Because God is perfected reason—that is, the totality or source of all rationality—he can't do anything irrational. He can't make 1 + 1 = 3 or override the Law of Contradiction (*pace* René Descartes, 1596–1650).[6] God can't act against his very nature.

Yet if God lacks nothing, why did he create people in the first place? Because God is the Creator, he acts in accordance with who he is: he loves to create, so he brings into existence many things, such as the billions of galaxies billions of light years away, simply for his delight. Moreover, because God is love itself, he deeply values friendship—one of the great forms of love.

Yet what does friendship entail? Friendship is meaningful only if it's *free*; love requires rational choice. It's a logical contradiction to say that God can *force* creatures to love him *freely*: he can't do that, for he can't do the logically impossible. So, God created humans (and possibly other rational creatures as well) because he loves to create but also, and far more to the point, *he made them to be friends with him.* One of the important revelations of the New Testament is that Jesus says to those who love him, "I have called you friends."[7] Our free choice to be friends with God is something that he can't bring about by his own power, but the human choice to love God freely is something of inestimable worth to the Creator.

In this way, prayer, one of the key ways humans can express their friendship with God, isn't some magical process that automatically causes certain things to come about: prayer is praising a divine friend for being such a good friend. It's asking a divine friend for help when one needs it; it's questioning—sometimes angrily—a divine friend about why such and such things happen; it's a mode of communicating with another, albeit a far greater, free being. Prayer takes God, and friendship with God, seriously. This we see not only with many famous biblical heroes, such as Abraham, David, and others, but also with Peter Parker—for instance, in *The Amazing Spider-Man*, vol. 2, #33 (2001), Peter questions God about 9/11; in #46 (2002), Doctor Strange recommends that Peter pray for guidance; and in #53 (2003), Peter thanks God for the blessing of a good wife.

"Can't You Respect Me Enough to Let Me Make My Own Decisions?": The Foundations of Christian Ethics

So according to Christian ethics, God gave people free will so that they could be friends with him, which, because God is the perfection of happiness and love, also means that God made people for infinite happiness and joy. Nevertheless, people have to *want* these things; they have to *choose* them. "Can't you," Mary Jane asks Peter in *Spider-Man 2*, "respect me enough to let me make my own decisions?" Peter, echoing God himself, of course says yes.

Yet here's the catch. Unlike Peter, God is also perfect holiness and perfect justice. He can't change who he is, so if people want to be friends with him and if they want to be happy, then they must be holy and just. No evil, not the smallest speck, can be in the presence of the burning purity that is God. As the Ark of the Covenant demonstrates (quite visibly in *Raiders of the Lost Ark*), the impure can't see the face of the Holy God and live. God *can't*—it's a logical contradiction to say that he could—put aside his holiness, and it's also impossible for him, because of his very nature, to ignore injustice.

Therefore, humans must use their rational minds—the image of God in man—to discern right and wrong, justice and injustice, and choose to do right if they want to be happy. Yet what is justice?

Justice means valuing each thing or person as they ought to be valued, wherein the value of each thing or person depends on either God's creative choice (that is, the value God assigned each thing or person he made) or God's own nature (where God's own value is a sheer fact or a given that he himself can't alter). Thus, for instance, although it's just for a man to love himself, it's unjust to love himself in the same way in which he would love an ape because this entails loving a greater thing, a rational animal, on the same level as a lesser thing, a nonrational animal. Or again, and more to the point, although it's just for man to love himself and his opinions, it's unjust for him to love himself and his opinions to the same extent as, or more than, God and his justice, because God (the uncreated being) is of far greater value than a man (a created being). So although justice is absolute, the rightness or wrongness of a given act depends on knowing the value of each thing considered and then choosing to act accordingly. The failure to choose to act in accordance with justice is known as injustice, evil, or sin.

All of this is crucial toward understanding both Jesus's maxim "to whom much has been given, much is required" and Uncle Ben's "with great power comes great responsibility." If a person has been given great power by God, then he or she is expected to do great acts of goodness with that power—if, for the moment, for no other reason than that the fulfillment of such an expectation is good for its own sake. If the person has been given limited power, then God expects lesser things of him or her: the justness of a given context varies according to what one is and has.

Some might complain and say, for instance, that God is unfair to make some people superheroes and others ordinary men (assuming the Marvel Universe and the existence of superheroes). Yet God doesn't act unjustly. Although the superhero might enjoy *more* unique pleasures, which are good in and of themselves (such as great strength), the superhero is also expected to use his power to benefit *more* people or, if not more people, at least to benefit people in *more* extraordinary ways. Thus, at the end of the movie *Spider-Man*, Peter rebuffs the offer of a romantic relationship with Mary Jane because, on top of his concern for her safety, he thinks that he can't both be with her and live up to the responsibility of his power. "This is my gift," he says. "This is my curse."

Consequently, it misses the point to think that being a superhero is always better than being an ordinary man. The point, according to Christian ethics, is that all people need to be just and act properly, which depends on what one is and has. If we are to follow Doctor Strange's advice and Peter's example, we should ask for God's help in doing so. Moral success is measured not by being the most powerful, but by doing what we should with what we are and have, such as the woman in the Gospels who gave both of her coins—a meager sum, but all she had—as opposed to the rich men who gave much larger amounts but a fraction of their wealth.[8] This is also why Dr. Otto Octavius is right when in *Spider-Man 2* he tells Peter, "intelligence is a gift and you use it for the good of mankind." In Octavius's case, the misuse of his great intelligence ultimately leads to terrible consequences: theft, the murder of the medical professionals seeking to help him, the terrorization of countless citizens, and ultimately his own death. It's only Peter's heartfelt persuasion of Octavius to reclaim his formerly held principle that prevents further disaster.

So, having great power is not simply better than having lesser power. What matters most is what a person chooses to *do* with that power. Furthermore, as we see in Peter's relationship with Mary Jane and the poverty he suffers because of his refusal either to steal or seek financial reward for his services to the city, the choice to act justly can be extremely painful at times. As Aunt May, Peter's font of moral wisdom and herself a committed Christian (as evidenced by her recital of the Lord's Prayer in *Spider-Man*), says in *Spider-Man 2*, "[Embracing the hero within means] sometimes we have to give up the thing we love the most . . . even our dreams." Nonetheless, the choice to do the right thing will, on top of being satisfying, in and of itself, *ultimately* result in happiness for the individual.

Consider, for example, the first *Spider-Man* movie. By reneging on his promise to Uncle Ben to paint the kitchen and by failing to stop the criminal who robs the manager at the wrestling event, Peter is initially shown to act according to his own distorted or purely selfish desires, instead of doing what he knows to be right. He's unjust because people ought to keep their promises (all things considered), and if people have the power to stop a criminal—especially with little trouble—people also have a duty to do that as well. Throughout the movie, however, Peter becomes more and more just, insofar as he chooses to focus on something greater than himself: justice and responsibility based on what he is and has been given. Thus, when Norman Osborne, in the guise of the Green Goblin, asks Peter why he bothers helping people, especially when they will eventually hate him for it, Peter replies simply and yet profoundly, "Because it is right." Osborne ridicules this sentiment because he denies the existence of a universal moral law, which Peter, helped by his belief in God, affirms.

Osborne sees morality as completely relative, claiming that the masses exist to lift "the few exceptional people on their shoulders." He's driven by dreams of power with which he can achieve his own selfish ends, implicitly rejecting the maxim "with great power comes great responsibility." Moreover, and to the point, it isn't a matter of Osborne choosing happiness, while Peter chooses duty. As I've said, acting justly and dutifully may require one to forgo certain pleasures at the moment, but because God is the source of both justice *and* happiness, he who acts justly will ultimately be the happiest. Thus, in *The Amazing Spider-Man* #500 (2003), the spirit of Uncle Ben asks Peter simply, "Whatever it is you do now, whatever it is you've become, tell me, Peter, are you happy?" To which Peter, who has acted justly and dutifully, replies, "It's the damnedest thing, but . . . I am. I'm happy."

"We Always Have a Choice": The Solution to the Problem of Evil

What about the problem of evil? Granting the Christian ethical claims that have already been made, what can be said to those who insist that the presence of evil precludes the existence of an omnipotent, omniscient, and perfectly good God? Let's follow the solution to this problem via Peter's own struggle with this dilemma, beginning with Peter's experience of the three key attributes of God that pertain to this problem: omnipotence, omniscience, and perfect goodness.

In *The Amazing Spider-Man*, vol. 2, #49 (2002), Peter and Mary Jane have been living apart for some time, which is taking a serious toll on their relationship. No matter what they themselves try to do, it appears as if nothing can prevent their final separation. Indeed, in this issue we see Peter flying to Los Angeles to meet up with Mary Jane at the exact same time that she flies to New York to meet up with him. Both desire to rebuild their marriage, but both, arriving in their respective cities, get the impression that the other isn't interested. The issue initially reads like a tragedy—a vivid demonstration of man's limited knowledge and power in a daunting, uncaring universe. Yet as both reboard their planes to head to their home cities, something beyond coincidence happens. A bolt of lightning strikes the plane that Peter is on, forcing it to land in Denver, where, remarkably, Mary Jane's plane has a stopover. Peter and Mary Jane somehow manage to bump into each other in the airport and from there take the initial steps to reconciliation. We can surmise that this brings home to Peter that not only is there a divine being who *knows* the future (including Peter's and Mary Jane's schedules and intentions) and has the *power* to use lightning to land an airplane and bring two individuals together at the exact same place and time, but one who also *cares* about Peter and Mary Jane. This being doesn't want them to get divorced, and when their best efforts to avoid divorce fail, he has the ability to step in and help out.

That's God, but what about evil? In *Peter Parker, Spider-Man*, vol. 2, #48 (2002), nicely titled "The Big Question," we see Peter explicitly asking God why he allows the people whom Peter loves—good people—to suffer. Peter's question is particularized, but we can extend it to ask why God allows evil to befall anyone. What is interesting in this issue is that God, as does God in the book of Job, appears to speak back to Peter, claiming that, "This is all part of my grand design" and that Peter gets "to figure it out for [himself]," which will "make all the difference in the world." Is God simply evading the issue, though? Is God playing with Peter, as a cat does with a mouse? Or does it suggest that God doesn't really know the answer and that there is no solution to the problem of evil? Does this finally suggest that God is not, after all, omnipotent, omniscient, and perfectly good?

The Christian ethicist would answer no to each of these questions. The solution to the problem of evil is implied in the very answer that God gives, namely that Peter gets "to figure it out for [himself]." How does this statement reveal the solution? Well, figuring out something requires not only a rational faculty capable of understanding, but also the *free will* to choose between possible beliefs that arise as a result of such knowledge. Free will makes "all the difference in the world." God, as perfect goodness, *wants* all people to be just and good, but he can't *force* people to *choose* to be good; he can't, once again, do the logically impossible.

Yet how is the presence of evil compatible with the existence of an omniscient, omnipotent, and perfectly good God? Strictly speaking, evil is simply the absence or privation of a good that should be present. Evil arises when we value a lesser thing—oneself or one's opinions—over a greater thing (God and his justice). This means that God didn't create *evil*. God created *free will*, which is one of the greatest things imaginable, yet the very goodness of this thing lies precisely in its *potential* to do one thing or another—to love a greater thing over a lesser thing (justice) or vice versa (injustice, evil, sin).

You might agree that this is a valid solution to the problem of *moral or chosen evil*, but what about so-called *natural evil*, such as disease, earthquakes, and the like? At least two of the three main solutions to this sort of evil flow from the concept of moral or chosen evil and are connected with Peter Parker's own struggle.

The first solution begins with the claim that human beings aren't the only types of free creatures that God made—that perhaps, among other things, he made angels, who are invisible and extremely powerful. As free creatures, these beings would, like humans, have the ability to choose to be just or unjust. Typically, the Christian tradition has maintained that some such beings chose their own way over God's and so became evil or "fallen." Because angels were originally closer to God than men were, their punishment was greater than ours—as is consistent with "with great power comes great responsibility." The result is that these fallen angels or demons exist within God's creation, and, because God respects their free will just as he respects ours (or else freedom wouldn't matter in the first place), they have some freedom to cause evil in the world; for instance, they can cause diseases, tidal waves, and so on. In this way, natural evil isn't natural at all: it's simply moral evil in the form of demonic activity.[9]

The second solution, which may be taken as an alternative to, or in conjunction with, the first, is that following on the principle of justice that states the higher is responsible for ruling the lower and the lower is dependent on the higher, when Adam, whom God made the ruler of the planet, rebelled against God (Adam's *superior*), God, acting justly, cursed Adam in kind, insofar as all that was *inferior* to Adam and those connected with him would henceforth be in rebellion against him and his own. Now man's emotions rebel against his reason, animals attack humans, and the entire natural world threatens us through storms, biological malfunctions (physical deformities, diseases, and death), and so on. In this way, all people suffer for the sin of their superior (Adam). While it would be unjust if this suffering made people evil (it doesn't, though people might have a greater disposition to do evil, which is known as "original sin"), there is no reason to think it unjust that people, as descendents of Adam, feel the effects of his choice. So once again, natural evil isn't natural at all if by *natural* we mean "the way God intended it." As before, natural evil is intimately connected with free choice and moral evil.

The third solution to natural evil, which, once again, may be taken on its own or with both or either of the previous solutions, states that when God made people, he made them separate from himself. Yet people can't exist in a vacuum; they have to be *somewhere*—in some plane of existence wherein action and interaction can take place. This plane is known as the physical world, which acts according to physical laws. Inherent in the very goodness of the physical world, however, is its potential for harm: the same tree that provides people with food can topple over and crush them; the same fire that gives humans light can burn them. God could, of course, intervene and prevent many of these evils (miracles are logically possible, after all), but if he were to do so every time, it would render the whole purpose of physical laws obsolete, thereby implying that such were not a good creation.

Dealing with Venom: How to Perfect or Pervert Justice

According to Christian ethics, then, evil exists precisely because God is good. That is, goodness is one of the things that motivated God to give people free will in the first place, and it's certainly the reason why he respects them enough to let them choose to do evil. Moreover, God, so the Gospels maintain, loves people enough to let them lock themselves in a place called Hell, which should be understood as the willed separation from He-Who-Is-The-Source-Of-All-Happiness-And-Existence. In simpler terms, Hell is the shadowy place on the very fringes of nonbeing, where the only thing that exists is the soul and its choices—nothing more.

Yet if this is the case and if, as I said, no evil can be in the presence of the burning purity that is God, then how can God, who can't act against his own nature, *logically* allow any who have sinned to be in Heaven? How can anyone who has chosen to imbibe the fatal drink of injustice be rescued?

The Christian solution to this ethical problem, which is very much connected with the third Spider-Man movie, is *mercy*. According to the law of justice, if someone sins against you, he or she must repay you in order for the debt to be no more. If he or she can't repay, then there is still the blemish or scar of injustice. Because human beings have—so Christians say—committed sins against God, they must repay him in order for their sins to be removed. The problem, though, is that no human can repay God without, in the process, creating more sin. For every wrong that people right, they commit two new wrongs; they bury themselves under the mountain of their own chosen injustice, and their only hope to be holy again—their only hope to be happy again—is for God to show them mercy. Yet because God is justice himself, he can't simply wave his hand and make injustice disappear; his very nature prevents him from dismissing injustice as if it weren't there. So God himself has to pay the price; he has to pay the human debt of sin. Therefore, God, so Christian ethics maintain, did this very thing through his son, Jesus.

Now Jesus, as man's superior, was able to represent all men just as Adam once did (thus, Jesus is called "the New Adam"), and as the Son of God, he was also able to live the morally perfect life.[10] As a result of this latter point, death could not hold him, because death represents the separation of man from God, which was brought about by man choosing injustice (that is, by choosing injustice, man also chose death or separation from true life, God). Because death couldn't bind Jesus, he was able to rebuild the bridge between man and God, and because Jesus, representing all people, paid the price of human injustice, he was also able—as the Debt Payer—to offer mercy to all who believe in him: by being perfectly *just*, he is able to give *mercy* to all who ask for it. Yet because Jesus loves justice and mercy, he also expects people to love these as well. The Christian, in other words, must be one who, mirroring Jesus, shows a proper love and understanding of mercy, which is the perfection, not the absence, of justice. This is what we see Peter Parker doing in *Spider-Man 3*.

The movie begins with Flint Marko (aka Sandman) fleeing from the police after accidentally killing Uncle Ben in an attempted carjacking. Marko's line throughout is, "I'm not a bad person; I just had bad luck." Of course, according to the law of justice, Marko is a bad person, not only for attempting to steal another's car but also for carrying around a loaded gun, which, accidentally or otherwise, ends up being used to kill an innocent man. Marko may not be as bad as people think, but he's still bad.

Meanwhile, a symbiotic alien entity known as "Venom" lands on Earth and attaches itself to Spider-Man's costume. This alien has the property of amplifying the emotions, in particular, the aggressive ones, of its host. Consequently, when Peter finds out that Marko is responsible for the death of Uncle Ben, Peter's anger exceeds the limits of justice and becomes its perversion: revenge. Revenge isn't the noble sentiment of justice, which demands that each thing be treated as it ought to be and that, failing just treatment, some debt for injustice must be repaid. No, revenge not only wants to repay in kind, but it wants to keep on attacking, keep on hating. For instance, justice demands that if a person steals my book, he return the book and compensate me for any additional suffering that results from the theft. Revenge, however, not only wants the book back and proper compensation given, but it also expresses a hatred for the perpetrator and yearns to see him suffer.

Near the end of the movie, Spider-Man gets the better of Marko and is thus faced with a choice: will he take revenge—thus signifying his own degeneration from the principle of justice "with great power comes great responsibility"—or will he show mercy, thus revealing his moral growth through the perfection of this principle. Of course, being a man who largely reflects Christian ethics, Spider-Man does as we expect him to, saying to Marko, "I've done terrible things too. . . . I forgive you."

"It's the Choices That Make Us Who We Are:" The Conclusion to the Matter

Throughout this chapter, I have tried to explain what Christian ethics entail by using the Spider-Man comics and movies as my example. At the heart of Christian ethics lies a particular recognition about the nature of God as the perfection of all things and a particular perspective on the free will of rational creatures. The solution to the problem of evil is provided in terms of these two principles. Rational creatures are given the choice—which, we are told in at least two Spider-Man movies, makes "us who we are"—to act in accordance with, or against, justice. That is, rational creatures are given the tremendous blessing of freedom, though this blessing can quickly become a self-made curse, because such creatures can choose to accept or reject a life lived according to the divine principle "with great power comes great responsibility." Spider-Man chooses to live up to this principle—most perfectly so at the end of *Spider-Man 3*, where he offers forgiveness to a man whom, were it not for Christian ethics, he would have every reason to hate.

NOTES

1. Luke 12:48.

2. *Amazing Fantasy* #15 (1962).

3. Some believe his ethics to have a Protestant, deontological slant. See Steven Waldman and Michael Kress, "Belief Watch: Good Fight," *Newsweek*, June 19, 2006.

4. Although Stan Lee, the creator of Spider-Man, is a nonobservant Jew, he appears to believe in something similar to a universal moral law and has applied this belief not only to Spider-Man but to most, if not all, of his Marvel creations. How and why Spider-Man took on Christian-specific overtones is a question that I can't answer, but just as Superman started out as a Moses figure and soon became a Christ type (see *Superman Returns*), Spider-Man started out generally moral and became something more.

5. C. S. Lewis, "On Ethics," in Lesley Walmsley, ed., *C. S. Lewis: Essay Collection & Other Short Pieces* (London: HarperCollins, 2000), 303–314, 305.

6. For more on this, see Descartes's *Meditations, Objections, and Replies*, ed. and trans. Roger Ariew and Donald A. Cress (Indianapolis, IN: Hackett Publishing Co., 2006).

7. John 15:14–15.

8. Mark 12:41–44.

9. For more on this, see Alvin Plantinga, *God, Freedom, and Evil* (Grand Rapids, MI: Eerdmans, 1996), 55–59.

10. Romans 5:12–21.

DOES GREAT POWER BRING GREAT RESPONSIBILITY?

Spider-Man and the Good Samaritan

J. Keeping

We all know the story: The bite of a radioactive (or sometimes genetically altered) spider gives high school student Peter Parker superpowers. When his spiteful refusal to stop a robber results in the death of his beloved Uncle Ben, Peter comes to understand that "with great power comes great responsibility" and vows that never again shall anyone come to harm because he failed to act.

As all great stories do, this tale not only entertains, but also resonates with us emotionally, illustrating its lesson with power and drama. To a philosopher, however, this is not quite good enough. Philosophers are in the business of taking claims of this sort—claims with strong intuitive and emotional appeal—and putting them to question. The point in doing this is not usually to undermine the claims or show that they are false, but simply to understand them better. So what I want to do in this chapter is ask just what does it *mean* to say "with great power comes great responsibility"? What is the nature and scope of the responsibility involved? Most important, if this is true, then *why* does great power bring great responsibility?

Responsibility Does as Responsibility Is

Responsibility comes in many flavors. Teachers have responsibilities to their students, doctors to their patients, parents to their children. These relationships clearly support a connection between power and responsibility. In each case, the individual in question has some power over those for whom he or she is responsible. In the case of the teacher, it is the power to determine the students' success or failure in the course. In the case of the doctor, it is the power to affect positively or negatively the patients' health. And in the case of a parent, the powers over his or her children are too numerous to list here. This kind of power is different from the power to bend steel bars or stick to walls, but it is a kind of power nevertheless.

So far, so good. Yet in each of these cases, the responsibility is owed to specific individuals for whom we have voluntarily assumed responsibility. We are responsible in this or that role only to those individuals with whom we have a particular relationship defined by that role. The thing about Spider-Man, though, the thing that makes him the Spidey we know and love, is that he helps *strangers*, people with whom he has no special relationship at all, people who often fear and hate him. This suggests that there may be more to responsibility than first meets the eye. Perhaps we can have a responsibility to people with whom we have no special relationship.

Spider-Man, Spider-Man, Does Whatever
a Samaritan Can

You're probably familiar with the story of the Good Samaritan: A man "fell among thieves, which stripped him of his raiment, and wounded him, and left him half dead." After two people had passed by without providing assistance, a Samaritan came along. This Samaritan "went to him, and bound up his wounds, pouring in oil and wine, and set him on his own beast, and brought him to an inn, and took care of him."[1] Because of this moving parable, the term *Good Samaritan* has come to mean anyone who voluntarily provides aid to a stranger.

Yet several conditions must be fulfilled for a situation to be one of "Good Samaritanism," as it is normally understood in philosophical discourse. "The paradigm of this duty is clearly the case of one person in peril whose only real chance of survival depends upon the action of one agent who has no special relationship to the victim other than the (accidental) fact that she happens to be on the scene."[2] Of course, you do not have to be the *only* person on the scene to qualify as a Good Samaritan, nor does there have to be only *one* person in peril. The defining criteria are as follows: (1) A person or persons are in *dire peril*, in danger of suffering death or serious injury; (2) the peril is *immediate*, meaning it is going to happen now, rather than in the future; (3) you are *aware* of the peril; (4) you have the *capacity* to provide aid; (5) you have no special relationship or commitment to the endangered individual(s).

Notice how Good Samaritanism differs from *charity*, in the sense of giving money to a homeless person or an organization such as UNICEF. The recipients of charity aren't normally in immediate, but are rather in *chronic*, need: the homeless person will not die if you don't give him your change *right now*, and your change will not relieve his need, except perhaps for a very short time. Instead, Good Samaritanism is usually considered to include such actions as saving a child who is drowning in a pool, calling an ambulance for an unconscious person, or calling the police when we witness a crime.[3]

Most, if not all, of Spider-Man's heroic exploits, such as saving a window washer falling from a building or apprehending a mugger, can be viewed as acts of Good Samaritanism. In some cases, the crimes that Spidey attempts to stop are crimes against property, rather than against persons, such as interrupting the Black Cat during a burglary. It could be argued that such deeds do not count as Good Samaritanism, because there is no one in immediate and dire peril, but I disagree, for two reasons. First, because loss of property constitutes indirect harm to persons. Being robbed of my means of sustenance harms me. Second, Spider-Man has no way of knowing, in advance, whether someone will be harmed or even killed during the execution of any particular crime. Perhaps the Black Cat finds someone at home during her burglary and violence ensues. Thus, whenever Spidey intervenes in a crime, he does so at least *potentially* in order to help someone in immediate and dire peril.

Your Friendly Neighborhood Samaritan

What do philosophers have to say about our duty to act as Good Samaritans? Well, some doubt that we have such a duty at all. Everyone agrees that it would be good of us to aid someone in need, but *duty* implies something stronger—it implies that we are morally deficient or blameworthy if we don't aid the person in question. The debate over this issue often takes the form of questioning whether we should pass laws requiring Good Samaritanism. To pursue this, let's delve a bit more deeply into the concept of duty.

To begin with, let's consider the question of why we have duties to others in the first place. What's wrong with living an exclusively self-interested life? Various philosophers have answered this question in different ways, but the answer I want

to develop here shares certain parallels with the parable of the
Good Samaritan.[4] I want to suggest that the ground of our
moral duties to others lies in the strong interdependence that
characterizes human existence. The most obvious case of this
interdependence is the family. As children, we are dependent on
our parents or other caregivers to provide us not only with food
and shelter, but also with affection, guidance, and a sense of who
we are and our place in the world. When we are grown and
our parents are aged, they in turn look to us to care for them.
Furthermore, within the well-functioning family, these relations
of mutual dependence are not typically thought of in terms of
reciprocal exchange (you scratch my back and I'll scratch yours),
but as a shared bond from which everyone benefits.

What is seldom appreciated is that the interdependence
that characterizes the family is also present to a lesser degree in
the larger units of social organization: local communities, cities, even nations. We rely on others, often others we have not
even met, in almost every facet of our lives. We rely on others
to grow, process, and transport our food. We rely on others to
maintain public utilities, such as electricity and telephone systems. We rely for our security on emergency services, such as
police and hospitals. And just as we rely on them, they rely on
us to perform our own roles, whether they be butcher, baker,
candlestick maker, or web slinger.

Yet this interdependence is not limited to the professional
world. Our society nurtures and sustains us in other ways, too.
It is from the larger community, via our families, social acquain-
tances, and the media, that we derive our culture; that is, our
language, customs, values, and possibilities for self-realization.
Culture, unlike the products of economic exchange, is something very much shared. Like the air we breathe, we are both
receiving from it and adding to it all of the time. Like the air we
breathe, it is essential to our existence. Imagine trying to function without a language or any of the other types of knowledge
and skills that we receive from our culture.

Finally, a community requires for its success some minimum of mutual respect among its members. Effective communication is possible only if, on the whole, people tell one another the truth. Driving is practical only on the condition that people generally obey the rules of the road. I can go about my business only if I do not expect to be the victim of random violence. As I rely on receiving this minimal level of respect in order to function effectively as a member of my community, others rely on me to give it to them.[5]

Of course, not all of us play by the rules all of the time. There are those who, like parasites, enjoy the benefits of community without giving back. The existence of such "free riders," however, does not negate the fact that a community's success depends on the cooperation of its members. The reason why most of us are not free riders is that we recognize that "what goes around comes around." Being lazy or dishonest or otherwise not fulfilling our obligations works only as long as we don't get caught. In the long run, the best way to ensure that others are good to us is to be good to them.

We are all, whether or not we realize it, contributors and beneficiaries in a web of shared interdependence whose continued success depends on each of us doing our part. We have duties to others because communities work only if we act in accordance with such duties, and humans can live only in communities. Jesus tells the parable of the Good Samaritan in response to the question, "Who is my neighbor?" Like Jesus's and Spidey's, our neighborhoods know no bounds.

The Do's and Don'ts of Duties

Philosophers sometimes distinguish between *positive* and *negative* duties. Simply put, positive duties tell us what we *should* do, and negative duties tell us what we *shouldn't* do. The sort of acts that negative duties forbid are those that harm other people, such as theft, kidnapping, extortion, and many of the other violent and nonviolent misdeeds that Spider-Man devotes himself to fighting. Positive duties, on the other hand, enjoin us to perform acts that benefit others; these include donating to charity, taking care of your neighbor's cat while she's away, and so on.

So, negative duties constrain us from doing harm, whereas positive duties enjoin us to do good. Negative duties are generally understood to be more stringent than positive duties are, meaning that we are *required* to observe negative duties, whereas we are only *asked* to observe positive duties. Let's consider an example. If a homeless person asks me for change on the street, most of us would agree that although it would be good of me to give it, I am not *obliged* to do so. It is morally permissible for me to pass him by and instead spend my change on the latest issue of *Amazing Spider-Man*. (Okay, we're imagining it's 1985.) On the other hand, most of us would also agree that it is *not* morally permissible for me to steal the change in his change cup. Even if the amount of money in each case is the same, the cases are not *morally* the same. I am permitted to deprive the homeless man of an *additional* 75 cents, but I am not by the same token permitted to take from him the 75 cents he already has. Positive duties are sometimes described as *supererogatory*, meaning that they are good to perform but not bad not to perform. Thus, giving money to the homeless man would be supererogatory.

There are a couple of reasons why our duty to refrain from harming others is thought to be more binding than our duty to help them. To begin with, it is much *easier* to refrain from doing harm than it is to do good actively. It's quite easy for me not to hold up a liquor store. Negative duties are less demanding, and their fulfillment can therefore be held to a higher standard. More important, if we were to hold positive duties to the same standard as negative duties, we would no longer be able to function effectively as autonomous agents. If the moral requirement to aid others were as stringent as that forbidding, say, murder or assault, then we'd have to devote all of our time and energy to the assistance of our fellow man, the excess of distress in the world being as great as it is. In fact, this is a choice Peter faces frequently—whether to pursue his own goals or come to the aid of others as Spider-Man. Of course, negative duties don't always override positive duties: no one would say that I can't shove you out of my way to save a child from being run over by a bus. Yet in general, the rule is that we are permitted to neglect our positive duties but not our negative duties. This is reflected in the legal statutes of most countries: it is usually criminal to harm others, whether by violence, fraud, or other means, but is not criminal to refrain from helping them.

Unmasking the Bad Samaritan

At first glance, Good Samaritanism appears to fall clearly within the scope of positive duties. It seems as if the case of saving a window washer from plunging to his death with a handy webline would be a clear example of rendering aid, rather than refraining from causing harm. If this is the case, though, then we would have to say that Spider-Man is not obliged to use his powers to protect others. In other words, with great power does *not* come great responsibility. It's certainly *nice* of Spidey to use his powers to save people, and we'd like him to keep it up, but it isn't strictly his *responsibility* to do so, according to this interpretation.

Is Peter wrong, then? Should we advise him to relax a little, stop taking his superhero duties so seriously? Well maybe,—but not everyone thinks that the duty to render emergency aid is a positive duty along the lines of donating to charity. The influential moral and political thinker John Stuart Mill (1806–1883), for example, claimed that it is our duty to render aid under certain circumstances because the failure to do so would *cause harm*.[6] So which is it? Are acts of Good Samaritanism best understood as doing good and therefore supererogatory, or as refraining from causing harm and therefore obligatory?

It all hinges on what we mean by *causing harm*.[7] Cause is a tricky matter. Although we are used to thinking of each event as having a unique cause, a cause is really just one of a set of conditions that have to come together for the event to occur. Imagine that you come home to your apartment at the end of a long day and decide to have a smoke. Unbeknownst to you, there is a gas leak in your apartment. You strike a match, and there is a terrible explosion. What is the cause of the explosion? Our first inclination might be to say the match, because it was the last condition to be fulfilled. When you sue the owner of the building for damages, however, your lawyer argues that the gas leak is the cause. Lighting a match in an apartment does not normally produce an explosion, after all. Your mother, who has been trying to get you to quit smoking for years, might claim that your addiction is the cause! This tells us that what we consider *the* cause of an event depends on our interests and background assumptions. There is no single, determinate factor that we can point to as *the* cause. It follows from this way of thinking about causality that a cause doesn't have to be an action at all! Instead, it could be a failure to act, what we call an *omission*. If I fail to turn off my stove and a fire results, I can justly be blamed for the fire. Yet note that it was not my action that was at fault, but my inaction.

Now let's apply this thinking to a case where someone fails to act as a Good Samaritan (commonly referred to in the literature as a Bad Samaritan). A window washer is working thirty stories up the side of a skyscraper. A rope snaps and he falls. Fortunately for him, Spider-Man is swinging by and could easily catch him with a webline. Unfortunately for him, Spider-Man decides it isn't his problem, and the poor window washer plunges to his death. What causes the window washer's death? Our first inclination is to say the breaking of the rope, but we could also cite gravity, his distance from the ground,

the hardness of the pavement, and so on. All of these conditions have to be fulfilled for his death to occur. If he had been
only one story up or if he had landed on a truckful of pillows,
for example, he wouldn't have died. Similarly, if Spidey had
caught him, he wouldn't have died. Knowing this, Spidey
didn't catch him. Would we be wrong in assigning Spider-Man
some of the blame for the window washer's death?

To be clear, we're not casting *all* of the blame on Spider-
Man. We're not arguing that in failing to save the window
washer, Peter is guilty of murder. Assessments of blame are sufficiently fine-grained that a person can be blameworthy even if
he or she is only *partly* responsible for someone's death. This
is reflected in laws that distinguish between murder and manslaughter, for example. The charge of manslaughter implies
some responsibility for causing death, but less responsibility
than the charge of murder, and the punishment accruing to
each reflects this. So a person can justly be blamed for a harm
so long as his or her action or inaction is a causal factor in that
harm and the individual could reasonably have predicted this.
The mental element is important. We could not blame Spidey
if he simply hadn't *seen* the window washer fall. Returning to
the example of the fire caused by my failure to turn off my
stove, the presence of the stove in my house is also a causal
factor in the fire, but we wouldn't blame the person who sold
me the stove. We wouldn't blame her because she could not
reasonably predict that I would use the stove so irresponsibly.

There are, no doubt, gray areas where it would be difficult
to assess whether someone's action or inaction is a blameworthy causal factor in someone else's misfortune. Yet cases of Bad
Samaritanism, where we are aware of the victim's distress and
have the capacity to relieve it but nevertheless choose not to, are
not such a gray area. Here our inaction can justly be described
as a harm-causing omission worthy of blame. So although we
don't have a positive duty to be Good Samaritans, we do have a
negative duty to refrain from being Bad Samaritans. Of course,

the only way we can avoid being Bad Samaritans is by being Good Samaritans! And because negative duties to refrain from causing harm are morally binding on us in a strong sense, we can conclude that we have a strong moral duty to act as Good Samaritans. It turns out that Peter Parker was right: great power really does bring great responsibility.[8]

Spider-Man: Hero or Menace?

Alright. We've established that Spider-Man does have a strong duty to provide emergency aid, but Spidey's actions pose a difficulty not present in classic cases of Good Samaritanism. Spider-Man is often accused of being a "vigilante," and vigilantism is illegal. So let's consider whether Spidey qualifies as a vigilante and, if so, to what degree this affects the moral status of his actions. Can one have a duty to do something illegal?

A vigilante is someone who takes it upon himself to enforce the law, usually by apprehending and/or punishing criminals, without the legal authority to do so.[9] By this definition, most superheroes, as well as the heroes of many films such as *Death Wish* and *Taxi Driver*, qualify as vigilantes. Depending on the jurisdiction, however, the law does permit private citizens some freedom to act against criminals without being guilty of vigilantism. Chief among these is the right to defend ourselves and others from criminals. If I am the victim of a holdup and I happen to know karate, the law permits me to use my skills to defend myself. Similarly, I'm also permitted to intervene on behalf of another person. What separates cases of self-defense and defense of others from vigilantism is that I don't, so to speak, go looking for trouble. I am not permitted to go out in search of crimes to stop.

Often Spider-Man intervenes in crimes that he just happens to come across in his day-to-day life as Peter Parker, but he also goes on "patrol" looking for criminal activity. Furthermore, he's quite diligent at tracking down opponents who may have eluded him during a first encounter, with or without the aid of a well-placed Spider-Tracer. So it seems that Spider-Man does qualify as a vigilante and therefore a lawbreaker.

Does this mean that Spidey is actually a bad guy, that, as J. Jonah Jameson would have us believe, he is a "menace" and little better than those he apprehends? There are, after all, sensible reasons why vigilantism is a crime in most jurisdictions. The police have the training and the resources to ensure that criminals are treated in a way that respects their civil rights. Vigilantes are much more likely to strike at innocent people and to use excessive force. Most important, law enforcement officials are *accountable* to the public. If they are found to be incompetent or corrupt, protocols exist by which they can be punished and redress made. By contrast, there are no facilities in place to supervise the activity of vigilantes, especially if they operate behind masks as Spider-Man does.

This is a complicated matter. To begin with, law and morality are separate, though related, realms. An act can be immoral without being illegal (cheating on your spouse) or illegal without being immoral (burning a CD for a friend). As Martin Luther King might remind us, it can be our moral duty to disobey unjust laws. Yet Spider-Man does not couch his superhero activities in terms of civil disobedience—he is not attempting to demonstrate the injustice of antivigilante legislation. Spidey doesn't seem to be in favor of vigilantism in general; he simply believes that his own obligations override restrictions on vigilantism. Can we have a moral duty to break an otherwise just law?

It might be helpful to consider what would happen if Peter chooses *not* to fight crime as Spider-Man. In fact, there are several stories where Peter throws in the tights, the most recent of which is the film *Spider-Man 2*. In each case, there is a sharp increase in crime, and police are helpless to stop whichever supervillain is featured in the story. This gives us a reason to think that the duty belonging to Spider-Man, and superheroes in general, overrides the otherwise very sensible prohibition on vigilantism. After all, superheroes are the only ones who can stop super*villains.* I think that something like this reasoning is implicit in the background of almost every superhero story—superheroes are tolerated precisely because they are *needed* in a way that vigilantes are *not* needed in the real world. With great power comes great responsibility, and if that responsibility is great enough, then it overrides the responsibility to act as a law-abiding citizen.

But wait, can't Peter fight super-baddies without breaking the law? Can't he join the police force or some sort of licensed superhero organization, as he does during the *Civil War* story arc? *Civil War* readers will already know the answer to this question. Any sort of official, publicly sanctioned status will entail that Spider-Man reveal his true identity. How else can the accountability crucial to public law-enforcement agencies be assured? When Spider-Man does unmask during *Civil War*, the results are predictable: he and his loved ones instantly become targets for just about every crime boss and supervillain whom he has previously brought down. The situation becomes so bad that Peter is forced to make a literal deal with the devil in order to undo the damage and make his identity secret again.

It appears that if Peter is to operate effectively, then he must keep his true identity hidden. Given a choice between betraying his duty to obey a generally just law and betraying his duty to protect the public from supervillains, it seems reasonable that he should choose what appears to be the lesser of two evils.

How Great Is That?

I would be remiss in my own duty if I didn't make it clear that our duty to act as Good Samaritans is limited. A would-be Good Samaritan isn't obliged to risk her own life to save another's, nor is she obliged to sacrifice large quantities of her time and resources to provide aid. She is certainly welcome to take on such risks and sacrifices, but her choice to do so is morally voluntary, rather than obligatory, and no one would blame her if she did not. If I witness someone being held up at knifepoint, I'm not obliged to intervene in the robbery at the risk of my own life. My responsibilities don't extend any further than calling the police. What if I had a gun? Then I could stop the robbery and perhaps even apprehend the robber at little risk to myself. So, according to the line of reasoning we have been following here, I would be morally obliged to stop the robbery. Clearly, what can fairly be demanded of me depends to some degree on my capacities at the time.

This brings us to the "great" part of "with great power comes great responsibility." Spider-Man has obligations that exceed those of a normal person because he has abilities that exceed those of a normal person. The analogy here is between superheroes and people in the real world who possess special skills. We hold people with relevant skills such as doctors and firemen up to a higher standard to provide aid when those skills are called for. There's a principle in moral philosophy that "ought implies can"—meaning that you can only be morally obliged to perform acts that you are capable of performing. In the case of Good Samaritanism, it can be said conversely that "can implies ought"—if you have the power to aid without incurring undue risk or loss to yourself, you also have the duty to aid.

Spider-Man, however, goes above and beyond even the enhanced duty that his great power confers. On a regular basis he risks his life against terrible odds, taking on opponents more powerful, such as Firelord, the former Herald of Galactus,[10] or more numerous, such as the Sinister Six, a team composed of six powerful super-villains.[11] His courage, persistence, and determination are extraordinary. He devotes large quantities of his time and energy to his superhero activities, often to the detriment of his job, studies, and personal life.

The duty of a Good Samaritan is always limited. There is so much suffering in the world that I could easily sacrifice all of my time and resources attempting to alleviate it, but this would effectively destroy my ability to live my own life. Our duties to act as Good Samaritans must be sufficiently limited to pursue our own lives, or else what is the point of having neighbors and a community at all? We must say, therefore, that Spidey is not obliged to make the large sacrifices of his time, health, and personal and professional relationships that he routinely makes in the pursuit of his superhero duties. The fact that he nevertheless makes these large sacrifices is part of the appeal of the character: by doing more than duty requires, Spider-Man shows himself to be not only exceptional in his abilities, but also exceptional in his morality. I like to think that by observing his example, we all become slightly better people.

NOTES

1. *King James Bible*, Luke 10:30, 34.

2. Patricia Smith, "The Duty to Rescue and the Slippery Slope Problem," *Social Theory and Practice* 16 (1990): 27.

3. The philosopher Peter Singer, on the other hand, claims that our duty to give aid to humanitarian organizations such as UNICEF is of the same degree and kind as our duty to act as Good Samaritans. See his book *Practical Ethics* (Cambridge, UK: Cambridge University Press, 1993).

4. The following argument is indebted to Alisdair MacIntyre, *Dependent Rational Animals: Why Human Beings Need the Virtues* (Chicago: Open Court, 2001).

5. This reasoning bears some resemblance to the notion of the "social contract," which is essentially the idea that moral and political obligations stem from the implicit or explicit agreement among the members of a community to abide by the restrictions of the contract in order to enjoy the benefits. There is an important difference, however, which is that social contract theorists normally hold that the social contract is a contingent feature of human social organization, in contrast to some "state of nature" in which we may have existed beforehand. MacIntyre instead argues that the interdependence which characterizes human communities is not simply an *agreement*, but part of our *nature*, part of what it means to be human.

6. John Stuart Mill, *On Liberty*, in *Utilitarianism and On Liberty*, ed. Mary Warnock (London: William Collins, 1962), 136–137.

7. The following argument is indebted to John Kleinig, "Good Samaritanism," *Philosophy and Public Affairs* 5 (1976): 382–407.

8. My conclusion therefore differs from that of Christopher Robichaud, "With Great Power Comes Great Responsibility: On the Moral Duties of the Super-Powerful and Super-Heroic," in Tom Morris and Matt Morris, *Superheroes and Philosophy* (Chicago: Open Court, 2005), 177–193. Robichaud argues that superhero duties are supererogatory.

9. The following discussion is indebted to Aeon J. Skoble and his article "Superhero Revisionism in *Watchmen* and *The Dark Knight Returns*," in Morris and Morris, *Superheroes and Philosophy*, 29–41.

10. See *Amazing Spider-Man* #269–270 (1985).

11. There have been several versions of the Sinister Six, but the original first appeared in *The Amazing Spider-Man* Annual #1 (1964).

WITH GREAT POWER COMES GREAT CULPABILITY

How Blameworthy Is Spider-Man for Uncle Ben's Death?

Philip Tallon

The death of Uncle Ben is essential to the story of Peter Parker. *Amazing Fantasy* #15 (1962), which features the first appearance of Spider-Man, also depicts the last appearance of Uncle Ben. Ben's death is not only an important event in the life of Peter Parker, it may also be the most famous fatality in all of comics—not to mention one of the only *final* fatalities. In a medium prone to resurrecting popular characters, the rule of thumb around Marvel Comics seems to be "No one stays dead except Uncle Ben."

Similar to the murder of Batman's parents (come to think of it, they stay dead permanently, too), the death of Peter Parker's uncle powerfully shapes his hero ethos and his desire to fight crime. Yet unlike Batman, Peter Parker's actions are partly responsible for the death of Uncle Ben, so Peter blames himself and feels ashamed, even keeping the secret of how Ben died from his Aunt May for many years. Given the importance of Uncle Ben's death for Peter's story, it's important to ask: how blameworthy is Spider-Man for his uncle's death?

Peter Parker's Good and Bad Luck

The Peter we meet first in *Amazing Fantasy* #15 is good at school, unlucky in love, and the unfortunate object of high-school scorn. In other words, he's a proxy for the teenage male readership of Marvel Comics. Slouching into a science exhibit after being ditched by the popular kids, Peter mutters, "Some day I'll show them! [Sob.] Some day they'll be sorry! Sorry that they laughed at me!" Three panels after muttering these words, Peter is bitten by a radioactive spider and is suddenly endowed with incredible powers: strength and speed far beyond the jocks who picked on him, plus a preternatural sense of danger and the ability to scale walls. Up to this point, the male teen-age readership of Spider-Man would like for Peter's story to be their story, but then Peter's fortune takes a turn for the worse.

Peter first uses his skills to win in the wrestling ring and become a television celebrity, wowing audiences with his spidey-skills and enjoying the money and attention. Peter's head begins to swell with this newfound fame when, after another successful show and turning down offers for agents and movie deals, Spidey watches coldly as a thief escapes from a security guard right in front of him. After the thief dashes into the ele-vator, the security guard upbraids Spider-Man, "What's the matter with you, mister? All you hadda do was trip him, or hold him for just a minute!" Spidey replies, "Sorry, pal! That's your job! I'm thru being pushed around—by anyone! From now on I just look out for number one—that means—me!"

Despite this callousness, Pete is still warmly attached to his Aunt May and Uncle Ben because they are, as he thinks to himself, "the only ones who've ever been kind to me." Fate's cruel twist soon follows when Peter is walking home one day after a performance and discovers that Uncle Ben has been murdered in his home by a burglar.[1] Spider-Man catches the burglar, only to discover it is the same thief he let escape a few pages earlier. After delivering the thief-turned-murderer to the police, Peter Parker pulls off his mask and weeps, saying, "My fault—all my fault—if only I had stopped him when I could have! But I didn't—and now Uncle Ben is dead."

Peter's serious angst is understandable. One of the two most important people in his life has just died. By all appearances, Peter probably could have prevented Uncle Ben's death if he had stopped the thief. Yet is Peter still suffering from an inflated sense of importance when he says Uncle Ben's death is "all" his fault? Is it really the case that Peter's act of selfishness makes him a principal person to blame for Uncle Ben's death?

Peter's situation is pretty unique. Rarely are we causally connected to the death of a loved one. Still more rarely can we clearly see how some regrettable action, through the twists and turns of fate, leads to an even more regrettable event down the line. So we need some help to explore the question of Peter's responsibility. For that, we turn to the work of Bernard Williams (1929–2003) and the contemporary philosopher Thomas Nagel, who have examined closely those places where morality and chance collide. The points where what we can be blamed for slams into the contingencies of fate result in what Williams called "moral luck." If Uncle Ben is one of the most famous fatalities in all of comics, Peter Parker is one of the most famous victims of moral luck.

The Web of Moral Luck

To understand moral luck, we need to begin with plain ol' luck. Some Marvel superheroes, such as Longshot, are said to have the ability to "control" luck, but what does this mean? Luck generally implies a situation where good or bad things are brought about by chance. So Longshot was said to be lucky, because he could improve the chances of good things happening with his "probability-altering powers." For instance, if you are at a casino at the blackjack table, the odds of getting blackjack are about 5 percent. This means that if you sit down at the table and are straightaway dealt a natural blackjack, we would call you lucky because what happened was improbable and fortunate. If Longshot walked up to the blackjack table, his odds would probably be much higher, making him more likely to "seem" lucky, when in fact he is not lucky in the same sense that you might have been. An unlucky occurrence is one that is improbable and unfortunate, as in the case of Uncle Ben's murder. It's unlikely that an innocent law-abiding citizen would be killed in a home invasion in contemporary America. It happens, but only infrequently. So we call victims such as Uncle Ben unlucky.

How does luck relate to morality? Can luck *change* a good action into a bad one, or vice versa? Can luck make an action more or less moral? Some philosophers have tried to keep these two ideas far apart, contending that morality is immune from the slings and arrows of outrageous fortune. In a famous passage, Immanuel Kant (1724–1804) suggested as much:

> A good will is not good by what it effects or accomplishes, because of its fitness to attain some proposed end, but only because of its volition, that is, it is good in itself and, regarded for itself, is to be valued incomparably higher than all that could merely be brought about by it in favor of some inclination and indeed, if you will, by the sum of all inclinations. Even if, by a special disfavor of fortune . . . this will should wholly lack the capacity to carry out its purpose—if with its greatest efforts it should yet achieve nothing and only the good will were left (not, of course, as a mere wish but as the summoning of all means insofar as they are in our control)—then, like a jewel, it would still shine by itself, as something that has full worth in itself.[2]

Kant here was suggesting that what really matters in morality is a good intention, a good will. He even went so far as to suggest that if by bad fortune your greatest efforts achieved nothing, the moral worth of your intentions would still have full worth in themselves. So morality is, according to Kant, immune from luck. Although Kant's ideas seem a bit extreme, we often do try to look into people's hearts in order to evaluate them morally. True, we might say, the Hulk causes a lot of damage, but deep down he has a good heart: *Hulk not want to smash, but sometimes Hulk smash.*

Yet there are times when we don't simply look at people's intentions to evaluate the morality of their actions. There seem to be times when luck surrounding an action can affect the way that we morally evaluate an agent. Our decisions do not take place in a vacuum but are surrounded by events that precede them and come after them, which are beyond our control. As Bernard Williams, in his famous essay "Moral Luck," noted, "One's history as an agent is a web in which anything that is the product of the will is surrounded and held up and partly formed by things that are not [products of the will]."[3] What's more, other events in the "web" can seem to change the way we think about and morally evaluate our decisions. Thomas Nagel defines the phenomenon in this way: "Where a significant aspect of what someone does depends on factors beyond his control, yet we continue to treat him in that respect as an object of moral judgment, it can be called moral luck. Such luck can be good or bad."[4] What Nagel means here is that moral luck refers to situations where our moral praise or blame depends, at least in part, on chance.

One example of moral luck might be a driver, we'll call him Driver A, who negligently procrastinates about getting the brakes on his car checked for a few months. During those few months, he drives around without incident, then finally gets his brakes checked. When he brings the car in, the mechanic clucks his tongue at the bad state of the brakes, and Driver

A scratches his head, shrugs, and admits he should have brought the car in sooner. Now imagine a different driver who does the exact same thing, except that during that same period before he takes his car to the mechanic, a child runs out in front of the driver. Driver B slams on the brakes, but the car doesn't stop soon enough, and the child is killed. In this case, not only would we likely blame Driver B more strongly than we would Driver A, the law would likely prosecute him for manslaughter, even though they both committed the same fundamental moral mistake (being lazy and careless with their brakes). Here Driver B is suffering from resultant luck, which is when chance affects "the way one's actions and projects turn out."[5] We see that in some cases, luck does affect the way we morally assess a person.

The Two Peter Parkers

Spider-Man is in a similar situation. Compare Peter Parker A, who selfishly lets a thief escape, only to discover that the same thief has killed his uncle, with Peter Parker B, who selfishly lets a thief escape and discovers later that the thief was apprehended while exiting the elevator. Both Peter Parkers would have performed the same action, letting the thief go, but Peter A seems *somehow* more morally blameworthy for his action than Peter B is.

At this point, you might be inclined to challenge the no-tion that moral luck should have any legitimate role in moral evaluations. To bolster the claim, let's consider more situations where we seem to use resultant luck as an indicator of how blameworthy a person is. Consider if someone tried to commit murder, but the intended victim tripped the moment the gun was fired, and therefore the bullet missed the target entirely. We would legally charge and morally blame the shooter only for "attempted murder." This indicates that despite his intent to murder, resultant luck reduces this would-be murderer's guilt. As another example, consider Paul Gauguin's abandonment of his family to facilitate his painting career.[6] If Gauguin fails to become a famous painter, then the abandonment seems to weigh more heavily around his neck, morally speaking. Yet if Gauguin succeeds, which he did, then he seems somehow less culpable for the act of abandoning his family for art's sake. So there do seem to be times when the way things turn out can increase or decrease the amount of moral blame we assign to someone. Perhaps this is not a good practice (more on that later), but we do sometimes adjust praise and blame based on luck.

Peter seems to do this himself. By all appearances, he willingly takes the blame for Ben's death. In *Amazing Spider-Man* #479, Peter finally confesses to Aunt May the secret of his identity and his involvement in her husband's death. "God help me, Aunt May . . . I'm the reason that Uncle Ben is dead." What Peter did was wrong, irrespective of the consequences: one should try to stop wrongdoing when it's in one's power to do so. Yet is Peter really the reason Uncle Ben is dead, in any morally meaningful sense? If moral luck holds true, then Peter is at least partly culpable, which is to say guilty, for the death of Uncle Ben. If moral luck does not hold true, however, then Peter is culpable only for letting a thief go, and he's been suffering from unnecessary feelings of guilt.

The Problem with Moral Luck

There are, of course, some potential problems with the idea of moral luck. Consider the moral assumption called the Control Principle. Though it sounds a bit like a scheme of Dr. Doom, it basically means that we are morally accountable for those affairs that are within our control. This was essentially Kant's position, which we discussed earlier. According to the Control Principle, for example, Spider-Man was not responsible for the death of Gwen Stacy, because he could not have saved her from the Green Goblin when the Goblin dropped her off the George Washington Bridge.

A corollary of the Control Principle is that two different people should not be judged differently if the only differences between them are "due to factors beyond their control."[7] If my two daughters were throwing rocks over a high wall at the same moment, and my older daughter's stone happened to strike an elderly woman (such as Aunt May), it would be strange for me as a parent to punish harshly my older daughter and leave my younger daughter completely unpunished. Because they were doing the same activity at the same time, it is even easier to see how they are both equally morally guilty, or at least as morally guilty as five- and three-year olds can be. (A side note: as a parent, I would also be partly culpable for *letting* them do this.)

Thus, we seem to have competing moral intuitions. On one hand, we may feel that the negligent driver who kills a child is more blameworthy than the one who doesn't, but, on the other hand, this cuts against the intuition we have that we should not judge people differently merely because of bad luck. So what do we do? As Williams and Nagel both noticed, recognizing moral luck not only uncovers a truth about common morality (we do evaluate people differently because of luck), but also cuts against some of our moral intuitions (we feel that people shouldn't be assessed differently for events beyond their control). This seems contradictory. Appropriately, then, because of the problems moral luck raises, there have been a number of attempts to show that moral luck is not as significant a phenomenon as Williams and Nagel suggested. If moral luck is really not that significant, then perhaps this will help us see how Peter isn't *more* to blame for letting the thief go because Uncle Ben died.

Peter Parker: Agent of Regret

Is there another way to explain the increased regret Peter feels for his bad action after Uncle Ben dies? I think that there is. By separating out the difference between the moral phenomenon of culpability and the moral phenomenon of responsibility for damage, we can help dislodge Peter from the web of moral luck and guilt in which he's trapped.

Peter unambiguously blames himself for the death of Uncle Ben, but what Peter is really experiencing here is a sense of *responsibility* for the damage that his inaction has allowed. Peter in no way intended or foresaw that allowing the thief to go would result in anyone's murder. If he had, he undoubtedly would have stopped the thief.

In his essay "Moral Luck," Bernard Williams helpfully described "agent regret," which is a certain kind of regret for something one has caused. One example might be a bus driver who accidentally struck and killed a child who ran out in the road. Everyone who saw the event would regret that it happened, but the person who did it would feel this regret in a first-person sense. He would regret that he did not stop the bus in time, even if he knew he was not negligent in his driving. Furthermore, the bus driver may rightly feel that he wants to do something to "make it up" to the family of the dead child, in the same way that Hulk might want to make it up to a family whose car he smashed, even if he could not have helped it. As Williams wrote, "We feel sorry for the driver, but that sentiment co-exists with, indeed presupposes, that there is something special about his relation to this happening, something which cannot merely be eliminated by the consideration that it was not his fault."[8]

In many cases, trying to repair the damage is the morally right thing to do, even when one is causally responsible but not culpable. Susan Wolf, in her response to the problem of moral luck, describes a "nameless virtue" that always aims to "tak[e] responsibility for one's actions and their consequences."[9] Peter's pain at the death of Uncle Ben and his sense of moral self-condemnation seem due to possession of this nameless virtue. Peter is a responsible person, who, in one moment of selfishness, acts against his better nature. Yet Peter's ability to repair his mistake is limited. In another response to the problem of moral luck, Judith Andre describes the problem death poses in these situations:

> Certainly there is moral defect if we fail to make good what we have destroyed when it is possible to make this good; furthermore, the defect is greater when the source of the damage is not just our action but our culpable action. But what about the cases where the damage cannot be repaired? Loss of life, most obviously, cannot be put right. There is at least a great sadness in having incurred a debt which one cannot meet, and therefore a feeling of inadequacy. As a result of that there is a sense of diminished worth. This is, however, distinguishable from moral fault in the sense of deserving punishment.[10]

Wolf and Andre, then, suggest that part of what it means to be a good person is to take responsibility for one's actions and the resultant consequences. A virtuous person aims to fix problems that result from her actions, even if she is not to blame for them. For instance, if I volunteer to cook dinner for a sick friend and then accidentally make my friend more sick (say, by accidentally buying tainted meat from the butcher), I would want to stay and devote even more care to my friend because of what I've inadvertently brought about (though my friend might understandably want me to leave before I cause even more damage). I would feel responsible, even if I did not feel guilty.

As Andre notes, though, if I cause some bad effect through culpable action (maybe I knew the butcher was a bit careless with cleanliness), then I would feel even more responsible, though not blameworthy. Following these ideas, then, we can see a bit more clearly that Peter is not necessarily more blameworthy if Uncle Ben is murdered than if the thief is immediately apprehended. There's a good explanation for the additional sense of regret and additional moral obligation Peter incurs, namely, that Peter is experiencing agent regret and an additional sense of responsibility for what his actions have led to.

It's distressing to lose a close family member, but it's even more painful when one is involved in the chain of events that led to the death and still more so when one's own immorality played a part in that chain. Yet these feelings should not necessarily be confused with guilt for the death of that loved one. What the challenging problem of moral luck shows us is how easily we can confuse different kinds of moral responsibility.

Aunt May's Dark Secret

Peter, however, is not the only person who has a misplaced sense of regret about Uncle Ben's death. In a 2002 issue of Spider-Man (*Amazing Spider-Man* #479), Aunt May confesses to Peter that she feels responsible for the death of Uncle Ben as well. In a tearful scene, Peter confesses his dark secret to Aunt May, saying, "Uncle Ben is dead. Because of me." Yet Aunt May replies, "You're not responsible, Peter. You're not. I am." Aunt May then confesses to causing Ben's death by having argued with Uncle Ben, which (in a case of retconned—or "retroactively changed"—Marvel continuity) caused him to leave the house, leading to his murder.

What Aunt May is feeling here, however, is a truly misguided sense of culpability for Uncle Ben's death. The normal arguments that happen between a husband and a wife have no relationship to being murdered by a criminal. Unlike Peter's connection to Uncle Ben's death, May's role in the causal chain is completely trivial. Yet because of the "web" of relationships between events, it can sometimes be easy to confuse involvement in the causal chain of events with responsibility or culpability for those events. Unfortunately, virtuous people who take responsibility for their actions seem especially susceptible to this kind of confusion.

Power and Responsibility

Philosophical thinking about ethics helps us disentangle ourselves from this web and see the different kinds of responsibility involved. Having distinguished between guilt and responsibility, then, we are able to get much closer to assessing Peter's culpability for his action. Peter Parker is partly responsible, but not in any deep sense culpable, for the death of Uncle Ben. He is culpable for wrongfully letting a thief go. Thievery is wrong, and because superheroes have it within their power safely to stop crooks who cross their paths, our intuition suggests that they should when given the chance. Yet does refusing to stop a thief one time make you responsible for all of his future crimes? Yes and no.

Most of us probably assume that Peter is not deeply responsible for the thief's future crimes. For one, Peter had nothing to do with the thief deciding to steal in the first place. Second, the murder of Uncle Ben was a distinct action, separated by time, space, and other factors from the crime Peter witnessed. *Novus agens interveniens* (Latin for "a new agent intervening") is a principle often invoked to show how one is much less responsible for events once the chain of causality one is responsible for is broken. Marilyn McCord Adams defines *novus agens interveniens* as when an "agent bears diminished or no responsibility for those consequences of his /her action that are produced by a new intervening agent."[11] In Peter's case, when the thief embarked on a second robbery (as told in the comic book), in one sense he began an essentially new chain of events to which Peter had little connection. Getting away with one crime does not *necessarily* entail that a criminal will commit another one.

Given what we know about criminals, however, it is likely that they will continue to commit crimes until caught. So, in that sense, the criminal's entire crime spree can be seen as a chain of events that Peter could have easily interrupted. This is why Peter is partly responsible for the death of Uncle Ben. One does not simply stop a crime. One stops a criminal.

Yet Peter's responsibility for the criminal's future crimes doesn't mean that Peter is, in fact, additionally guilty for letting the thief go if the thief chooses to commit more crimes. That would land us back in the sticky web of moral luck. Peter does not become more guilty as the criminal's rap sheet lengthens. Allowing the thief to go on committing crimes is part of what is entailed in the wrongness of the single bad action of letting a criminal escape. It's part of what was already morally wrong with Peter's selfish refusal to help catch a criminal.

In the strict sense, I think, the Control Principle holds true. Driving full speed when you know your brakes are bad already entails full moral culpability for recklessness, whether or not you get in an accident. It is only in, say, hitting a small child that one becomes responsible for the result of that culpable choice. Peter's bad decision is what he's guilty of, but with the murder of Uncle Ben, the decision "activates" his (small) responsibility for the thief's future crimes. Peter acknowledges this responsibility and, being unable to bring his uncle back to life, vows never to make the same mistake again. Thus, Peter seems to learn the right lesson from his experience. Instead of using his expanded powers for selfish ends, he uses them selflessly, taking full responsibility for his actions.

Peter's pain at the death of his uncle, then, is best understood as a mixture of personal agony at his own loss, guilt about his earlier bad action, and the kind of responsible agent regret that calls for taking responsibility for the results of one's actions (in this case, honoring his uncle's advice and example and caring for his uncle's widow—all of which Peter does). These are three distinct responses, which Peter unfortunately (but understandably) collapses into one ball of shame and guilt. If Peter had been a philosopher, instead of a scientist, he might have experienced less guilt and shame, though maybe he wouldn't have taken to the streets to fight crime with quite the same determination. He might have been a happier person but perhaps a less driven superhero. Bad luck for him. Good luck for New York City.

NOTES

1. There are three notable differences between the film and the comic versions of the Spider-Man origin. The first is that in the comic, Peter Parker was not provoked in any way to allow the thief to escape (as he was in the film by the rude behavior of the promoter). The second is that in *Amazing Fantasy #15*, Uncle Ben never utters the phrase "With great power comes great responsibility." Rather, this line is stated in the final narration. The third is that in the film, Uncle Ben is killed while waiting for Peter in the car, but in the comic, he's killed in a home invasion. Notably, in more recent issues of the comic, Uncle Ben's murder and the origin of the "great responsibility" line have been retroactively changed ("retconned") to fit with the movie version.

2. Immanuel Kant, *Groundwork of the Metaphysic of Morals*, trans. and ed. Mary Gregor (Cambridge, UK: Cambridge University Press, 1997), 8.

3. Bernard Williams, "Moral Luck," in *Moral Luck: Philosophical Papers 1973–1980* (Cambridge, UK: Cambridge University Press, 1981), 21–39, 29.

4. Thomas Nagel, "Moral Luck," in *Mortal Questions* (Cambridge, UK: Cambridge University Press, 1979), 24–38, 26.

5. Ibid., 28.

6. Bernard Williams, "Moral Luck," 25.

7. Dana K. Nelkin, "Moral Luck," in Edward N. Zalta, ed., *The Stanford Encyclopedia of Philosophy* (Winter 2009), (Stanford, CA: Stanford University Press, 2009), http://plato.stanford.edu/entries/moral-luck/, accessed December 29, 2009.

8. Bernard Williams, "Moral Luck," 43.

9. Susan Wolf, "The Moral of Moral Luck," *Philosophic Exchange* 31 (2001): 13.

10. Judith Andre, "Nagel, Williams, and Moral Luck," *Analysis* 43:4 (1983): 206.

11. Marilyn McCord Adams, *Horrendous Evils and the Goodness of God* (Ithaca, NY: Cornell University Press, 1999), 34.

PART THREE

SPIDER-SENSE AND THE SELF

WHY IS MY SPIDER-SENSE TINGLING?

Andrew Terjesen

Spider-sense is essential to Spider-Man. This ability to sense danger compensates for a complete lack of training in acrobatics and the martial arts. It also has some less obvious uses, enabling him to change out of costume without fear of someone stumbling upon him and guaranteeing that he can quickly web-swing through the city without having to calibrate his web anchors. Given the usefulness of this danger-sense and Spider-Man's popularity, one would think that there'd be many imitations of this power in the comic-book world, but that's not the case. Compared to all of the Superman-like superheroes who popped up in the 1940s and the number of comic book characters, such as Norman Osborn, who mimic Wolverine's "healing factor," relatively few characters share Spider-Man's special ability. I suspect that one reason this is so is because spider-sense is so hard to explain.

The official Marvel attempt at a cogent explanation of Spider-Man's special power limps along: "The precise nature of this sense is unknown. It appears to be a simultaneous

clairvoyant response to a wide variety of phenomena (everything from falling safes to speeding bullets to thrown punches).
. . . The sense can also create a general response within several minutes; he cannot judge the nature of the threat by the sensation."[1] This vague account leaves us scratching our heads. Yet there is a good reason why this and other explanations of the spider-sense are so vague, namely, because important philosophical issues about the traditional five senses haven't been worked out sufficiently. If we don't yet understand how our own senses work, how could we possibly expect to understand the ability to sense something outside our normal range of perception?

Getting the Sense of Things, Directly

For a long time, the predominant view of perception was *direct realism*. Many classical philosophers thought our senses were similar to cameras that directly received the imprint of physical objects in the world. This is a form of realism because it holds that what we perceive exists independently of our perception of it; we uncover these objects when our senses are confronted by them. It's a direct form of realism because the primary objects of our perceptions are actual objects in the world. According to this view, when Spidey sees the Green Goblin flying toward him, he's seeing the Green Goblin himself and not an image of the Green Goblin that his mind creates.

One problem with direct realism is that if it's true, then it's not clear how to explain visual illusions and hallucinations. Let's assume the Marvel Universe is real, but that the Green Goblin doesn't really exist in it. Rather, he is only a figment of Spider-Man's imagination. If the Green Goblin doesn't exist, then according to direct realism, there shouldn't be anything for Spider-Man to perceive when he "sees" the Goblin flying toward him. Direct realists do have ways of getting around this problem, but most seventeenth- and eighteenth-century philosophers found those solutions to be too complicated or implausible. A good philosophical account of perception should enable us to understand what happens when we make perceptual mistakes. Even better, it should help us determine when we're actually perceiving things in the world, as opposed to when we're hallucinating, dreaming, or having some other false perception of the world. Such a theory would allow us to know when to rely on our senses and when not to do so.

What Danger Looks Like

The first major alternative to direct realism is a view known as *indirect realism*, and philosopher John Locke (1632–1704) was one of its foremost proponents. According to Locke, objects in the world have certain properties that cause our sensory organs to produce perceptual experiences in our minds. This is an indirect perception—the "Green Goblin" that Spider-Man sees is really something created by his brain (based on information gathered by his sense organs) to resemble the actual Green Goblin in the world. The Green Goblin in Spidey's head—which merely resembles the real Green Goblin—is an example of a *sense datum*.

In the indirect realist view, we perceive sense data, not the actual objects. The sense data are produced in our minds by the interactions between objects in the world and our sensory organs, so they still tell us about objects in the world. Sense data are suited to the sensory organ that produces them. For sight, it would be a picture of the Green Goblin. For hearing, it would be the sound of his maniacal laugh and the noise produced by his glider, and so on. Yet what sense datum is appropriate for a danger-sense? What looks like danger?

The 1970s live-action television series about Spider-Man represented his spider-sense as providing pictures of events that seemed to take place in the near future. Peter Parker has a vision of someone about to be attacked, and he rushes to investigate as Spider-Man. The more recent Sam Raimi Spider-Man movies retain elements of this interpretation. The genetically engineered spider that bites Peter Parker is described as having reflexes so fast they "border on precognition." The acquired power in Peter is represented by the "bullet-time" sequence when Flash Thompson tries to hit Peter, only to find Peter effortlessly dodging his fists.

The idea that spider-sense is a form of precognition is very tempting, but it goes against most depictions of Spider-Man. Even in that encounter with Flash from Raimi's first film, Spidey doesn't know the nature of the threat that sets off his spider-sense. If he were seeing pictures of the future, he would have a better idea of the danger. He would know, for example, that it was Flash's fist coming at him. Instead, he feels a buzzing in the back of his head. The sense datum for his spider-sense seems to be a generic feeling, not a specific image of some event in the future.

On the other hand, it's possible that what happens in the future causes his spider-sense to go off, but he's unable to process the information beyond perceiving it as an imminent and threatening event. This would be like hearing someone whispering but not being able to make out the words. It's just noise—but noise to which we've become attentive. We don't need to think about our lack of precision regarding future events to recognize difficulties in perceiving. As we'll see in the next section, it's always difficult to describe what the things we perceive are "really" like, if, as Locke suggested, we don't really perceive the objects that are the sources of our perceptions.

Even though we can't say for certain, there are good reasons to think that Spider-Man's special sense is not about the future, but is some way of knowing about things in the present. It makes him especially attentive to whatever might harm himself or others. We can think of Spider-Man, then, as sensitive to a special quality of things, their *dangerousness*. Dangerousness would be the quality in things or events of potential harm, and this quality is present whether or not actual harm is to be experienced from the dangerous things and events. Electro's electrical bursts, for instance, are dangerous even if one is wearing protective clothing to prevent electrocution. If, moreover, dangerousness concerned only future dangers, then Spidey's spider-sense wouldn't tingle whenever villains pass by him in disguise.

The Relative Nature of Danger

Locke identified two kinds of properties that can produce sense data: primary qualities and secondary qualities. *Primary qualities* are those such as shape or solidity that are built into the object itself. More important, primary qualities produce sense data that resemble the property that produced them. For example, the Rhino is a Spider-Man villain who is enormous and thick-skinned, and has a large amount of mass. Size, texture, and mass are all primary qualities. The size of the Rhino in our mind's visual field relative to other objects parallels the size of the Rhino in the actual world relative to those same objects. If he looks bigger than a refrigerator, then he really is bigger than a refrigerator. Because primary qualities are built into the objects, the sense data they produce can change only if the object itself is changed. So, the rough, leathery texture of Rhino's "skin" (actually an exoskeleton bonded to his epidermis) will feel differently only if we sand it down or find some way to get the suit off his body.

A *secondary quality* is a property that doesn't exist in the object but rather comes about when a perceiving subject encounters the primary qualities of an object. The notion of secondary qualities enabled Locke to explain perceptual illusions without giving up on his perceptual realism. Secondary qualities are all of the properties that we can make mistakes about, the color of something, the way something smells, and so on. Because secondary qualities aren't a part of the object, they can change without changing the object in any way. What does change when secondary qualities change is how primary qualities interact with the person perceiving them. Mysterio is a villain who uses special effects to create convincing illusions. For example, he can make Spidey think he's falling off a bridge by simulating the appearance of a bridge and the "feel" of falling. What he's doing is using objects that have certain primary qualities that activate Spider-Man's sense organs in just the right way to create the sense data of a bridge shape or a feeling of weightlessness.

Locke illustrated the nature of secondary qualities with an experiment you can try at home. Stick your left hand under hot water while you put your right hand in a bowl of ice, then stick both hands into lukewarm water at the same time. As Locke pointed out, "It is impossible that the same water . . . should at the same time be both hot and cold."[2] Locke thought that heat had something to do with motion. We now know that heat is the energy of molecular motion. The two hands would be in different states of molecular motion before being plunged into the water, thus their motions would be differently affected by the same stimulus. The left hand's molecules would slow down, creating a cooling sensation, while the right hand's molecules would speed up, producing a warming sensation. Secondary qualities depend on the state the perceiver is in and will vary as the perceiver's state changes.

Is dangerousness a primary quality or a secondary quality? If dangerousness was a primary quality, that would mean that there's something about an object that inherently makes it dangerous. The only way it would cease to be dangerous would be if we changed its physical configuration somehow. If you think about the things that normally set off the spider-sense, it seems unlikely that dangerousness is a primary quality.

Aside from imminent danger, such as a falling object, the spider-sense alerts Spider-Man to potential dangers (such as bombs or traps), hostile thoughts, criminals in disguise, and so on.[3] Spider-Man can use his spider-sense to navigate a dark room, and he can also use it as a form of radar-sense after he has been blinded. As Spider-Man describes it, he begins to "see" the danger of the wall in front of him, as opposed merely to feeling it.[4] Most of these examples involve things that are only dangerous in specific circumstances. A wall that Spidey is about to walk into can be physically identical to a wall in my house; the only difference is the relationship the wall bears to Spidey (the perceiver). The robot arm that Doc Ock is swinging at Spider-Man is no different than the other three robot arms, except for the fact that it's moving toward Spidey. So dangerousness would have to be a secondary quality. The danger of a bomb is a function of the structure of the bomb (primary qualities), which allows for an explosive reaction under certain circumstances that would cause a force (another primary quality) to be created that could alter the primary qualities of nearby objects. Most bombs are very dangerous to someone such as Spider-Man, but not to the Hulk. Danger is relative to the perceiver's circumstances, thus making it a prime example of a secondary quality.

Is It *Really* Dangerous?

Before we close the book on the spider-sense, we need to consider a basic problem with indirect realism. How can we be sure that the buzzing in Spidey's head is being caused by something that is really dangerous? According to indirect realism, we do not gain access to the world directly. Everything we learn about the world comes from the sense data that we perceive. We assume that there's an underlying causal mechanism because our perceptions follow certain regular patterns. For example, J. Jonah Jameson always smells of cigar smoke, and he's often seen with a cigar in his mouth, so we assume he smells like cigars because he smokes them. Yet we can't look at the world directly in order to see whether our sense data are representing things in a reliable way. Trying to verify the accuracy of our perceptions through our perceptions would be like trying to determine whether the *Daily Bugle* is accurate in its coverage of Spider-Man using only the *Bugle's* editorials.

One strength of indirect realism is that it seems to be consistent with what we do know about our perceptual system. Our sense organs are designed to receive certain limited stimuli (such as light waves or pressure) and convert them to electrochemical signals that travel through the brain until they reach a processing center. The more we learn about the way the brain works, the harder and harder it is to be a direct realist. These days, direct realists are in the minority. The problems of indirect realism produced some interesting responses. The most obvious response was *idealism*, which holds that nothing but our perceptions exist. (This has nothing to do with being idealistic in the sense of pursuing ideals.) The idealist George Berkeley (1685–1753) challenged the distinction between primary qualities and secondary qualities. After all, our knowledge of the size or the mass of an object is dependent on the appearances of our measurements, but those can be mistaken. Mysterio can trick Spider-Man into thinking he's only two inches tall by playing with Spidey's frame of reference to throw off his sense of perspective. If we can be deceived about these primary qualities, then there's no reason to think that they are any more accurate than secondary qualities. From that point, Berkeley argued that it makes more sense to think that our perceptions of the world are all that there is.[5]

Berkeley intended his idealism to be an antidote to the skepticism that he argued was inherent in indirect realism. Depending on the lighting, Silver Sable's hair can look silver, white, gray, or even platinum blond. Knowing that he can only say it appears silver, Spider-Man will always wonder whether it's really silver. Berkeley solved this by reuniting our perceptions with objects in the world, but he did this by denying the existence of a physical world independent of perception. Berkeley's theory of perception was direct but not a form of realism, so how could Berkeley be sure there was no physical world? A younger contemporary of Berkeley suggested a different approach. David Hume (1711–1776) agreed with Berkeley that we don't have grounds for distinguishing between primary and secondary qualities. The difference is that Hume thought we had no grounds for drawing any conclusions about the world beyond our sense perceptions.

Hume's view of perception is called *phenomenalism*, in order to distinguish it from indirect realism and idealism. The difference between the three views can be found in their various notions of what sense data are. Indirect realists regard sense data as internal representations of the external objects that caused them (and the causal process is reliable so that it produces the same sense data under the same circumstances). Idealists deny the distinction between sense data and the objects in the world. Phenomenalists think of sense data as those that appear to us (*phenomena* comes from a Greek word meaning "appearing"). According to phenomenalism, the existence of anything beyond those phenomena, including the mechanisms that produce the phenomena, cannot be known or understood by us. Any attempt to describe the "true nature" of the world is idle speculation, including the claim that there's nothing beyond our experiences. After all, how could one prove that negative claim? So, does spider-sense point a way out of phenomenalism?

When the Spider-Sense Fails

The spider-sense doesn't give false positives, but there are a few instances where it has failed to detect a specific danger.[6] The most obvious example is when Spider-Man gets hit over the head by Aunt May after she sneaks up behind him in Doc Ock's house. To his surprise, Spider-Man doesn't feel the slightest tingle of his spider-sense. The narrator even mocks Spidey's confusion, saying, "Forget it, wall-crawler! After all, the eerie sixth-sense of yours reacts only to the nearness of sworn foemen—of hidden menace. Why should it have sounded the clarion call of deadly danger—when the one who has struck you down—is none other than Aunt May herself."[7]

The Aunt May example suggests a way of thinking about dangerousness that might help us untangle the nature of the spider-sense. Normally, we might think of dangerousness as something that has the potential to cause harm. Yet if that were the case, then Spider-Man wouldn't be fooled by a vase-wielding Aunt May. It's not that danger is something that will cause harm as much as it's some harm that we are afraid will befall us. Vases have the property of hurting someone's skull when used as a weapon. That's not what makes us see them as dangerous. It's the fear we have of the pain that would be caused by our getting hit with a vase that makes us regard a vase as dangerous. Spider-Man is always worried that his archenemies are going to kill him, but he would never believe that the woman who raised him has any intention of harming him.

This way of thinking is actually very close to what Hume said about morality, namely, that all of our moral judgments are the result of sentiments, which are responses to the things we see. So, if MJ sees Spidey kissing the Black Cat, her judgment that this is a bad thing is the result of her pained reaction to seeing a violation of her trust in Peter. Hume's argument for this kind of moral sense is summed up in the following passage:

> Take any action allow'd to be vicious: Wilful murder, for instance. Examine it in all lights, and see if you can find that matter of fact, or real existence, which you call vice. In which-ever way you take it, you find only certain passions, motives, volitions and thoughts. There

is no other matter of fact in the case. The vice entirely escapes you, as long as you consider the object. You never can find it, till you turn your reflection into your own breast, and find a sentiment of disapprobation, which arises in you, towards this action. Here is a matter of fact; but 'tis the object of feeling, not of reason. It lies in yourself, not in the object.[8]

What Hume was saying is that if we examine any action that we deem to be wrong, there's nothing in the action itself that we could call its "wrongness." In the Black Cat example, it's not the act of kissing that's inherently wrong. Nor is it the passion felt by either of them. Nor is it the fact that Spider-Man has a relationship with MJ. Any individual aspect of the situation is a physical fact—neither good nor bad. If you take away all of the features of the situation, there'll be nothing left behind in the act to call wrong. Instead, it's the disapproval of what Spider-Man is doing that makes MJ judge it to be wrong.

You might argue that the wrongness is Peter's intention to kiss Black Cat, even though he's committed to someone else. Yet Hume would have pointed out that depending on what society she lived in, MJ might not be offended by Peter's action or think it wrong. The French Araignée-Homme kissing La Chatte Noir might only cause Marie-Jeanne to shrug her shoulders and walk out of the room. To further illustrate his point, Hume pointed out how we judge differently the same situation in the human world and the natural world. Patricide is a crime for human beings, but when an acorn grows into a tree and chokes off the roots of its parent, no one is outraged. Similarly, incest is taboo among human beings, but no one minds it among dogs and cats.

Dangerousness seems to operate in the same way. This shouldn't be too surprising, because dangerous things are objects and situations we *ought* to avoid—and morality is all about the way we *ought* to act. Spider-Man's spider-sense doesn't warn him about Aunt May because he doesn't react to her as a threat. She doesn't produce fear or caution, but rather the opposite emotional responses. The other time Spider-Man is hit from behind is by the Jackal, who is his beloved mentor Professor Miles Warren in disguise.[9] When Spider-Man expresses surprise that the Jackal has sneaked up on him, the Jackal tears off his mask and gloats, "Your famed spider-sense only protects you against enemies, not 'friends,' and dear boy haven't I always been your friend?" His emotional reaction to Miles Warren is positive, so Spider-Man doesn't interpret his presence as threatening.

Spider-Sense, Spider-Judgment, or Both?

If the spider-sense is a kind of moral sense, that would explain a lot of the idiosyncrasies of Spider-Man's experiences. For example, it alerts Peter to "emotional danger" when Brad Davis starts chatting up MJ.[10] To determine that someone is crossing a line in a relationship requires some sort of moral determination of what's appropriate. It's nothing like recognizing the danger a bomb poses. Nevertheless, we should be careful about following Hume's account too closely.

By equating our moral sense with our emotional responses, Hume was driving a wedge between the things we can be certain about and morality. Hume's phenomenalism means that he could speak with certainty only about what appeared to him in his perceptions. Emotions are reactions to our perceptions and therefore go beyond what we can be certain about. Hume's moral theory leaves open the possibility that our moral judgments are simply our desires about the way the world should be and not an objective fact about the world.[11] In other words, if Venom goes on a rampage and kills people, it's wrong only because people disapprove of what he did. If he killed only people whom everyone wanted to see dead, there'd be nothing wrong with what he did (because no one would mind). Or if the Hypno Hustler used mass hypnosis to make everyone approve of infant sacrifice, it would cease to be wrong. These implications of Hume's theory are unacceptable because they can't do justice to the reach of our moral judgments.

One critic of Hume's phenomenalism was Thomas Reid (1710–1796). Reid's philosophy has become known as the Common Sense School because it embraced the idea that our perceptions of the world always contain some basic, reliable judgments produced by the common sense that all sentient beings possess. (Reid's common sense is not, however, the same as what people normally mean by "using your common sense.") According to Reid, it's a mistake to claim that we simply take in what we perceive as a video camera does. We must make sense of what we're perceiving as we're experiencing it. Spidey doesn't simply see patches of green mixed with patches of orange and hear a maniacal laugh. His common sense puts them together as a single entity known as the Green Goblin. Moreover, when he sees the Green Goblin coming at him, he recognizes that it's an act of hostility. It's possible that Spidey could be mistaken, thinking that the Green Goblin in question is Norman Osborn (the man who killed his first love), when it's really Phil Urich trying to be a heroic Green Goblin. Mistakes can happen when one makes a judgment, but we've seen that Spider-Man's spider-sense is not immune from making mistakes about the level of danger.

Reid didn't claim that we never make mistakes in our judgments about the world. His point was that some things are pretty obvious to anyone who takes time to consider the matter. For example, based on his experiences, it would make sense for Spidey to conclude that the tingling sensation indicates the presence of danger. Something must be causing such a reliable reaction, just as something must be causing the Green Goblin to appear in front of him holding a pumpkin bomb. Common sense tells Spidey that the Green Goblin exists independently of his mind. Much like the spider-sense, the operations of common sense are so complex that we can't explain how they work. We can only say that they're at work, and they both work quite reliably. Reid thought, moreover, that we can usually tell when someone is using common sense to judge what they're perceiving: "It is easily discerned by its effects in men's actions, in their speeches, and even in their looks; and when it is made a question, whether a man has this natural gift or not, a judge or a jury, upon a short conversation with him, can for the most part determine the question with great assurance."[12]

Did We Learn Anything?

It may seem that we're no closer to understanding the spider-sense than we were before, but our journey through the developments in the philosophy of perception in the seventeenth and eighteenth centuries has highlighted some important points. Perception is not simply the act of being confronted with some property in the world. There's no sense datum that perfectly represents our perception. Our perceptions are inextricably mixed with judgments, just as Reid pointed out, "in common language, sense always implies judgment"—as in the phrase "knock some sense into you."[13] Spidey's danger-sense is not some sort of Geiger counter for danger. Rather, it mixes some information he gathers about the world—how this gathering takes place is not explained—with his judgments concerning which things ought to be avoided. Recognizing that our perceptions always involve some judgment means that we can't simply accept things as they appear and so must strive to hone our senses through careful reflection.

Despite what Hume might suggest, spider-sense, common sense, moral sense, and color vision are not distinct perceptual faculties. Rather, they represent a continuum of judgments about the world around us. Vision, for example, is thought to have evolved to enable animals to perform certain tasks necessary for their survival. Being able to see that a fruit is ripe because it appears red is extremely helpful for creatures that survive by gathering food from trees. Likewise, social cognition, such as detecting someone's emotion based on nonverbal cues, is important for effective group cooperation. Reid's own comment on how we determine the presence of common sense also invokes the criterion of success in dealing with the world. In a way, all of our senses are a form of spider-sense, because they take input from the world in order to make a judgment about what is good or bad for us and give us the information we need to navigate this dangerous world.[14]

NOTES

1. *The Official Handbook of the Marvel Universe: Spider-Man 2004* (June 2004), 35. One finds the same wording in both the deluxe edition from the 1980s and more recent handbooks.

2. John Locke, *An Essay Concerning Human Understanding*, II, viii, 21. Reprinted in Roger Ariew and Eric Watkins, eds., *Readings in Modern Philosophy, Vol. II: Locke, Berkeley, Hume and Associated Texts* (Indianapolis, IN: Hackett, 2000), 21.

3. For example, a bomb in a bank satchel (Amazing Spider-Man #42 [November 1966]), a truck filled with villains (*Amazing Spider-Man* #299 [April 1988]), Stilt-man out of costume (*Amazing Spider-Man* #237 [February 1983]—only a moment later he detects that someone is picking his pocket when his attention is on Stilt-man), and the "criminal" Rocket Racer when visiting his mother (*Amazing Spider-Man* #183 [August 1978]).

4. This happens in *Spectacular Spider-Man*, vol. 1, #26–28 (January–March 1979).

5. Idealism opens the door to the possibility that things don't exist when we're not around to perceive them or that they constantly change with each new perceiver. Berkeley avoided these relativistic conclusions because he believed that one perceiver (God) was always watching everything.

6. I'm not talking here about those times when his spider-sense has been canceled out by Mysterio's gas or the gas used by both the Green Goblin and the Hobgoblin. In those instances, it seems as if Spider-Man has lost touch with his spider-sense, just as someone might block my pain receptors. This is shown when he realizes that the Hobgoblin's gas didn't take his spider-sense away; the gas simply made it difficult for him to hear his spider-sense —although it did break through when he came across a galactic threat (*Amazing Spider-Man* #250 [March 1984]).

7. *Amazing Spider-Man* #114 (November 1972).

8. David Hume, *A Treatise of Human Nature*, ed. David Fate Norton and Mary J. Norton (Oxford, UK: Oxford University Press, 2000), III, i, 1, 301.

9. *Amazing Spider-Man* #148 (September 1975).

10. *Amazing Spider-Man* #188 (January 1979).

11. There's disagreement about whether Hume himself thought our emotional reactions were culturally relative or shared by all humanity. I tend to think the latter.

12. Thomas Reid, *Essay on the Intellectual Powers of Man*, also in Ariew and Watkins, *Readings in Modern Philosophy*, 445.

13. Reid, *Essay on the Intellectual Powers of Man*, 444.

14. I can find no official confirmation of it (and you couldn't pay me enough to reread the Clone Saga to find it), but in discussion forums and on Wikipedia I have seen it remarked that Spider-Man's spider-sense doesn't react to his clones and that it is because they register as "self" (because they are genetic copies), and no one would regard his or her self as a danger. What I can confirm is that the clone Ben Reilly's spider-sense is identical to Peter Parker's, except that Venom activates Ben's spider-sense (*Official Handbook of the Marvel Universe: Spiderman 2005* (April 2005)). The reason given is that Ben never bonded with the Venom symbiote, which presumably means there was no mixing of the "self." If accurate, the clone examples give greater credence to the idea that the criterion is individual survival.

RED OR BLACK

Perception, Identity, and Self

Meaghan P. Godwin

There's much ado about identity in all hero stories, super and otherwise. According to Stan Lee, Spider-Man was created to fill a special niche—the identity of the super-teen. Teenagers are a special breed, as psychologist Erik Erikson (1902–1994) noted, because not only are they in a stage of development where they're trying to figure out what to do with their lives, they're also "primarily concerned with what they appear to be in the eyes of others as compared with what they feel they are."[1]

Peter Parker has been variously portrayed as a high schooler, a college student, a scientist, a geek, a photographer, a good kid, a smart alec, a boy next door, an idealist, a romantic, a comic, and a moral hero. Yet a stunning turnabout of identity happens when Spidey encounters the alien symbiote—a parasitic life form seeking a host to transform. Peter's sense of self changes, both inside and out—physically, emotionally, superficially, and essentially—once he's infected by this invader. Confidence becomes arrogance. Romance becomes womanizing. Braving the fight turns to murderous rage. Still, even with his newfound power of a stronger, more dangerous persona, *something* of the original Peter recognizes that the changes are not for the better. So we are left to wonder, What is it in Peter that changes because of the symbiote, and what is it that doesn't change? When we say that our "selves" change or are affected in some way, what is it that we are talking about? What is the *self*? What is identity? And how do we know who we are?

These questions are of interest to philosophers from all schools of thought, but in this chapter we'll look at them from the perspective of pragmatism. Pragmatism is a philosophical point of view that attempts to gain a better understanding of our understandings (yeah, that's right, understanding our understandings) by investigating our use of language, our perceptions, our various mental capabilities such as imagination, and different combinations of these—all considered from the vantage point of their practical consequences.

A Hero Transformed

> This suit, where'd this come from? The power, feels good. . . . But you lose yourself to it.[2]
>
> —Peter Parker, *Spider-Man 3*

So, you awaken hanging upside down from a Manhattan skyscraper. You already have superpowers, so this isn't *completely* off-the-charts weird, but there's something different— your costume. Wait. It's not *just* the costume, it's something more, something internal. You feel stronger, more powerful, more confident, more forceful, more angry, but somehow it's still you. What's going on? Is it the new threads? Or is the new costume allowing you to see yourself in a different way? How much does your perspective or outlook influence who you are?

For Peter Parker, the influence of his new perspective, however *alien*, is palpable.

Super fans, the comic book and cartoon crowd, know that the symbiote has its own agenda, being sent from an alternate dimension. This is a good thing for us to keep in mind because the changes in Peter are not passive. The symbiote is an active agent, feeding on and amplifying the negative aspects of human nature: anger, jealousy, vengefulness. These traits are more obvious in Eddie Brock, the symbiote's ultimate mate, than they are in Peter—yet they are there in Peter. These negative traits exist in all human beings, to some degree, but *where* in human beings are they? In the self?

When first under the symbiote's influence, Peter recognizes the changes and deliberates about how to handle them. He chooses to take off the new suit, the better in him trumping the worse, at least at first. Yet he also chooses to put it back on because he *enjoys* the new power. Perhaps this is in part because whether as Red-and-Blue Spidey or Black Spidey, Peter seems to be constantly at odds with his world. Every time he gets into a groove (spider powers, new jobs, dating MJ, key to the city, doing well in school), something arises to create trouble (Green Goblin, no sleep, New Goblin, cosmic ooze). Then there's the whole Flint-Marco-being-the-man-responsible-for-Uncle-Ben's-death-but-who-is-also-a-person-caught-up-in-life's-whirlwinds-so-does-Spidey-kill-him-or-not thing. It's all very confusing. Thank God for Aunt May, who finds a way to plant a simple and profound truth in the midst of these storms, "Uncle Ben wouldn't want us living with revenge in our hearts, it's like a poison. It can take you over and turn us into something ugly."[3]

Yet who is this Peter Parker whom Aunt May warns against being taken over by revenge? For that matter—who are you? Who am I? (And is that Daltry and Townshend on the radio, singing—"Whooo are you? Who who, who who?") Are we who *we* think we are or are we who *others* think we are? Perhaps we're some combination of our own ideas and the ideas others have about us. Perhaps who we are is not a matter of self-perception or the perceptions of others. *Maybe*, and just stay with me here, maybe the question isn't about *who* we are but about *what* we are. What's a self?

Philosophers such as the noted Scottish smarty-pants David Hume (1711–1776) and the famous Indian sage Siddhartha Gautama (ca. 560–480), aka. the Buddha, claimed that a self is nothing more than a product of both imagination and language.[4] Hume and the Buddha each spoke about the self in terms of aggregates and composites, little bits of things held together to form a whole. Their idea was that what we think of as a self is really just a bundle of things, such as thoughts, feelings, and sensations that we tie together as an imagined whole and call *the self.* This may seem crazy, but think about it: what does your *self* look like? Is it what you see in the mirror? The reflection is something we directly experience, but isn't your *self* something more? That mirror reflection, the physical you, grows and changes constantly. If the self was only your mirror image, then how could we say that you are the same self now that you were as an infant? You've stopped wearing diapers by now, but you're still you, right? When we watch Spider-Man, we know that it's still Peter Parker under that mask, and when his suit changes from red and blue to black, we know that it's still Spidey, still Peter there, too. If we want to find a self, we apparently need to look deeper than appearance. We need to look to our inner experiences. Yet that doesn't mean there has to be some single, stable, unified thing. Perhaps the self is really the combination of all of those inner experiences.

When I ask people—okay, college students, but they're people, too—what they think of when they think of their "selves," I usually get a list that includes appearance, preferences, and feelings. We already covered appearance. What are preferences? Are they desires? A class of thoughts?

What about thoughts? Can we say that we identify our *selves* with our thoughts? Maybe, but when we speak of thoughts, don't we speak of ourselves as *having* thoughts? We can't both *have* something and *be* that something at the same time, can we? When you think about having a pizza, are you at the same time being a pizza? When Peter thinks about Mary Jane, he doesn't somehow become Mary Jane, he has a thought about her. When he thinks about Flint Marco being responsible for Uncle Ben's death, the thought angers him. He becomes angry, but he doesn't become the thought. So the self isn't thought.

Let's go back to the anger thing. Peter does become angry. Very angry. Angry enough to kill . . . almost. Angry enough to scrape Sandman's face against a moving subway car, anyway. So perhaps a self is more like feelings, emotions. When we speak about emotions, we say someone *is* angry or happy or sad or whatever. In these cases, though, the subject of the sentence is still the person, the self to which we are referring. Emotions are modifiers—oh, no, grammar!—of the person or the thing having the emotion. Peter is angry, he's not anger itself. In the black suit, he seems to enjoy his anger and feels powerful enough to do something serious about it. Yet it's still Peter under there, not anger and power as distinct, separate entities packed into Spidey's suit as if they were clowns in a car.

What then, you ask, about the mind? Can the self be identified as a mind, as some combination of thoughts and feelings? I in turn may ask you, is there a difference between the mind and the brain? What exactly is the mind? Hm, you say . . . good questions. We usually want to think the mind is something else, something other, but we can easily get ourselves into a dispute about the definition of mind, much as we are in now concerning the definition of the self. When we talk about our minds, we do so as something we have, as we did with thoughts and emotions. "I've made up my mind" seems more correct than saying, "I've made up myself." Perhaps this is just a turn of phrase, a language problem, and the self really is the mind. After all, if you lose your mind, we sometimes say that you're *not yourself*. We may say that, but when we visit our grandparents who suffer from Alzheimer's, are we visiting someone else or are we visiting them? Fair enough, you may argue, but who gets to define a self: the self in question, or others who exist in relation with that self, such as family, friends, coworkers? Excellent question! We'll return to it a little later.

A lot has been said so far about what a self isn't, but it still seems as though the idea of a self can't be shaken. This fact was enough for another Scotsman, Thomas Reid (1710–1796), to say that the self exists as a simple, unchanging thing.[5] Reid didn't need proof of what the self looked like or of what it was made. It was enough for him that it felt real. Peter Parker is Peter Parker because we can refer to Peter Parker and know who and what we mean. 'Nuff said. It's common sense, a phrase that also happens to be the name of the school of philosophy Reid helped found.

Maybe Peter would agree with Reid. After all, he said that the suit was something to which you could lose yourself. He even warned Eddie Brock about it in *Spider-Man 3*.

> Peter: "Eddie, the suit, you've got to take it off."
> Eddie: "Oh, you'd like that, wouldn't you?"
> Peter: "I know what it feels like. It feels good. The power. Everything. But you'll lose yourself. It'll destroy you. Let it go."

If Reid is correct, Peter may be right—your self is lost when the parasite takes over. If Hume and the Buddha are right, then it isn't a matter so much of losing yourself as it is perhaps a matter of redescribing yourself. If you do that, then maybe you can even redescribe what a self is.

Selves Transformed

It's a funny feeling, not knowing who you are. I get a
bump on the head and I'm as free as a bird.

—Harry Osborn

Can you bump me on the head?

—MJ, *Spider-Man 3*

Who gets to define a self: the self, or others who exist
in relation to the self? Prior to being clothes-lined by Peter,
Harry was a seething pile of rich-boy anger. Postconcussion, he
was back to his old self—funny, charming, relaxed. Did Harry
change, or did his perception of his relationships change?
Peter was suddenly just Peter again, not a spandex-wearing
father killer. Yet didn't the concussion have something to do
with this change in perception? Should the self of a human
being be thought of as including biology, psychology, and sociology? Is Peter only Peter, or is he Spider-Man *and* an orphan
and Aunt May's nephew *and* Dr. Connors's student *and* MJ's
boyfriend *and* Harry's best friend *and* a spandex-wearing father
killer *and* therefore Harry's sworn enemy?

Pragmatic philosophy may give us a way to incorporate all
of those "ands." A uniquely American philosophical school, it
was formulated, refined, and informed by the American spirit,
a spirit of change and of choice. Pragmatic philosophy, or
pragmatism—developed in the 1880s by the likes of Charles
Sanders Peirce (1839–1914) and William James (1842–1910)—
was born into a time when academic pursuits were not as distinct from one another as they are today. Many of the fathers
(sorry, Ladies, no mothers here, but there were some aunts
and there's a bevy of daughters) of this movement also studied
psychology, sociology, medicine, and education. These inter-
disciplinary interests helped form a different understanding of
what a self might be. What they came up with is known today

as the "social self." The idea is that our understanding of who and what we are is shaped by our relationships with our environment.[6] Rather than assume a simple self or some psychological ego whose discrete actions control choice, thought, and emotion, pragmatists such as John Dewey (1859–1952) and George Herbert Mead (1863–1931) thought that a *web* of conditions, as it were, contributes to our notions of what a self is and how it functions. This web consists of factors that include biology, psychology, socioeconomic status, environment, and on, and on, and on.

The psychologist George Engel (1913–1999) summed up this web with the term *biopsychosocial*. Though Engel was primarily concerned about developing a holistic approach to medical diagnoses, rather than lending overt support to pragmatism, his ideas do provide that support. Let's break down Engel's word: "Bio" recognizes that the human self is composed in part of genetics and the fleshy bits that express them. "Psycho" refers to the psychological component of the human self, and, more important, it acknowledges that our mental processes affect our physical and social processes, as well as vice versa. "Social" works in the same way, serving as prop to the idea that our socioeconomic environment affects who and what we are, as much as do our biology and psychology. These three influences exert pressure on one another to create the self that we think we know and feel so intimately. Yet because the biopsychosocial factors are susceptible to change, so, too, is the self that they produce susceptible to change. The biopsychosocial model of the self recognizes that the nature-versus-nurture debate has been wrong all along. It's not an either/or, it's both and more (rhyme time!).

The biopsychosocial self, or BPS self, for short, composed as it is of the biological brain, the psychological mind, and a social identity, reveals itself to be the result of the ways that it is variously affected by other selves and things, and that affects them in turn. It is, then, a pragmatic definition of what we are as selves. It succeeds as a general description of selves considered as a species of animal on this planet, but is that enough? What about *who* we are as individual selves? Peter Parker may be a BPS self, but who exactly is *he*? How do we determine the identity of a self?

The Transforming Self

I don't know what to do. . . .

—Peter Parker

I'm sure you'll find it within yourself to do the right thing.

—Aunt May, *Spider-Man 3*

The question of self-identity puts Peter's struggle with the symbiote and Eddie Brock's eventual succumbing to it into perspective. How can Peter maintain his sense of identity, his sense of who he is, while Eddie seems to lose his? The symbiote feeds on anger and frustration, sensations present in both young men. Yet in Pete's case, his biopsychosocial self seems to identify more with the positive side of human nature than it does with the angry, destructive side. A BPS profile of Pete would show strong relationships with good people, such as Aunt May, MJ, and Harry, as well as a good biology (scientist parents, spider stuff). Eddie seems to be a loner, full of piss and vinegar, but even he does not completely allow the symbiote to entirely control his sense of who he is. In later versions of the story, Venom (whom Eddie becomes) never loses his hatred for Spidey, but he refuses to harm innocent beings (unlike his cousin Carnage, but that's a different story). Assuming that getting a full BPS profile of everyone we know is not possible, how can we truly distinguish someone's self? How do we identify someone? How are we identified? In other words, what comprises identity?

Perhaps we are best identified by our actions. Action aids in the identification of a person—the individually identifiable BPS self. After all, actions speak louder than words, right? This is always how the "real" superhero is distinguished from a villainous doppelganger when such a ne'er-do-well has disguised him- or herself as the hero. The villain always does something out of character, something the hero wouldn't do.

In fact, character, the sum of a person's actions, is a good way of thinking about self-identification. What makes up Peter's character? By and large, he is a good guy. Smart and unassuming pre–spider bite, then smart and still pretty unassuming post–spider bite, he works hard, studies, helps out around the house. He does get a little full of himself after a while, but isn't it convenient that the symbiote comes along to show him (and us) how dangerous that kind of behavior can be?

The pragmatist John Dewey told us that "Plato once defined a slave as the person who executes the purposes of another, and, a person is also a slave who is enslaved to his own blind desires."[7] Here the slave is defined by action, by doing what others want or what the undisciplined self wants. Eddie as Venom is a slave in both senses: doing the anger-driven bidding of the symbiote by continuing to bond with it, while giving in to his blind hatred for Peter. He also pursues Gwen Stacy blindly, entirely unaware of her lack of affection for him. An important part of Eddie's identity, then, would be someone who acts out of blind desire, and this would be one distinguishing mark of who he is, of his *self*. If Eddie should come to his senses at some point and stop behaving in this way, we could still identify him as Eddie who has changed or bettered him*self*. Perhaps at this point, we can state that identity is the mark or outward expression of self.

Elsewhere, Dewey wrote, "[T]he identity of an individual is constituted by continued absorption and incorporation of materials previously external."[8] Identity is who we are, whereas self is what we are. We are selves that have identities. You may hear a new parent freak out because there is a "little stranger" in the house. Babies do not seem to have completed identities, if identity includes the incorporation of external qualities, such as what colors and toys they like, what kinds of clothes they prefer, how they respond to good news and bad news. Still, babies do have some identifying characteristics. Even if they do not know themselves, we know them, as the child of so and so, as being fussy or quiet, and so on. If identity is the expression of a self, then we'd have to say that an infant has a BPS self. The point is that a self is a thing that is constantly molded and remolded into a complex and mutable identity.

This seems to be what we have with Peter Parker, a complex identity. Eddie's identity is more closely aligned with the symbiote, making them a good match as Venom, but Peter never really gets into being Black Spidey. He toys with it until he realizes that it's consuming his identity, and he manages to save his *self* before it's too late. Who knew church bells could be so helpful?

If Peter was only and simply good, he would likely not have put the black suit back on after taking it off the first time. An identity or a social self is, as Dewey wrote, "a shifting mixture of vice and virtue" because we are constantly dealing with an environment in flux.[9] This is a pretty good description for each of us, including Peter Parker. He grows up in the care of an aunt and an uncle because his own parents die in a plane crash. He is bullied. He loses his uncle in an act of violence. He struggles with a love interest who is a product of an unseemly environment. The seeds of Black Spidey are planted early, but so, too, are the seeds of Red-and-Blue Spidey. His aunt and uncle give him a loving environment. He has a best friend who stays with him, despite their different economic situations. His intelligence and drive give him the wherewithal to succeed despite the odds. Although the black of retribution follows him, the red and blue of hope and encouragement are also there cheering him on.

In the movie, the conflict between Red and Blue Spidey and Black Spidey is more about a conflict between the best and the worst in Peter Parker. Such a struggle can help depict how difficult it is to pin down the nature of the self. When something such as your*self*, something that seems too obvious to be doubted, is suddenly pointed out to be elusive and perhaps not at all what you thought it to be, what other sorts of things might you be taking for granted? When in *Spider-Man 3* MJ asks the struggling Peter, "Who are you?" he answers honestly, "I don't know." Sorting out the transforming identity of our *selves* is an ongoing process, and it's also the central task for living a reflective life.

NOTES

1. Erik Erikson, "Eight Ages of Man," in R. Diessner and J. Tiegs, eds., *Sources: Notable Selections in Human Development* (New York: McGraw Hill/ Dushkin, 2001), 22.

2. All quotes from *Spider-Man 3*, www.imdb.com/title/tt0413300/quotes.

3. *Spider-Man 3*.

4. David Hume, *A Treatise of Human Nature* (Oxford: Clarendon Press, 1896); John J. Holder, ed., *Early Buddhist Discourses* (Indianapolis, IN: Hackett, 2006).

5. Thomas Reid, *Thomas Reid's Inquiry and Essays* (Indianapolis, IN: Bobbs-Merril, 1975), 212–215.

6. George Herbert Mead, *The Philosophy of the Act* (Chicago: The University of Chicago Press, 1972), 215.

7. John Dewey, *Experience and Education* (New York: Collier Press, 1973), 67.

8. John Dewey, *The Quest for Certainty* (New York: Capricorn Press, 1960), 189.

9. John Dewey, *Human Nature and Conduct* (New York: Modern Library, 1957), 55.

WITH GREAT POWER

Heroism, Villainy, and Bodily Transformation

Mark K. Spencer

Some of the most harrowing scenes in the *Spider-Man* films are when ordinary people are transformed into superhuman beings, capable of spectacular feats of strength and agility. Watching Peter Parker transform into Spider-Man or Norman Osborn into the Green Goblin brings a thrill of excitement—perhaps we wish to undergo such amazing bodily transformations, or perhaps we fear doing so because it could mean the end of our personal identities. Yet Spider-Man and his adversaries still have very human concerns after their transformations: desires for power, love, pleasure, and safety. They are still caught up in the same moral struggles that we all find ourselves in—but unlike us, they destroy sections of Manhattan while engaged in those struggles. So, despite the differences, the bodily transformations of Parker and company have analogues in our own ordinary lives. Our quests to become more fulfilled people involve decisions that both cause and are influenced by bodily changes, which, though not as spectacular as those in the films, are nevertheless as decisive for our lives as Parker's transformation was for his.

Changing the World

Phenomenology is a school of thought that has its origin in the work of the German philosopher Edmund Husserl (1859–1938). It focuses not on theories about how we think or act but tries to describe very precisely our actual experiences of the world and the ways that our experiences are structured. Two French phenomenologists, Maurice Merleau-Ponty (1908–1961) and Emmanuel Levinas (1906–1995), focused on the ways in which we experience our bodies and how these experiences form the basis of many of our other experiences. They also analyzed the passive aspects of our lives, such as our bodiliness and our affectivity, aspects of ourselves over which we don't have total control but that have a lot of impact on who we are. By focusing on their descriptions of experience, along with the holistic view of our ethical lives given by virtue ethics, we can see how the spectacular bodily transformations undergone by Parker and others in the Marvel Universe have a significance for our lives and how ethics is much deeper—and more exciting—than simply following rules.

Prior to his bodily transformation, Parker is a weak, timid, and awkward teenager, despite having basically good intentions and desires. Many situations that he encounters—from being late for the bus to seeing Mary Jane's boyfriend—present obstacles to the achievement of his goals. Merleau-Ponty pointed out that things that we encounter as obstacles are experienced as such because of how our bodies, with their abilities and weaknesses, meet up with the world.[1] We do not experience the world as pure minds that impassively gather data via the senses. Rather, every experience of the world that we have involves a meeting of our bodies, feelings, and interests with the situations in which we find ourselves. Our senses, desires, and thoughts all involve bodily reactions and movements, though often we are not aware of them, and our bodies either harmonize or fail to harmonize with the structures that are encountered through the senses. Changes to our bodies—both wounds and enhancements—also involve changes in the world as we perceive it. One's world of experience is always structured in terms of ideas and concepts, which turn the flux of sensory experience into concrete, definable objects. An infant's world is very narrow, but as our senses and abilities for movement become better developed and as we learn concepts and a language, the world expands. We become aware of things as the things that they are. Greater knowledge and greater sensory and affective acuity yield a richer world with more detailed objects. Having a larger world gives one new opportunities for movement and action, and these in turn expand one's perceptions and knowledge.

With Parker's new abilities, things that were an obstacle prior to his transformation no longer are: a wall is no longer just the side of a building for him, but a thing to be climbed, a new possibility for movement. The very *meanings* that walls and dangerous people have for Parker have changed through his bodily transformation and his new motile possibilities. The same thing happens to us when we grow in virtue or vice: a transformation of bodily abilities and of the way in which we perceive and understand certain objects in the world presents new possibilities for action.

Bodily modification and transformation of perception also requires, according to Merleau-Ponty, a sort of knowledge that is different from knowledge that can be put in the form of propositions. Merleau-Ponty pointed out that our bodily movements all have a sort of meaning, and as we develop new abilities, we develop a "motor knowledge" or "bodily knowledge" in our very actions. We see this in the way that Spider-Man is able to move at high speeds, knowing where next to shoot his webs without calculating and using his spider-sense to avoid danger. We also see this in any athlete whose body "knows" how to move to accomplish a play, without requiring an explicit scientific analysis of the situation. Merleau-Ponty argued that this bodily knowledge underlies all other forms of knowledge, for it is the way that our bodies mesh with or fit into specific situations in the world. This sort of knowledge gives to us a world, a feel for that world, and it develops when we undergo bodily transformation in the development of abilities and habits.

Transformation, Virtue, and Vice

Changes to the body involve taking on or losing ways of perceiving, feeling, and acting in the world. Through these changes, the world also appears differently. Interest and feeling cause us to see aspects of things that we didn't see before, and new abilities cause us to perceive things as obstacles or opportunities in new ways. Yet these modifications to the body and the corresponding changes to our perceptions of the world always contribute to our goodness or badness because they also involve choices in real situations. Through the new opportunities it presents to us, bodily transformation is not just a matter of *what* we are, but a matter of what we *ought* or *ought not* to do. The way in which bodily transformations change the whole person points us to the holistic vision of virtue ethics.[2]

Spider-Man's bodily transformation doesn't, in and of itself, make him a superhero, just as Norman Osborn's gaining new strength doesn't by itself make him evil. Their transformations are not only a matter of organic changes but involve choices, reasons, and an interplay between the new abilities, the situations in which they find themselves, and their previous character. To take on his new abilities fully, Parker must practice them, so that they become habits, and so that his body really gains the motor knowledge necessary for him to act as Spider-Man. This practice takes place in concrete situations, some of which he chooses and others that are forced on him. Parker chooses to use his new abilities in different situations, which help him develop virtues, rather than vices. Likewise, Osborn's new strength helps make him vicious because of the choices that led to his taking on a bodily transformation in the first place.

Thomas Aquinas (1225–1274) described virtue as "the perfection of a power."[3] We have several natural powers— our emotions and desires (such as love, anger, joy, sadness); our senses and our ability to move; our intellectual abilities to know things in various ways; and our volitional abilities to deliberate and choose. Each of these powers is oriented toward goals in the world, and it takes practice and the formation of a habit to make sure that these powers reach their proper goals. Indeed, it is a struggle to discover what our proper goals are and to perform actions that will enable us to reach those goals consistently. Virtue shapes and strengthens our desires so that we want to reach those goals, are motivated to reach them, and actually have the ability to reach them. Developing virtue requires developing one's bodily abilities and feelings so that one has the intuition to know what to do in a given situation (Aquinas called this prudence) and so that one has the bodily knowledge and ability necessary to carry out virtuous action.

Spider-Man struggles a great deal with deciding what will bring him fulfillment and with choosing the right thing to do. Each choice he makes leads to a further modification of his bodily abilities and his perception of the world, as well as to growth in virtue or vice. This is dramatically portrayed when his choices modify his bodily abilities to the point where he loses and then regains his superheroic powers in *Spider-Man 2*. In this, we see an idea put forward by both virtue ethicists and phenomenologists: ethics is not simply a matter of isolated acts, but the drama of an entire life. We also see this drama in the lives of the supervillains, such as when Doc Ock's bodily transformation, combined with his weak and sentimental will and his pain at his wife's death, make it so difficult for him to do what's right. We learn from this that bodily transformations can contribute significantly to changes in our character, especially when we're just swept along by the changes.

We also learn from Doc Ock that the conscience can nevertheless reassert itself no matter how deeply it is buried. The best condition, though, involves one's feelings and desires working together with reason. Reason can't absolutely control feelings through rules but must mesh with the passive and chancy aspects of the person—the body and the feelings. All of this must be worked out during the course of an entire life—and there is the possibility of reversing one's direction, as we see with Parker's turn toward evil in *Spider-Man 3*, as well as with Doc Ock's and the Sandman's conversions toward goodness. New bodily abilities are required for and flow from choices made to pursue virtue or vice, but they don't necessitate such choices. Still, the more one sets oneself on the path of virtue or vice, the harder it is to change.

The passive and vulnerable dimensions of our emotional and bodily lives play an important role in Aquinas's understanding of virtue and vice and of human nature.[4] Parker in no way chooses his new abilities; they are thrust on him in a freak accident. When Norman Osborn, on the other hand, seizes superpowers for himself, he combines new bodily abilities with a pride that goes beyond his power to control. Osborn's inner conflicts depict the dangers that virtue ethicists see in seizing power for oneself, rather than working with the passive and uncontrollable elements we meet in life. Virtue entails harmony among all of the aspects of your life; vice is a result of one part of your life overruling and destroying the others. When ethics focuses only on rules and acts, rather than on paying attention to the fact that our bodies are subject to forces beyond our total control, it risks the evils to which Osborn subjects himself, and it also brings about lives that are neither as good nor as fulfilling as a life that is open to vulnerability, such as the one that Spider-Man leads.

Great Responsibility

How does Parker know he's doing good when he's saving people as Spider-Man? The Green Goblin seems to have a point when he argues that those who have more advanced bodily abilities ought to rule the weaker members of society. Those with greater bodily abilities see more of the world and have fewer obstacles. Perhaps the great responsibility that comes with great power is a responsibility to oneself, to furthering one's own goals, and building up one's strength even further. Yet Spider-Man rejects this proposal. He believes that he has a responsibility to others not because it makes him feel good, but because that is what his bodily powers enable and call him to do. In *Spider-Man 3*, when he uses his powers pridefully it leads to misery, for he *does* feel a call to serve others with the great power that he has been given. Just consider the evident pain he feels when he chooses to ignore a mugging and fails to respond to the call for help.

The call to goodness is experienced bodily, and this is overlooked by the likes of the Green Goblin and others who claim that one's abilities are to be used for mastery over others. Levinas agreed with Aquinas and Merleau-Ponty that our human lives do not simply consist of collecting and acting on facts. Our bodily interaction with the world involves a feeling of being alive, of sensing our own vitality, and this is a matter of enjoyment or suffering. When Spider-Man is swinging through Manhattan and doing the other extraordinary things he can, not only do we see his special bodily abilities and knowledge being exercised virtuously, but we see him fully engaged in the activities and experiencing either intense pleasure or suffering. This full engagement points to a distinctively human aspect of the films—that is, a distinctively bodily aspect—for it is through the ways that our bodies fit into a situation that we enjoy life or suffer.[5]

Levinas thought that this enjoyment or suffering was decisive for experiencing the call to goodness.[6] We don't merely feel our own enjoyment or suffering. Rather, when we encounter others, we feel for them, we experience their enjoyment or suffering sympathetically. When we encounter another person, we are called out of ourselves into a state of sociality with that other person. We feel a call to help others in their suffering— ideally, Levinas thought—even to the detriment of ourselves. Levinas described this experience as one of "being substituted for the other," of being oriented toward serving others before oneself. He argued that if it were not for the way that others affect us bodily and emotionally, calling us out of ourselves in responsibility, there would be no language or ability to discover anything about the world. Rather, we would remain trapped in ourselves; our experiences would then be infantile, merely oriented toward the satisfaction of our own needs. The fact that we communicate shows, he thought, that we are first and foremost oriented toward others, and this orientation is the essence of ethics. This is the ethical call, the basis of all of the goodness and meaning in our lives.

To refuse to listen to this call is to fail to realize something fundamental about what we are as bodily beings: it is a failure to be the human beings we are. Despite his claims to the contrary, the Green Goblin has already been called out of himself by others; by pretending not to have heard this call, he is living a self-contradiction. The presence of others makes me realize that I can't enjoy myself unrestrictedly—and if I try to, I can't enjoy myself at all. Spider-Man experiences this call when he loses his abilities in *Spider-Man 2*, yet nevertheless rushes into a burning building. There we see that the call to serve can go beyond even what one is bodily able to do.

The call to serve others is an element of life over which we have no control. Spider-Man can't say when his powers will be needed, but he must be responsive to the call of the other person whenever it comes. The call is the foundation for all meaning in our actions, for it is what draws us out of ourselves into society. Levinas pointed out that once we have experienced in the face of another person a call to serve, we must respond not blindly, but with deliberation about how best to act. Doing so successfully requires growth in virtue and a concomitant growth in bodily ability, and this moral development is never really finished.

Human fulfillment comes not only from enjoyment, but from the often painful experience of sacrificing oneself for others. The cycle of enjoying one's bodily abilities and having them constantly implicated in the need to serve others is the very glory of human life—the quest for goodness that ennobles us.

A Story about a Girl

Aquinas argued that eros, or the love of attraction, draws us out of ourselves toward others. It is not only a force attracting us romantically to another human person, but an emotion that can lead us to zeal and action for higher causes and even for the divine. Merleau-Ponty pointed out that love, especially sexual love, colors every aspect of our lives, including all of our seemingly unrelated bodily abilities and movements; love is part of the bodily system of meaning that underlies the rest of our understanding of the world. Levinas said that romantic eros is dangerous because it can blind us to the needs of others beyond the one to whom we are attracted. Yet romantic eros allows ethical goodness to go on in the future because its sexual expression between a man and a woman leads to children, who carry on the quest for goodness.

Parker's love for Mary Jane does at times lead to conflict with his listening to the call to serve others; however, this conflict is another essentially human aspect of the story, something with which we all struggle in our quests for good, fulfilled lives. Unlike Norman Osborn, whose self-centered love for his son blinds him to the needs of others, Parker continues to strive for virtue, trying to find the right place in his life for his love for Mary Jane and for his superheroic abilities. He allows love to draw him to higher callings, rather than blinding him to the world. This quest, which is always messy and never complete, is a major part of the quest for virtue and necessarily involves mediating among various aspects of our bodies.

It is telling that the first *Spider-Man* film opens with Parker saying that his story is about a girl, Mary Jane. The drama of his relationship with her is the drama of Parker becoming a superhero and a virtuous human being. There is a sexual and erotic tonality to everything that Parker does, because that is part of being human, part of being a bodily being, and that tonality must be taken into account if one is to have a truly good, flourishing life.

The concluding scenes of *Spider-Man 3* sum up these bodily aspects that come into play when we consider the point of our lives. Parker has, in his final battle with Sandman and Venom, tested his bodily powers to their fullest. He experiences the conflicting pulls of virtue and vice in the context of his bodily abilities, and at great cost to himself and his friends he discovers that love of his friends can *both* draw him out of himself *and* blind him to the ethical call of others. We see him realize the conflicting tragic and comic aspects to being a body. We see him discover that life is not about formulating and following moral rules, but about coordinating and harmonizing aspects of bodily life by properly using reason and his other powers. We see him profoundly suffering and profoundly happy; we see him flourishing as a human being. Spider-Man's story depicts in vibrant fashion these conflicted, vulnerable, emotional, erotic truths about our lives, thus calling us to pay more attention to the roles our bodies play in our lives so that we might become the unique heroes we are called to be.

NOTES

1. See his *Phenomenology of Perception*, trans. Colin Smith (London: Routledge, 1958), particularly part 1, chaps. 3–4; part 2, chap. 3; and part 3, chap. 3. See also his *The Structure of Behavior*, trans. Alden L. Fisher (Boston: Beacon Press, 1963), especially part 3.

2. For more on virtue theory, see White's "The Sound and the Fury behind 'One More Day,'" as well as Sanford's chapter, "Spider-Man and the Importance of Getting Your Story Straight," both in this volume.

3. Throughout this chapter, I am drawing on Thomas Aquinas's discussions of the appetites or emotions, habits, and virtues throughout the first part of the second part of his *Summa Theologiae*, translated by the Fathers of the English Dominican Province. See I-II, q.55 for his definition of virtue.

4. For a beautiful and compelling discussion of these aspects of Aquinas's thought, see Thomas Hibbs, *Aquinas, Ethics, and Philosophy of Religion: Metaphysics and Practice* (Bloomington: Indiana University Press, 2007), especially chaps. 8 and 9. For a discussion of the place of vulnerability in virtue ethics, see Martha Nussbaum, *The Fragility of Goodness: Luck and Ethics in Greek Tragedy and Philosophy* (Cambridge, UK: Cambridge University Press, 1986), especially part 3.

5. Levinas discussed enjoyment in *Totality and Infinity: An Essay on Exteriority*, trans. Alphonso Lingis (Pittsburgh: Duquesne University Press, 1969), part 2; and in *Otherwise Than Being or Beyond Essence*, trans. Alphonso Lingis (Pittsburgh: Duquesne University Press, 1998), chap. 3.

6. The call to goodness is discussed in *Totality and Infinity*, part 3, and in *Otherwise Than Being*, chap. 4.

PART FOUR

ARACHNIDS "R" US: TECHNOLOGY AND THE HUMAN, ALL TOO HUMAN

TRANSHUMANISM

Or, Is It Right to Make a Spider-Man?

Ron Novy

> Four-hundred thousand years of evolution and we've
> barely even tapped the vastness of human potential.
>
> —Norman Osborn, *Spider-Man*

Aunt May is a cyborg. Her visual acuity far exceeds that of any member of her bridge club. Her access to stored information is incalculably greater than that of her ancestors. Her body's metabolism is alterable more or less at will. All of this fantastical manipulation of her otherwise normal human body—yet it's just another Sunday morning for Aunt May, sipping coffee and peering through her bifocals at the *Daily Bugle*.

The glasses, the newspaper, and the coffee are all technologies that dramatically enhance the capacities of Aunt May's aging body. She may also require insulin injections, have a titanium hip, take Prozac, and slip into a sweater when the temperature falls. Yet for any of these integrations of technology with her body, Aunt May is hardly unusual in her Queens neighborhood.

Few of us would begrudge Aunt May's use of these technologies, but she's not the sort of person who usually comes to mind when we think about human enhancement. In the New York of the Marvel Universe, we likely conjure images of Doc Ock with his four mechanically integrated arms or of Green Goblin pumped up on military-grade super steroids or of Lizard's human genius fused to a reptilian body, or—on a more positive note—of that web-slinging gymnast with the Spidey senses.[1] Unlike those of Aunt May, many of Spider-Man's abilities exceed typical human capacities. What are we to make of deliberately altering a human (or a human deliberately altering herself) in order to gain such superpowers? In other words, is it right to make a Spider-Man?

Enhancement Anxieties

Current and emerging technologies (gene therapy, neuroenhancement, nanotechnology, superprosthetics, and so on) that stretch our cognitive and physical capacities beyond a merely biological conception of being human add a distinct "biopolitical axis" to any discussion of the place of technology in human well-being.[2] At one end of the spectrum we find transhumanism, a movement that advocates the development and use of human enhancement technologies. At the other end, we find "bio-conservatives," critics of the use and development of such technologies.

Among the many criticisms of deliberate enhancement beyond the normal human range, three related themes stand out: that enhancement requires one to play God with the natural order; that it will destroy the equality of persons that underpins liberal democracy; and that it deprives the enhanced being of his or her *pure* human essence. Francis Fukuyama, a former member of the President's Council on Bioethics and a critic of transhumanism, says, "We do not want to disrupt either the unity or the continuity of human nature, and thereby the human rights that are based on it."[3] Though well-intentioned, much of the anxiety expressed by such bio-conservatives, as we shall see, amounts to hand-wringing based on a series of false dichotomies involving humans, technology, and nature.

Like a God among Men

> Any sufficiently advanced technology is indistinguishable from magic.
>
> —Arthur C. Clarke, Third Law of Prediction

Opposition to superhuman enhancement has a history longer than Doc Ock's sleeves. In *The Republic*, Glaucon, acting as Socrates's foil in their dialogue on the nature of morality and justice, argues that given the power of invisibility, even the most virtuous person would become a monster:

> No man can be imagined to be of such an iron nature that he would stand fast in justice. No man would keep his hands off what was not his own when he could safely take what he liked out of the market, or go into houses and lie with any one at his pleasure, or kill or release from prison whom he would, and in all respects be like a god among men.[4]

Here, Glaucon touches on all three challenges to human enhancement: this man would "be like a god among men," would lose his human nature, and would destroy any notion that he was the equal of other men. If Glaucon is correct, no person given powers that greatly exceed the norm—say, invisibility or the ability to sling webs—would be able to resist abusing that power. Put more strongly, lack of opportunity and fear of punishment hold our selfish—or at least self-interested—desires in check. With superpowers, these constraints are loosened so that one's underlying desire to exploit, steal, or be generally naughty can run free. To twist a phrase, "With great power comes great corruptibility."

Although Spider-Man may stand out as an exemplar of radical human enhancement, many of the objections raised to pursuing just such technologies are made flesh in the range of Spidey-villains: deliberate physical modification leads down the path of criminality and madness—or, as in Dr. Michael Morbius's transformation into "Morbius, the Living Vampire," both.[5] As Glaucon might have predicted, Morbius's effort to escape his "natural" limitations leads to the loss of all but a trace of his humanity, while simultaneously reducing the rest of us to the status of cattle.

Doc Ock—like Spider-Man—is who he is due largely to fundamental modifications to an otherwise unexceptional human body: pudgy physicist Otto Octavius's cerebellum is linked via nano-wires to four powerful and intelligent mechanical arms. Similar sorts of modifications to other more or less normal people are essential to the back story of many Spidey-villains. Lizard, Jackal, Morbius, and the like came to exist as a consequence of someone trying to catapult himself (and it is usually *him*self) beyond the existential constraints of a "normal life." Octavius's megalomania led him to risk destroying a large portion of Manhattan; Norman Osborn is driven insane by forgoing safety protocols in pursuit of profit; Curtis Conners becomes Lizard in his efforts to use reptilian DNA to regrow a lost limb.

Spider-Man is as radically altered as any member of his rogues' gallery, but how Peter Parker came to have his genetic makeup scrambled with that of a spider is quite different. Peter's enhancement came about unintentionally—a scrawny high school kid in the wrong place at the wrong time. Unlike Octavius or Osborn, Parker is a decent kid playing within society's rules. When Peter is transformed, his moral character is also Spider-Man's character. Otto and Norman, on the other hand, are ambitious and already quite sure of their superiority to other individuals. When they cause themselves to transform, their moral character becomes that of Dr. Octopus and Green Goblin, respectively. Their superpowers eliminate many of the previous barriers to fulfilling their egoistic and narcissistic desires, desires that do not dominate Peter's character.

Though not denying the possibility of abuse, the growing transhumanist movement is held together by the beliefs that cutting-edge technology properly applied can significantly improve our individual and collective well-being, and that we have an ethical obligation to pursue such improvements. As contemporary philosopher Nick Bostrom puts it,

> Transhumanism has its roots in secular humanist thinking, yet is more radical in that it advocates not only traditional means (such as education and cultural refinement) of improving human nature, but also direct application of medicine and technology to overcome some of our basic biological limits.[6]

Transhumanists favor the development of technological means both to achieve human capabilities and to expand on them, even if this leads to our surpassing what have been taken to be human limits. These enhancement possibilities are generally seen as a continuation of the traditional function of medicine and technology: to improve physical, cognitive, and emotional well-being and to provide for the possibility of surpassing limits. In short, to develop what the funny papers call "superpowers."

A Lucky Guy

What seems to separate Spider-Man from the villains he fights is the character of the individuals prior to their transition. Peter Parker is a modest guy changed by an *accidental* spider bite, whereas most villains begin as overly ambitious, self-important persons who *deliberately* attempt to make themselves "like a god among men." Supervillainhood is thus often the result of meddling where perhaps humans ought not to meddle.

In *Spider-Man* (2002), Peter Parker is bitten by a "super spider" that has escaped from its cage at Columbia University's Genetic Research Institute.[7] The bite, rather than causing necrosis or neurotoxic shock, adds certain of the spider's characteristics to our soon-to-be hero. This could have been quite a horrible event, given his literary predecessors—recall the fate of Andre Delambre in *The Fly* or the Samsa family's reaction to Gregor's transformation in *The Metamorphosis*.[8] It turns out that Pete is a very lucky guy.

The spider that bit Peter had been genetically engineered to combine the jumping ability of *delana sparassidea*, the net webbing of *filistatidea kukukcania*, and the "almost precognizant" reaction time (the famed "Spidey-sense") of the grass spider, an unspecified species of the family *agelenidae*. Its venom spliced bits of its mutated genes into Peter Parker's DNA, giving him those same abilities. Apart from the obvious "superpower" benefits, we see Peter transformed overnight from a near-sighted, ninety-eight-pound weakling to a sharp-eyed, six-pack-wielding Charles Atlas.

A Strange Liberation Movement

I beheld the wretch—the miserable monster whom
I had created.

—Victor Frankenstein, *Frankenstein*

In a 2004 article, "The World's Most Dangerous Idea: Transhumanism," Fukuyama touches on a number of points critical of the deliberate altering of persons and characterizes transhumanism as "a strange liberation movement" that aims for "nothing less than to liberate the human race from its biological constraints."[9] As a critic of enhancing human beings in ways that pale by comparison to Spider-Man, Doc Ock, or

Green Goblin, Fukuyama holds that designing and imposing a genetic makeup on a person would in some way force him or her into an attitude, a lifestyle, or a career chosen by the designer, rather than by the recipient.

In response to Fukuyama, we might say that because each human necessarily has a genetic composition, it hardly seems responsible to leave such an important matter to chance when one need not. Refusing to intervene when able to do so is to embrace a status quo that may include wholly avoidable hardships. Why not simply remove the problem from the person's life? All things being equal, it seems obvious to most of us that if we can act to bring about lives in which we are healthier and more functionally capable, we ought to do so.[10]

Consider a trait such as athletic ability: certain enhancements might require that a decision to modify be made prior to an individual's birth (say, altering genes to avoid a predisposition toward arthritis or to increase endurance).[11] Other enhancements might occur only after the individual has been born; such modifications may be a simple addition (something akin to a cochlear implant to boost one's sensory range or an insulin pump to regulate endorphin levels) or an outright substitution of one part for another, as we already do for damaged hips and knees.[12] Either way, there is a decision made that limits or expands the individual's capabilities.

So, in response to Fukuyama calling transhumanism a "strange liberation movement," we might say "yes, it is, and a good thing, too." The ongoing effort to free ourselves from the biological inheritance of our ancestors is a defining condition of human history—from the first pointy stick to the latest antibiotics. According to Fukuyama, this effort to wrestle "biological destiny from evolution's blind process of random variation and adaptation and move to the next stage as a species" is something to be feared and avoided.[13] On the contrary, given the trajectory of human technology and medicine, it not only seems inevitable that we will continue to push against whatever limits to our abilities, thoughts, emotions, and duration exist, we actually have a responsibility to do so. We may never be quite "like a god among men" as Glaucon expresses it, but nonetheless humans have continually met and broadened those limits to good effect.

Equality and Biology

> There are eight million people in this city. And those teeming masses exist for the sole purpose of lifting the few exceptional people onto their shoulders. You and me, we're exceptional.
>
> —Green Goblin, *Spider-Man*

Fukuyama argues that transhumanism will damage the traditional Enlightenment principle of human equality. As he puts it,

> Underlying this idea of the equality of rights is the belief that we all possess a human essence that dwarfs manifest differences of skin color, beauty, and even intelligence. This essence, and the view that individuals therefore have inherent value, is at the heart of political liberalism. But modifying that essence is the core of the transhumanist project.[14]

If Fukuyama is correct, human enhancement is a very real threat to the egalitarian ideals of liberal democracy because radical modification of the body will fundamentally alter our "human essence." Writing against expanding our use of enhancement technologies, Fukuyama asks, "If we start transforming ourselves into something superior, what rights will these enhanced creatures claim, and what rights will they possess when compared to those left behind?" He fears that "the first victim of transhumanism might be equality."[15]

Historically, human biology has not contributed positively to our notion of political equality. We need only look at the chattel status of women, the forced relocation of Native Peoples, the existence of an "untouchable" caste, and the persistence of Jim Crow to see that gender and skin color have often served as markers of social and political inequality. Equality under political liberalism is simply not a matter of possessing this or that biological characteristic, as Fukuyama suggests, but of possessing the capacity for moral agency: political rights are held without regard to physical difference. As such, transhumanism would seem actually to increase equality, because many of those whose capacity to participate in society had been limited—say, by autism or physical disability—may become able to exercise full membership.

Fukuyama is right to point out that enhancement technologies—as happened with electricity, literacy, and smelting ore—would likely suffer a distribution problem, with disproportional access for wealthy countries and wealthy individuals. Yet this criticism is nothing peculiar to enhancement technologies, but rather to the sort of socioeconomic system under which these technologies have come to exist. Such an objection in fact places enhancement technology squarely within traditional social justice concerns regarding distribution of and access to those resources necessary for human flourishing.

Enhancing People and Creating Monsters

I will not die a monster.

—Doc Ock, *Spider-Man 2*

The technological "improvement" of us (or at least some of us) has generally been uncontroversial so long as the results either restore an individual to "normal" (such as providing physical therapy and prosthetics for war veterans) or permit an individual to "catch up" to that standard (such as by providing glasses to the nearsighted or speech therapy for a child who stutters).

For many people, things start to get ethically messy when these "fixes" involve the deliberate alteration of our mental or emotional status—consider the controversy over the wide-spread use of Ritalin among children in elementary school. Things get messier still when we apply our technology in order to alter ourselves in ways that exceed the normal range of human abilities—consider the Olympic medals stripped from athletes who were found to have used artificial steroids to bulk up or blood doping to boost endurance. Enhancement, regardless of the specific technology under consideration, is by definition a form of modifying an existing system, and so always is constrained by earlier design. After all, Peter Parker is the same person, despite the new Spider-Man body (hence the need for a mask!). While biological history may limit certain options (for instance, an unmodified human cannot "spin a web, any size, or catch thieves just like flies"), it cannot determine what must happen (say, that we all have the type-A personality and flat-top hair of J. Jonah Jameson). So, although physics prevents Godzilla from doing the two-step on Tokyo, the basic biological blueprint can generate both the tiny gecko and the nine-foot-long Komodo dragon.

Those concerned that transhumanism will undermine our human nature usually have in mind something to the effect that we all share a set of biological features that are necessary and sufficient for having this nature. As such, our human biology, as vessel for our "human essence," is sacrosanct. Unfortunately, a quick scan of the staff at the *Daily Bugle* Christmas party shows that the human gene pool is far from static—it is modified ever so slightly from generation to generation and individual to individual. To be enhanced is a difference of degree, not of kind.

Perhaps the uneasiness with the use of enhancement technologies is the age-old fear of creating monsters. Zombies, Dr. Moreau's "children," and Victor Frankenstein's creation all violate the divide between human and nonhuman. Although such creatures may have a monstrous appearance (think of

Morbius and Green Goblin), they needn't. Teratogenesis—the creation of monsters—seems to terrify us for just the reason that Fukuyama indicates: it produces creatures recognizable as "us" but with the soul of "them."[16] Nonetheless, any claim such as Fukuyama's that radical enhancements will undermine a human essence relies on a number of assumptions. Perhaps most important, that a human essence exists and that only those creatures imbued with it deserve equal rights. By these lights, enhancement technologies would create monsters without a human essence—Jackal and Lizard would be not mere supervillains, but also abominations.

In the realm of Marvel, such an assumption would have a hard time getting by: nonhuman races such as Kree and Skrull and nonhuman individuals such as the Asgardian Thor and the android the Vision all seem to be—and are treated as—persons, just as much as their biologically human counterparts are. Those humans enhanced with machine parts, animal genes, or anything else are grouped into the categories of "hero" and "villain" in the same way as their wholly human and wholly nonhuman counterparts: by examining their behavior. To be monstrous is not about biology, but about actions.

The origin stories of our villains tell us a lot about the risks many of us associate with technologically enhancing humans—we can keep a running tally of deaths, assaults, thefts, extortions, and incidents of littering for which Spidey's criminal menagerie is responsible. Yet it isn't their enhanced bodies that make them supervillains—after all, Spider-Man is an enhanced good guy. Instead, Green Goblin, Doc Ock, and the rest result from piling superhuman enhancements onto individuals with seriously flawed moral characters.

As for Fukuyama and Glaucon's third concern—that of the evils of "playing God," isn't that what human technology has always done? We modify our world and ourselves in order to thrive. Vaccines, turtlenecks, and the printing press are as much a manipulation of the natural world as are mechanical arms, pumpkin bombs, or mixing genes across species. The drive to alter the world around us (and so altering ourselves as well) may be the closest thing to a human essence we can find.

Creating MJ's Smile

Face it, Tiger . . . you just hit the jackpot!

—Mary Jane Watson, *Amazing Spider-Man #42*, 1966

We can imagine that Mary Jane Watson was not always the beautiful redhead next door, that she, like many of us, endured an awkward stage of acne and braces. To counter the acne, she was prescribed Accutane; to correct the gaps in her teeth, she had orthodontic work and wore the middle-schooler's most dreaded device, headgear.

Like the Watsons, other parents also attempt to alter a whole range of undesirable characteristics in their children, and we would likely condemn any parent who was able but unwilling to do so. If it is worthwhile to have a child endure the discomfort of an orthodontist cutting into her jaw and installing an Escher maze of bands and wires, would any responsible parent not opt to achieve the same results without causing pain to the child? Similarly, assuming a genetic fix were possible, why not give Mary Jane teeth that are not only straight but also twice as resistant to chipping? Or perhaps even teeth that would not stain, regardless of how much coffee or how many cigarettes she consumes when nervously waiting for a theater callback? It's hard to see why giving MJ a chance at a good smile—or even a "super smile"—would be objectionable or even less than obligatory. And so, if not super teeth, why not super strength, super agility, super vision, and so on. Why not superpowers?

Although we may squirm at the deliberate creation of a Spider-Man from a Peter Parker or of a Doc Ock from an Otto Octavius, it seems we have an obligation to pursue at least some of our options regarding human enhancement so that Aunt May, Mary Jane, and the rest of us may have healthier, happier lives.[17]

NOTES

1. In *Spider-Man* (2002), Norman Osborn tests a "human performance enhancer" on himself. Under development by Oscorp for the military, "CX00009" had increased the strength in "rodent subjects" by 800 percent, as well as led to "violence, aggression, and insanity."

2. A term borrowed from James Hughes's *Citizen Cyborg: Why Democratic Societies Must Respond to the Redesigned Human of the Future* (Boulder, CO: Westview Press, 2004). Hughes is the executive director of the Institute for Ethics and Emerging Technologies, a hotbed of transhumanist thought.

3. Francis Fukuyama, *Our Posthuman Future: Consequences of the Biotechnology Revolution* (New York, NY: Picador, 2002). Criticism of transhumanism is not limited to the political right; for instance, see Jurgen Habermas's *The Future of Human Nature* (Cambridge, UK: Polity, 2003).

4. See Plato's *The Republic*, trans. B. Jowett (Mineola, NY: Dover Publications, 2000), 2.359a–2.360d for the full "Ring of Gyges" discussion. This theme continues to be popular in both books and films. See, for instance, J. R. R. Tolkein's *The Lord of the Rings* trilogy or H. G. Wells's *The Invisible Man*.

5. In an effort to combat his own rare blood disease, Morbius, a Nobel-winning biochemist, undergoes a treatment of his own design involving electroshock and vampire bats. The process invests him with many attributes traditionally associated with vampires: great strength, flight, hemophagia, and so on.

6. Nick Bostrom, "Transhumanist Values," at www.transhumanism.org/index.php/ WTA/more/transhumanist-values.2003, last accessed June 19, 2010. In 1998, Bostrom was a cofounder of the World Transhumanist Association (renamed "Humanity+" in 2008). In 2004, Bostrom and James Hughes founded the Institute for Ethics and Emerging Technologies.

7. The film updates the spider from one that has accidentally absorbed "a fantastic amount of radiation" during a science experiment (*Amazing Fantasy* #15, 1962), to one that has been deliberately genetically modified.

8. Andre Delambre is the name of the title character in both the original short story (1957) and the first film version of *The Fly* (1958). In David Cronenberg's 1986 remake, we follow scientist Seth Brundle (played by Jeff Goldblum) as he transforms into "Brundlefly."

9. Francis Fukuyama, "The World's Most Dangerous Idea: Transhumanism," *Foreign Policy* 144 (September–October 2004): 42–43.

10. Although this "capabilities approach" can trace its philosophical roots to Aristotle's concern for human flourishing, economist Amartya Sen and philosopher Martha Nussbaum are credited with its contemporary incarnation and popularization.

11. For instance, the ACE (angiotensin-converting enzyme) gene pair has four different configurations. Having two "long genes" causes a person's muscles to act more efficiently than if she has two short genes or one long and one short. Other things being equal, a person with the long ACE form responds better to physical conditioning.

12. In March 2009, *Science Magazine* announced the creation of an "artificial muscle" that is faster, stronger, and more flexible than human muscle tissue; see Ali Aliev et al., "Giant-Stroke, Superelastic Carbon Nanotube Aerogel Muscles," *Science* 323 (March 20, 2009): 1575–1578.

13. Fukuyama, "The World's Most Dangerous Idea: Transhumanism."

14. Ibid.

15. Ibid.

16. Today, the term *teratogenesis* is rarely used outside of medical embryology to refer to the study of the development of defects in an embryo.

17. Thanks to Dawn Jakubowski, Jacob Held, and J. J. Sanford for many helpful comments on earlier drafts.

MAXIMUM CLONAGE

What the *Clone Saga* Can Teach Us about Human Cloning

Jason Southworth and John Timm

In July 1994, Marvel Comics published *Web of Spider-Man* #114, and with it began the longest-running event of comic book history—the *Clone Saga*. The premise of the story was that a long-forgotten and believed-to-be-dead clone of Spider-Man was alive and had returned to New York. At least for the first year of the story, things were exciting. Those of us who remembered the clone wanted to know how it could be that he was alive; those unfamiliar with him wanted to know who he was; and everyone wanted to see what trouble he'd stir up for ol' webhead. If you ask Spider-fans today what they think of the *Clone Saga*, however, they are likely to have less-than-positive things to say. Some of this has to do with how the story began to drag on as it progressed into its second year, but more has to do with the mishandling of the science (and that's saying something when it's coming from fans who can accept cosmic rays turning someone into a rock monster!). In this chapter, we'll take a close look at how cloning is treated in the *Clone Saga*, and in doing so, we'll separate the science from the fiction. With a clearer understanding of what a clone is and how cloning works, we'll be in a position to evaluate the reactions of various characters in the *Clone Saga* to the revelation that they or someone they love is a clone.

Gwen Stacy Is Alive . . . and, Well . . . ?!

Although the *Clone Saga* took place during the 1990s, the roots of the story go back to *Amazing Spider-Man* #144, published in May 1975. This issue ends with the revelation of a living Gwen Stacy—who'd been killed by the Green Goblin in *Amazing Spider-Man* #121 (1973)! During the course of the next several issues and in *Giant-Size Spider-Man* #5, Peter Parker struggles to figure out how Gwen could possibly be alive. The answer finally comes in *Amazing Spider-Man* #148, when Ned Leeds explains to Peter that she must be a clone. As the story progresses, we learn that Ned is right, and that Gwen was cloned by Peter and Gwen's former biology teacher, Professor Warren—now known as the villainous Jackal. It seems that Warren had his students give "cell samples for some project or other."[1] Whatever his initial intention for these cell samples, overwhelmed by grief after the death of Gwen, he used them to clone her. As the story arc comes to a close in *Amazing Spider-Man* #149, we learn that Warren has also cloned Spider-Man, and much of the issue is devoted to a battle of the Spider-Men. The fight ends when the cloned Gwen makes Professor Warren feel guilty for his actions. Remorse comes too late, however, and Warren and the Spider-Clone appear to be killed in an explosion that Warren had arranged earlier. The last plot thread from this story arc is wrapped up in issue #151, when Spider-Man drops the dead body of the clone down the chimney of an incinerating plant. Good-bye, Spider-Clone . . . or so it seemed.

As any long-time reader of the Webbed Wonder knows, nothing comes easy, and this proves to be no exception. Years after thinking his problems with clones were over, Peter comes face-to-face with his clone while visiting Aunt May in the hospital.[2] After a spectacular and obligatory fight, the clone explains that he goes by the name of Ben Reilly—a mash-up of Peter's uncle's first name and his aunt's maiden name.[3] Ben and Peter find that they can get along, and Ben decides to stay in New York. To protect Peter's identity, Ben makes a superhero identity for himself—the Scarlet Spider. Soon after his debut, we discover he was not the first clone of Spider-Man made by Professor Warren—that was a man known only as Kane.[4] Kane is an "imperfect clone," horribly disfigured and degenerating. To slow this effect, he wears a chemically treated costume of his own.[5] The arc turns even more convoluted: we learn that MJ is pregnant,[6] a third spider clone is revealed—Spidercide,[7] and a scientist announces that the man we thought was Peter Parker is actually a clone, and that Ben is the original.[8]

Things reach their absolute silliest in the *Maximum Clonage* arc. In this story, Peter sides with the Jackal to fight Ben because he is upset at the revelation that he is a clone. Thankfully, Peter comes to his senses just in time to help Ben fight an army of hundreds of Spider-Clones.[9] The *Clone Saga* finally comes to an end with the revelation that Norman Osborn (Green Goblin) is alive and has masterminded all of the events of the *Saga*. The final fight with the Green Goblin results in the death of Ben Reilly, and he dissolves into a puddle of goo.[10] This convinces Peter that he was not the clone after all, and his life moves on to the next cloneless tragedy.

The Shattering Secret of Cloning

Before we can evaluate the claims about cloning in the *Clone Saga*, we need to get clear about what cloning is. In general terms, to clone something means to create a cell or an organism that is genetically identical to the original individual. There are three types of cloning—molecular, therapeutic, and reproductive. Molecular cloning is a common laboratory technique primarily used to examine DNA fragments. It is often easier to study a particular gene after isolating and amplifying it. Once the gene and its location have been identified, it needs to be isolated by cutting it away from the rest of the DNA. The DNA fragment is next shuttled into bacteria by splicing it into a plasmid, a small circular piece of DNA that bacteria naturally pass between one another. The bacteria are then grown in a culture dish, where they will continue to make copies of the DNA as they grow. When the bacteria have grown enough to yield appropriate amounts of DNA, it is collected for study. After DNA is amplified through molecular cloning, it has numerous uses. For instance, the DNA could be sequenced, where the exact nucleotide order is determined. This is useful to forensic scientists in genetic fingerprinting—DNA testing.

Although the science is more in keeping with the mighty Marvel tradition than reality, the origin of one of Spider-Man's first villains, the Lizard, provides a close enough example to illustrate molecular cloning. The Lizard was born Curtis Connors, a soldier who loses an arm while serving in the army. In his work as a research technologist, he obsessively studies reptilian limb regeneration in the hope of regrowing his arm, and he develops an experimental serum taken from reptilian DNA. The reptilian DNA is isolated and put into a serum, which acts as a means of shuttling the new DNA into his body, similar to the way that plasmids work with bacteria in a lab setting. Curtis ingests the serum and his limb grows back, but the process also turns him into a reptilian monster.[11] This is something like the process of bacteria taking up a plasmid and using the cloning product along with their native DNA.

Therapeutic cloning is the creation of embryos in order to harvest stem cells for use in research. The stem cells are not used to produce adult clones, but to study their early development in the hope of finding ways to treat diseases such as Alzheimer's and Parkinson's. The process that results in therapeutic cloning is called somatic cell nuclear transfer. The way it works is that you take an ovum—that's an egg cell, for those who don't remember health class—from a female and remove its nucleus, including its DNA. You next remove the DNA from an adult cell taken from another member of the same species and insert it in the ovum. The ovum is then either treated with chemicals or a small electric charge is applied, and if the process is successful you have a pre-embryo that develops, producing stem cells. The stem cells are harvested less than a week after they begin dividing, at which point the embryo is a mass of cells that wouldn't yet have attached to the wall of a uterus, were it the product of natural conception.[12] Researchers are then able to coax the stem cells into growing a variety of types of tissues and organs.[13]

The type of cloning most commonly discussed outside of a biology laboratory is reproductive cloning, which is what occurs in the *Clone Saga*. One of the most famous examples of this is Dolly the sheep, cloned in 1997, one year after the *Clone Saga* concluded. Reproductive cloning of the type that resulted in Dolly begins the same way as therapeutic cloning: Ovum minus nucleus plus new DNA plus chemicals or electrical charge results in an embryo. Rather than removing stem cells from the embryo after several days, the embryo is allowed to develop for a time and then it is implanted in the uterus of a host mother—not necessarily genetically related, this could be a surrogate or the cell donor. If successful, the mother will carry the fetus to term and give birth.[14]

The Game of Life—What the *Saga* Gets Wrong (and Right) about Cloning

Now that we have a handle on just what's meant by cloning, how does all of this relate to the *Clone Saga*? First, let's acknowledge that the *Clone Saga* is a work of imaginative fiction, written before there were any documented cases of somatic cell nuclear transfer using an adult mammal cell. We can't expect the authors to have gotten every detail correct, but we can use some examples of technology from the story to illustrate how cloning works in the real world.

In the *Clone Saga*, the Jackal/Professor Warren was able to take cells from Peter and Gwen, put them in a "clone casket," and in just a short time out came adult clones with latent memories—and the same haircuts—of the originals intact.[15] We're supposed to consider the clone casket as something like an artificial womb (despite the morbid connotations of "casket"!), but those don't exist. If this were to happen in real life, the cloned cells would have to be moved from a test tube to the uterus of a human being (or a ewe). Once implanted in a uterus, an embryo would develop at exactly the same rate as a normal member of that species. This means Warren would be waiting nine months for his clone, and all that he would have at the end of that time is a baby. As you might expect, that baby would develop at the same rate as a normal member of that species, making it a double bummer for the professor. Not only would he have to raise a child, he would either be dead or a very old man by the time the Gwen clone reaches the age of consent. Leaving aside the problem of aging, there's no guarantee the clone would look the way Warren had hoped anyway. Identical twins often have variations in their appearance, and genetically identical calves often have different color patterns and spotting.

Worse than expecting a clone to be physically identical is hoping a clone will have the same memories as its genetic predecessor. There's no reason to think that this might happen. Memories are not passed along with DNA; otherwise, we would have innate memories of parts of our parents' lives, and their parents' lives, and so on, until we have memories of Adam's first glance at Eve. The Gwen clone would be born as any other baby is, forming its own sense of identity as she grows up. There's also no mystic link between clones, where they can share thoughts or dreams. This is pure science fiction.

Two things the story gets wrong that you probably haven't considered are the chances of bringing a successful clone to term and the cost of doing so. This is cutting-edge science, and there's plenty of trial and error. Dolly was one of only three births out of 277 attempts to clone a sheep.[16] Even if we expect the same success rate as Dolly, Warren would've had to find donors for all of those eggs, as well as surrogate mothers for any clones that were successfully dividing. We're looking at major corporate underwriting for this project and a lifetime commitment—not the type of thing you secretly do over the weekend in a university basement.

Obviously, we're having a little fun here at the expense of "Merry" Gerry Conway, his editor Stan "the Man" Lee, and a smorgasbord of respected but adjectiveless writers from the 1990s, correcting what seem like silly beliefs about clones to a reader as intelligent as you. That said, we're not just taking the wind from the sails of these comic legends, for we've had the pleasure of hearing these malformed opinions expressed semester after semester by college students in bioethics classes. The air is full of an overwhelming number of false beliefs about clones, so it's well worth the time to set the record straight.

Given the emphasis we just placed on what the writers got wrong, it's important to give them credit for what they got right. In the *Clone Saga*, there's a dramatic moment where Peter Parker is revealed to be the clone, and Ben Reilly is shown to be the genetic predecessor through a blood test.[17] This is one aspect of the science of cloning that the writers got perfectly right. Both Spider-Men would have identical nuclear DNA, but their mitochondrial DNA would be different. The mitochondrial DNA comes from the donated egg, and because Peter Parker has no living blood relatives, the egg donor couldn't have had the same mitochondrial DNA as Peter. If both Ben and Peter donated a blood sample to be compared to an older sample of Spider-Man's from before the cloning, it would be simple to match the mitochondrial DNA of the sample to one of the two Spider-Men—which shouldn't be too hard to come by, considering all of the blood that Spider-Man has shed throughout his career.

Another point the writers got right is the familial relationship of Peter and his clones. A clone and his genetic predecessor are genetically related in the same way as identical twins, although they'd be different ages and would have different mitochondrial DNA, unless the surrogate mother of the clone was a blood relative of the person being cloned. Naturally occurring identical twins get half of their nuclear DNA from each parent, while a clone gets all of his nuclear DNA from his genetic predecessor. The authors got this correct in the scene where everyone's favorite wall-crawler throws Ben Reilly's corpse into an incinerator and says, "Goodbye, Brother."[18]

The Worth of a Clone

Now that we've debunked many of the misconceptions people have about human cloning, we can evaluate the rationality and appropriateness of the reactions of the characters in the story to the news that they or people they know are clones. It's important to keep in mind that these characters, similar to people in real life, don't act only for the sake of acting. Underlying the way the characters in the *Clone Saga* behave are beliefs about what clones are and how they deserve to be treated. So, to come to a decision about who acts appropriately and who doesn't, we'll have to look past mere behavior and evaluate people's underlying beliefs.

At the far negative end of the spectrum is Kane, the first Spider-Clone, who seems rife with self-hatred. Throughout the *Clone Saga*, Kane is singularly committed to no other goal than killing all other clones and everyone associated with his own creation. The oldest story about Kane is the three issue miniseries *Spider-Man: Lost Years* (1996). In this story, we see him hunt and attempt to kill Ben Reilly—a recurring trope in the *Saga*. He also attempts to kill his cloner, Professor Warren, several times. When dealing with nonclones, however, he appears uninterested in a fight. In one of his early appearances we see him run from a fight with Peter, even though he's already tried to kill Ben on several occasions.[19] Likewise, the only time we see him go after Mary Jane (an easy target) is when he wants to test her fetus to ensure that it's not a clone.[20] What little dialogue Kane indulges in centers on his underlying desire to end all clone life. We see that desire take form when in *Spider-Man: Redemption* #4 (1996) he rescues everyone trapped in a burning building except for Ben Reilly. Rather than rescue him, Kane states that he's going to "perish with him."

Peter's reaction to clones is not as violent or suicidal as Kane's, but it's nevertheless negative. When Peter is told that he's a clone (which turns out to be false), he gets very angry. He runs from his wife and tells Ben that he's lost everything.[21] Peter goes as far as to team up with the Jackal to fight the Scarlet Spider because of a misplaced belief that clones shouldn't or can't be good. Further evidence of Peter's beliefs can be found in how he handles the apparent death of the Spider-Clone in *Amazing Spider-Man* #149 (1975). Peter typically holds himself responsible for all injuries and deaths that come from fights he has as Spider-Man, but the only time he pays the Spider-Clone another thought is when he realizes he needs to destroy the body to protect his secret identity.

On the other hand, neither Ben nor Mary Jane sees anything wrong with being a clone. When Peter reacts negatively to the news that he's the clone, MJ tries to comfort him, explaining that it doesn't change anything. They still love each other; they still did nearly all of the things they remember doing together, and these are the things that matter.[22] On numerous occasions, she suggests that they just go back to living their lives the way things were before the news, because there's no good reason not to. Ben's reaction is much the same as MJ's. He doesn't want Peter's life, and he doesn't feel as if he's entitled to anything other than what he already has.

Who's right, Kane and Peter, or MJ and Ben? In "The Wisdom of Repugnance," Leon Kass offers an argument against human reproductive cloning that captures the philosophical underpinnings of both Kane's and Peter's reactions. Kass begins by suggesting that the visceral hostility many people have toward cloning is appropriate. The reason people react this way, according to Kass, is that cloning is not only wrong, but it's so wrong that it's "beyond reason's power fully to articulate it."[23] In this sense, he sees it belonging in a category with father-daughter incest and bestiality (in fact, Kass thinks most cases of cloning will *be* incest). If Kass is right about this, it would explain why Peter and Kane do more grunting and yelling than giving reasons when others try to engage them in a conversation about clones.[24]

Even though reason can't fully explain what's wrong with cloning, Kass goes on to offer an argument against it. He says that cloning denies a sense of life's purpose to the clone because clones and those around them will recognize that their genotypes have "already lived," which leads to certain expectations about how their lives ought to be lived, based on the lives of their genetic predecessors. If this happens, the clone won't see his life as something with a purpose of its own, but that of another. Being denied the ability to establish one's own purpose is such an evil for Kass that he holds no clone should ever be born.[25]

For Kass, the expectations that others have for the clone are inextricably connected to the expectations a clone will have for itself:

> The child is given a genotype that has already lived, with full expectation that this blueprint of a past life ought to be controlling of the life that is to come. Cloning is inherently despotic, for it seeks to make one's children (or someone else's children) after one's own image (or an image of one's choosing) and their future according to one's will. In some cases, the despotism may be mild and benevolent. In other cases, it will be mischievous and downright tyrannical. But despotism—the control of another through one's will—it inevitably will be.[26]

With others expecting the clone to behave in a certain way, he'll feel as if he's supposed to confirm those expectations, and if he happens to share any preferences or desires with his genetic predecessor, this will lead others to expect further similarities.[27] The amount of distress caused by this identity confusion will be so great, in Kass's account, that to bring such a person into existence would constitute a great wrong.

Something similar to Kass's argument seems to be behind both Peter's and Kane's reactions. Kane wants every clone of Peter dead, and he wants Peter left unharmed, seeing his purpose and the purpose of the other clones as in service to Peter. Likewise, Peter claims that everything has been taken away from him when he's told he's a clone. It doesn't matter that he has a wife who loves him, or that he has been a hero for decades. Peter suddenly sees that life as belonging to Ben.

Kane and Peter part ways with Kass, though, when they extend his conclusion from it being better that clones not be born at all to it being morally permissible to kill or otherwise physically assault clones.

On the other side, Ben and MJ have no problem with cloning, and we can understand why by considering the work of the contemporary philosopher Gregory Pence. Pence argues against Kass's claim that the fact that a clone's genotype has already lived provides an argument against cloning. To make his case, Pence considers identical twins, who share 99.9 percent of their genes. The types of expectations Kass suggests people will have for clones already exist for twins. Many (foolish) people think that identical twins necessarily have the same likes and dislikes, tastes, and expectations for the future. If Kass is right that such expectations make it wrong to clone, then it seems as if he ought to be in favor of the termination of identical twin pregnancies (or at least committed to it being a grave wrong to give birth to twins). The problem here is with the people who are judging the clones, not with the clones themselves. These people conflate individuals' genes with their identities.

Notice that in Pence's view, Kass's objection also fails concerning a clone's expectation of self. A clone who believes he ought to have the same likes, dislikes, tastes, and expectations for the future as his genetic predecessor would be as irrational as a person having the same belief concerning his identical twin.[28] It's the recognition that Peter is conflating these different things that leads MJ to tell Peter that the news that he's a clone doesn't change anything in their lives. It's also what's behind Ben's shock that Peter seems to think that if he is Ben's clone, then Ben is entitled to Peter's life.

According to Pence, any attempt to draw a distinction between the worth of clones and the worth of their genetic predecessors is going to fail because the only serious difference is that of origin. This, however, would not be a legitimate reason to treat them differently. To argue as Kass does—that cloning is wrong because nonclones will be bothered and will have inappropriate expectations of them—is akin to arguing that interracial couples ought not to have children. The analogy should be clear. Some people feel repugnance toward these children and have expectations based on false beliefs, but that is a problem with the racists, not with the children or their parents. The same should hold for clones.

This argument can be further extended to cover Kass's concern that clones have analogous feelings about themselves. These clones are like people of mixed race with negative self-perceptions. We don't think that such misplaced self-perceptions really mean there is something inherently wrong with being biracial, and we hope they can overcome their negative self-conceptions. It should be clear at this point that the problem with all of Kass's concerns is that he has not shown there's something wrong with clones or cloning; rather, he has only shown that ignorance about cloning can lead to inappropriate expectations, which can result in harmful outcomes. This makes it all the more important that we take the time to correct such false beliefs, such as those discussed earlier, no matter how silly they may seem to us.[29]

Kane and Peter are self-loathing and feel inferior and worthless because they have a skewed sense of what gives someone moral worth. MJ and Ben recognize that what a person has accomplished in life is what's important, and that genetic origin is irrelevant to the issue of moral worth. They recognize that Kane's and Peter's self-hatred is irrational. If cloning is wrong, we'll have to look to arguments other than those offered in the *Clone Saga* to figure out why.

Game's End

So, true believers, what have we learned? For starters, we learned that Gerry Conway got a surprising amount right about human cloning when he wrote the original *Clone*

Saga in the 1970s. It's true that Professor Warren would have access to enough genetic material to make a clone of Gwen and Peter. He also got the familial relation between Peter and the clone right—they're brothers. Some of the things he got wrong are excusable. For instance, artificial wombs are possible, even though they don't yet exist. We have also learned that the writers of the 1990s *Saga* got quite a bit wrong, given how much later it came out. For example, it's a bit silly to think that clones age at an accelerated rate until they reach the same age as their genetic predecessor. Given how handily Pence rejects Kass's arguments, we also know that Kane and Peter react irrationally when told they are clones. This does not mean that the moral permissibility of human reproductive cloning is now a settled issue, however.

This chapter has presented and responded to only one objection to human reproductive cloning—albeit one of the most common objections. There are plenty of other objections out there. Some state that it's unnatural and thus immoral; others argue from a theological perspective that we ought not to play games with the process God created for reproduction; still others say that it will lead to what they consider harmful consequences to society, from it being easier for homosexuals and single women to have children to the creation of human-animal hybrids.

On the other hand, there are arguments that human reproductive cloning isn't simply permissible, but that it leads to serious moral goods. These goods include making it easier for infertile couples to have children, allowing couples to have children with the guarantee that they'll not have a genetic disease carried by one of the parents, and libertarian appeals that it's none of the government's business what you do with your genetic material. For every argument on both sides of this issue, there are countless objections.

It's your job to go investigate these arguments and objections further and to make up your own mind. What would be the fun in the two of us standing on Stan's Soapbox and telling you what to think?[30]

NOTES

1. *Amazing Spider-Man* #148 (1973).

2. *Web of Spider-Man* #114 (1994).

3. *Web of Spider-Man* #117, *Amazing Spider-Man* # 394, *Spider-Man* #51, *Spectacular Spider-Man* #217 (all 1994).

4. *Web of Spider-Man* #118, *Spider-Man* #52, *Web of Spider-Man* #119, *Spider-Man* #53 (all 1994).

5. *Web of Spider-Man* #120, *Spider-Man* #54, *Web of Spider-Man* #121, *Spider-Man* #55 (all 1995).

6. *Spectacular Spider-Man* #220 (1995).

7. Spectacular Spider-Man #222, Web of Spider-Man #123 (both 1995).

8. Ibid.

9. *Amazing Spider-Man* #404 (1995).

10. *Amazing Spider-Man* #418 (1996).

11. *Amazing Spider-Man* #6 (1963).

12. This description of size is not meant to carry with it any suggestion about the morality of the process. The moral permissibility or impermissibility of therapeutic cloning in the case of humans hinges on three questions well beyond the scope of a paper about Spider-Man. First, should this collection of cells be considered a human being? Second, is it ever morally permissible to take a human life? And third, if the answer to the first two questions is yes, do the particulars concerning therapeutic cloning justify the loss of life?

13. Kathi Hanna, "Cloning/Embryonic Stem Cells," www.genome.gov/10004765, accessed September 20, 2009.

14. Deborah Barnes, "Research in the News: Creating a Cloned Sheep Named Dolly," http://science-education.nih.gov/home2.nsf/Educational+Resources/Grade+Levels/ +High+School/BC5086E34E4DBA0085256CCD006F01CB, accessed September 20, 2009).

15. *Amazing Spider-Man* #148 (1975).

16. Barnes, "Research in the News: Creating a Cloned Sheep Named Dolly."

17. *Spectacular Spider-Man* # 226 (1995).

18. *Amazing Spider-Man* #151 (1975).

19. *Web of Spider-Man* #123 (1995).

20. *Web of Spider-Man* #124 (1995).

21. *Amazing Spider-Man* #404.

22. *Maximum Clonage Omega* (1995).

23. Leon R. Kass, "The Wisdom of Repugnance," *New Republic* 216, no. 22 (June 2, 1997): 17–26.

24. Ibid.

25. Ibid.

26. Ibid.

27. Ibid.

28. Gregory Pence, *Medical Ethics: Accounts of the Cases That Shaped and Define Medical Ethics*, 5th ed. (New York: McGraw Hill, 2008), 147.

29. Ibid., 143.

30. We would like to thank Ruth Tallman for her excellent comments on this paper.

PART FIVE

YOUR FRIENDLY
NEIGHBORHOOD
SPIDER-MAN

JUSTICE VERSUS ROMANTIC LOVE

Can Spider-Man Champion Justice and Be with Mary Jane at the Same Time?

Charles Taliaferro and Tricia Little

Who am I? You sure you want to know? The story of my life is not for the faint of heart. If somebody said it was a happy little tale . . . if somebody told you I was just your average ordinary guy, not a care in the world . . . somebody lied.

–Peter Parker, *Spider-Man*

In both the comics (beginning with issue #42, *The Amazing Spider-Man*) and the films (beginning with the first film, *Spider-Man*), Mary Jane Watson (MJ) raises a serious challenge for Peter Parker as Peter, as well as for the superhero Spider-Man: Is the heroic fight for justice compatible with a romantic, committed relationship between Peter/Spider-Man and MJ? MJ is in peril to the extent that Spider-Man's enemies realize she is Spider-Man's partner. So when, if ever, is it fair or right for MJ to be in such a vulnerable state?

Neither the films nor the Marvel comic books deliver a clear answer of when, if ever, the call to fight for justice takes precedence over the desire for a romantic, committed relationship. In 1987, it appeared that the answer was "yes," for in *Amazing Spider-Man*, vol. 1, Annual #2, Peter and MJ marry (she changes her surname to Watson-Parker). Yet their life and happiness come under constant attack until, in 2007, in Spider-Man's dubious deal with Mephisto and in his effort to save Aunt May, MJ's memory of her marriage is (apparently) obliterated. We are even left wondering whether the marriage really took place when, in *Amazing Spider-Man* #545, we are given an alternative history of our hero and MJ and are told that they never married.

If we turn to the films, at the end of *Spider-Man 3*, it appears that Peter and MJ are together again, but only after Spider-Man has freed MJ from Sandman. Although MJ and Peter are reconciled, both characters may well wonder whether the relationship can work. Maybe someone like Venom will kidnap MJ again. Maybe Spider-Man will not be successful in freeing her, fighting crime, and taking care of another family duty: looking after Aunt May. Then there's the possibility that MJ and Spider-Man will have children. They, too, may become targets of Spider-Man's enemies.

Spider-Man and MJ's struggle over romantic love versus the heroic pursuit of justice is part of a general problem that was noted by Nelson Mandela, the great opponent of apartheid in South Africa. Mandela maintained that each person has an obligation to her family, as well as to her community. In a just society, Mandela thought that one can fulfill both obligations. In an unjust society, however, meeting both obligations is profoundly difficult and sometimes impossible. The case of

Spider-Man and MJ represents an instance of such a troubling tension of (potential) obligations.

The Primacy of Justice

> You're so mysterious all the time. Tell me, would it be so dangerous to let Mary Jane know how much you care?
>
> —Aunt May to Peter Parker, *Spider-Man*

> Then you know why we can't be together. Spider-Man will always have enemies. I can't let you take that risk. I will always be Spider-Man. You and I can never be . . .
>
> —Spider-Man to Mary Jane, *Spider-Man 2*

Imagine that you're very much in love with Pat Watson (a gender-neutral name, call him/her PW), and the feelings are mutual. You may not be a superhero, but you are proficient in the martial arts. One night while you are both strolling to your apartment, hand in hand, you witness an altercation. You recognize that the assailant is a serious criminal who has a knife and has killed before. He's attacking Kris, someone whom you've known for years as a coworker. You and Kris are *not* friends; you and Kris don't dislike each other, but there's no strong friendship or bond between the two of you.

Consider, now, three scenarios.

Option A: You and PW keep walking but phone the police right away. You don't know whether the police will arrive in time to rescue Kris.

Option B: Making sure that PW is safe, you go to the rescue of Kris and disarm the assailant, then hand him over to the police when they arrive. It becomes apparent that due to the late arrival of the police, if you had not intervened Kris would've been killed.

Option C: Making sure that PW is safe, you go to the rescue of Kris. You manage to make sure Kris escapes, but in the process you are mortally wounded. You still manage to keep the assailant under your control so that the police can arrest him, but then you die in the arms of PW, who tells you that he/she loves you.

Maybe option A is morally acceptable. You'll have done better than the bystanders in the Kitty Genovese case who simply looked on when she was killed, while no one took the time to call the police. Clearly, option B is the best, in the sense that it produces the best results in terms of a rescue and heroism, but in real life we can't be so sure of the outcome. What are the chances that you (unarmed) have acquired such a skill set that you know with certainty that you can defeat an attacker with a knife? Even so, doesn't the desire or call to fight for justice require aiming for success (B) but being willing to suffer death (C)? If C is the outcome, wouldn't it be natural for PW and others to see your sacrifice as heroic?

If so, this would be a case of subordinating romantic love to justice. The rescue of an innocent person with whom you have no romance can and perhaps (if you're heroic) inevitably will involve serious sacrifice and thus the possible sacrifice of a long-term romantic life with PW. We believe that aiming for B but having to accept the possibility of C is the hero's choice, whether or not the skills you have in order to bring about the just outcome are the result of intentional acquisition (you developed your martial arts skills by enduring years of training) or by accident (while in high school you were bitten by a spider and, through no choice of your own, you suddenly acquired fighting skills). We've been referring to "the hero's choice," but although option A may not be blameworthy, we think aiming for option B also seems the right choice for someone who simply wants to do the right thing.

Under some circumstances, justice can trump romantic love, in the sense that occasions may arise when doing the right thing might involve putting romantic love in jeopardy. If you aimed at B but wound up with option C, PW might still love you for the rest of PW's life (so, in a sense, her romantic love would remain), but your shared life of romance with PW would be at an end.

Spider-Man's powers and skills have sometimes enabled him not to have to choose between MJ and saving lives. In the first film, Spider-Man manages to save a cable car full of children and MJ at once, rather than face a terrible choice between the two. He did make the choice to secure the children first, but it turned out that he was able to save MJ, too. Can our hero always be so lucky? Consider the moral dilemmas that we might face without superpowers. Imagine that you're with your romantic partner, PW, during the collapse of a bridge. A school bus full of children seems as if it's headed into the river, but now imagine that you're the only one who can jump into the driver's seat and steer the bus to safety. To do so, however, you must leave PW in a reckless, highly dangerous position where (s)he might be killed. Under these circumstances, when you don't have superhuman powers, don't you think there are good enough reasons why you should save the children first? Imagine that there are at least twenty children and that it's highly likely that (unless you intervene) they'll drown, whereas although PW is in danger, (s)he knows how to swim.

Sometimes a hero has to make sacrifices so that others can enjoy the benefits that the hero can't. Consider, for example, Frodo in *The Lord of the Rings*. He tells Sam, "I tried to save the Shire, and it has been saved, but not for me. It must often be so, Sam, when things are in danger: someone has to give them up, lose them, so that others may keep them." It's partly because of Peter's giving primacy to justice that he's reluctant to follow up on his intention to propose to MJ at one point in the film *Spider-Man 3*.

Aunt May: How's Mary Jane?

Peter Parker: I don't know.

Aunt May: I never heard from you. Did you ever propose?

Peter Parker: You said a husband's gotta put his wife before himself. [*puts the ring in her hand*]

Peter Parker: I'm not ready.

Just as Frodo puts the good of the Shire over his own good, Peter is faced with putting MJ's good (safety, well-being) over his own.

Now let's consider the opposite position, when romantic love takes precedence over the call to fight for justice.

The Primacy of the Romantic

She looks at me everyday. Mary Jane Watson. Oh boy! If she only knew how I felt about her. But she can never know. I made a choice once to live a life of responsibility. A life she can never be a part of. Who am I? I'm Spider-Man, given a job to do. And I'm Peter Parker, and I too have a job.

—Spider-Man, *Spider-Man 2*

Some cultures seem to recognize the primacy of marriage over justice, or they appear to recognize that marriage can count as an important value that overrides civic duty. In ancient Israel, for example, when a man married, he didn't have to serve in the military or have any other civic duties. According to Deuteronomy 24:5, "When a man takes a new wife, he shall not go out with the army nor be charged with any duty; he shall be free at home one year and shall give happiness to his wife" (New American Standard translation). Yet this is only for a year and seems to be for the sake of pleasing his wife, as well as to have sufficient time to produce an offspring. Although not all marriages privilege romantic love, there is a presumption of romance in Hebrew tradition, as is made evident in *The Song of Songs* and elsewhere (for example, Proverbs 5:15–19). There is no suggestion in this biblical precept that the newly married man can postpone military duty only during times of maximum security. It may be argued that this relief from military duty is really just part of one's duty to the community: ensure that the wife is pregnant so that there will be progeny for future armies, lest the man die in battle before having offspring. This may be, although we can imagine encouraging population growth in many different ways (conjugal visits, the man serving in the army in a reduced fashion, and so on).

The primacy of romance may be apparent in the following scenario. Again, let's imagine you're in love with PW and the feeling is 100 percent shared. You're contemplating two careers: as a member of an elite crime-fighting unit with an honorable, proven code of conduct or becoming a surgeon. Imagine that you have equally good skills for either vocation. Imagine, too, that you might save a roughly equal number of lives in either vocation, but if you go with the crime-fighting unit, you substantially risk crippling wounds and death. Putting a number on it, imagine that the unit consists of twenty members and each year at least one member is killed. Now imagine that PW makes this claim on you: "Tiger, I know you would be a superior officer fighting crime, rescuing the innocent, but I beg you to become a surgeon instead. Sure, performing surgery may not be as glamorous as rescuing hostages, preventing kidnapping, and capturing homicidal maniacs, but I love you and need you. I need to be able to count on you and your health! If you become a surgeon, maybe there'll be a greater chance you and I can live together to parent a child! Look, if you inadvertently come across a bank robbery and can stop it without risking your life: do it! But as long as that elite crime-fighting unit has enough fit and willing members, it's not cowardly for you to choose the path of healing. If you choose medicine, you would be choosing a life with me, Love." In this case, wouldn't romantic love take precedence over the desire to fight for justice?

We believe the answer is yes, whether or not the skills you have to become either a surgeon or a crime fighter are natural or instilled in you by an external agent—for example, by means of a radioactive spider. (As a side point, we are using a case in which the fight for justice involves violence/physical force, but a similar dilemma can be devised in which the fight for justice is nonviolent. PW might ask you to become a surgeon instead of being a police administrator who does not serve on the front lines.)

Consider another case in which it appears that justice is subordinate to romantic love. Imagine that an evil villain whom you put in prison has managed to escape, and he takes vengeance on you by killing PW's beloved aged father. Perhaps you (quite rightly) feel a call to justice in tracking down the villain in the name of PW, but imagine that you can't do this and, at the same time, help PW pick up the pieces of her life and cope with the loss of her father in a civil manner. Perhaps you have some evidence that the villain has escaped to a different spatio-temporal dimension and won't be able to inflict more harm. Imagine further that PW asks you to let the villain go and concentrate on your relationship together; PW begs you to look forward to future goals, which may include goals that PW's father held dear. Under those conditions, wouldn't romantic love trump the call to fight for justice? This would be a case similar to Mandela's description of how family obligations (in this case, we are imagining it is a family obligation founded on romantic love) can come into conflict with one's obligation to one's community.

We think this is a case when romantic love can trump justice, and it would actually be a possible scenario with Peter Parker, who shows signs that he's not always driven by revenge. Peter is initially fueled to use his new powers (super strength, web slinging, wall climbing, and so on) to seek revenge for the murder of Uncle Ben, but later he realizes that he should always use his powers for the good.

Romantic Justice or Just Romantic

I know you think we can't be together, but can't you respect me enough to let me make my own decision? I know there'll be risks but I want to face them with you. It's wrong that we should be only half alive . . . half of ourselves. I love you. So here I am—standing in your doorway. I have always been standing in your doorway. Isn't it about time somebody saved your life?

—Mary Jane Watson to Spider-Man, *Spider-Man 2*

The scenarios we have considered establish that there are cases when the call to fight for justice takes precedence over romance, and there are also times when romance takes precedence over the desire to fight for justice. We suggest that in the name of romantic love, you should comply with your lover's plea to be a surgeon, but we also suggest that (as in the first scenario) if you and PW are confronted with the case of Kris, you should (if you are a hero) put the desire to fight for justice first. The difference between the cases lies, in part, in the difference between choosing a career versus choosing what to do under circumstances you didn't seek out. Romantic love can keep you from actively seeking a career of doing good in the face of clear, imminent danger, but it can't relieve your duty (if you're a hero) to save the innocent when there's no one else available, even at great personal cost to you and your beloved.

So, what about Spider-Man and MJ? As we admitted at the outset, the answer isn't obvious. If Peter and MJ are together and Peter's identity as Spider-Man is widely known, MJ will face danger (as we have seen). Under these circumstances, would Peter be responsible for deliberately putting her at risk? Or could MJ resolve matters by pleading that Peter seek to do good by other means than crime fighting (as in our second scenario)? Even further, if Peter did comply and find another, safer occupation, would MJ still love him if he lacked the flair and secrecy of Spider-Man? We don't see these as genuine options.

In the end, we think that Spider-Man and MJ are in an unavoidable, yet not undesirable, conflict about whether they can be successfully married, but in their case *this is not a conflict between justice and romantic love.* If MJ truly loves Peter—Spider-Man—she cannot plead for him to give up what he has dedicated his life to be. After all, it's partly because of his commitment to justice that she falls in love with him. Spider-Man also can't cease to fight for justice and yet be confident that the world (including MJ) will live in safety. If he truly loves MJ (romantically), he needs to fight for justice so that MJ can live in safety. In this way, romantic love can intensify the call to fight for justice.

Back to the question in our title: Can Spider-Man champion justice and be with Mary Jane at the same time? Our answer is: only with a great deal of difficulty and luck. This is a choice made by both partners, not by Spider-Man in isolation (as it was at the end of the first movie). Spider-Man was not so lucky when it came to rescuing his first major girlfriend, Gwen Stacy, who was killed by the Green Goblin. The fiend threw Gwen off a bridge. When Spider-Man went to save her, she was falling so fast that when he pulled her up with his webbing, she experienced whiplash and her neck was snapped. Here we see Spider-Man acting for justice in order to save his love, but ultimately he fails at both. Given this tragedy, we cannot offer a confident, unqualified "yes" to the question raised by our chapter.

Let's rephrase the question, though: can Spider-Man champion justice and be in love with Mary Jane at the same time? Our answer is yes! Indeed, it's partly out of romantic love that he feels called to champion justice, come what may. If he ceased to champion justice, this would not only be a failure to be heroic, it would be a failure to be romantic, making MJ's world less safe and less exciting.[1]

> It's me, Peter Parker. Your friendly neighborhood—you know. I've come a long way since I was the boy bit by a spider. Back then nothing seemed to go right for me. Now people really like me. The city is safe and sound. Guess I had a little something to do with that. My uncle Ben would be proud. I still go to school. Top of my class. And I'm in love. With the girl of my dreams.
>
> —Peter Parker, *Spider-Man 3*[2]

---

[1]We thank Charlie Biskupic and Samuel Dunn for helpful comments and conversations on Spider-Man, justice, and romantic love.

[2]All quotes are derived from the International Movie Database (www.imdb.com).

LOVE, FRIENDSHIP, AND BEING SPIDER-MAN

Tony Spanakos

Why is the wisecracking webhead called our "friendly neighbor-hood Spider-Man?" The Spider-Man part is obvious, though deeper than it appears. As for the neighborhood, although he saves the world several times, Peter Parker remains that unas-suming geeky boy from Queens. The real mystery is why he's called friendly. Is he just an affable guy? Is he a friend to all? Is it friendship that motivates him to risk his life to save others, including those who try to kill him? Is this different from the friendship that Mary Jane Watson and Harry Osborn feel for him? What *is* friendship anyway?

Philosophers have long seen friendship as a form of love, so our question is really: do Peter, MJ, and Harry love one another? Philosophers such as Eddie Van Halen and Sammy Hagar wonder, "If it's got what it takes," then "why can't this be love?" Yet what does it mean to have what it takes? The two main types of love we'll need to consider are *philia* (pronounced phil-ee-a), which means reciprocated love between a few fellows, and *agape* (pronounced a-GA-pee), which means sacrificial love directed to all.[1] The first type was made popular by Greek philosophers, and the second by early Christian apologists. Both feed into what we can learn about love and friendship from Spider-Man. Of course, what we can learn about love and friendship from Spider-Man depends on which story arcs we look at—there are many, and they are not all consistent. To make our task manageable, we'll focus on the comics *Mary Jane (MJ)*, *Mary Jane: Homecoming (MJH)*, *Spider-Man Loves Mary Jane (SMLMJ)*, *The Death of Gwen Stacy (DOGS)*, and the movie *Spider-Man 3 (S3)*.

A Fine Fellow

Aristotle (384–322 BCE) told us that "the man who is isolated—who is unable to share in the benefits of political association, or has no need to share because he is already self-sufficient—is no part of the polis, and must therefore be either a beast or a god."[2] Unlike herding animals or bees in a hive, human beings are rational animals and live together not simply out of need but also because of the rational goods that can be obtained from communal living. *Philia*, which can be translated either as "fellowship" or "friendship," makes those communal goods possible.

Aristotle believed there are three types of *philia*, and what motivates each is different.[3] Fellowship may exist because two people gain pleasure from each other, or because they find mutual advantage from their relationship. These first two kinds of fellowship are incomplete and imperfect because they are based on convenience and temporary factors.

The third and most complete fellowship is between people who are motivated by a shared admiration for virtuous living, who wish to spend time together doing good things, and who see one another as "other selves." These kinds of fellowship make the individual friends better, and if there are many fellowships of this sort in a community, the whole community is made good by them.

Can superheroes be our friends? Aristotle considered situations where one friend is superior to the other, whether in natural powers, virtue, or station in life, and argued that love can overcome the inequality, "in all friendships based on inequality, the love on either side should be proportional—I mean that the better of the two . . . should receive more love than he gives; for when love is proportioned to desert, then there is established a sort of equality."[4] Call this the Aristotelian principle of proportionality; it entails that the lesser friend ought to give more love to the greater than does the greater to the lesser. Yet maybe it doesn't apply in cases such as Spider-Man's, because superheroes are more like the gods and goddesses of old, about which Aristotle wrote, "[T]he gods . . . have the greatest superiority in all good things . . . [and] if a person be very far removed, as God is . . . [there] can no longer be [friendship]."[5] The principle of proportionality can't stretch far enough in those cases.

So, what's a boy bitten by a radioactive spider to do? Can MJ love him? And why does Harry hate him so much?

Sacrificial Love

Christian *agape*, like *philia*, is translated as "love," but it seems worlds apart from Aristotle's *philia*. St. Basil (330–379) explained that *agape* requires that we live in communities so we can serve one another. While *philia* attracts friends to each other, *agape* sends us out to serve all we meet.[6] St. John the Evangelist characterized the heart of *agape* best when he wrote, "In this is love, not that we loved God, but that He Himself loved us, and sent forth His Son to be an expiation for our sins."[7] Aristotle's principle of proportionality is inverted here.

The difference between these two sorts of love is further highlighted in these words of Jesus to His disciples, "This is My commandment, that ye be loving one another, even as I loved you. Greater love [*agape*] hath no one than this, that one should lay down his life for his friends [*philoi*]. Ye are My friends [*philous*] if ye be doing whatsoever I command you."[8] Not only is Christian *agape* different from pagan *philia*, it transforms the meaning of *philia*. While Aristotle's ideal *philia* was fellowship of equals, Christ called His disciples friends, *philous*, despite the greatest of inequalities—that between human and Divine. Yet this *philia* comes with the price of showing *agape* for one another, as Jesus has done toward them.

C. S. Lewis (1898–1963), in *Four Loves*, distinguished *agape* and *philia* from two other Greek words for love: *storge* (attraction) and *eros* (sensual love). In the latter three, the rule holds that "only the lovable can be naturally loved."[9] We are attracted to the things we find attractive, not repulsive. We seek fellowship with our fellows, not with people we can't get along with, and we seek *eros* in that which arouses our senses, not in the opposite. Yet it is only "Divine Gift-love [*agape*] in the man [that] enables him to love what is not naturally lovable; lepers, criminals, enemies, morons, the sulky, the superior and the sneering."[10]

Spidey may not be a Christian, but the "great responsibilities" that come with his "great powers" are built on ideas of sacrificing himself for others, a secularized version of *agape* centered on unconditional love for individuals for their own sake. This concept of the self-sacrificing hero who protects those who fight against him has been absorbed into popular culture, including comic books. The creators and the fans of Spider-Man value *agape*, even if they are unaware of its Christian essence.[11]

MJ Hearts Spider-Man

The comics *MJ*, *MJH*, and *SMLMJ* focus on MJ, her friendship with Liz Allen, and their consultation and competition over boys, one of whom happens to be our friendly neighborhood Spider-Man. *MJ* begins with MJ dreaming of dating Spidey and dealing with the reality of Harry Osborn, one of her best friends, who is suddenly wanting to be more than that.

Ever the earthy one, Liz tells MJ she should stop "daydreaming about a certain someone in red-and-blue tights." MJ defends herself, saying, "Hey! Every girl has the right to fantasize."[12] Does she? Aristotle would have written off fantastic "loves" for two reasons. First, the fantasy element implies that the object of fantasy is so distant from the other that the two are not and could not be fellows. That is, they could not be "other selves" for each other. Second, *philia* is not possible in such a relationship because *philia* is a habit that is formed over time and through proximity. So, fantasies cannot involve fellowship.[13]

In a rare moment of contact between the two in the series, Spidey saves MJ in issue #1, then swings with her home to Queens, prompting her to ask, "How did you know where I live?" He stammers, claiming it is one of his powers, in an attempt to make the distance between them greater than it truly is.[14] Later, MJ has what would otherwise be an ideal date with a very romantic and mature Harry, but she confesses, "I just don't think Harry's the right guy for me, you know?" He's a good guy, but she wants Spider-Man as her "homecoming date."[15] Understandable, but we're still in fantasy land here, good for Mysterio, but not for Aristotle.

Later, Harry realizes the situation and says, "You don't have to say anything, MJ. I know. You like me fine. We're great friends . . . but I'm just second place. Your heart belongs to Spider-Man."[16] This turns out to be exactly the right thing to say, and MJ accepts him as a boyfriend. Yet the spider-crush doesn't go away, and when she sees Spidey leaving her school one morning, she asks him to homecoming. He says he can't. Still, she wants to know who he is. Spidey declines revealing himself, saying that he can't be sure he can trust her.

Spider-Man's honesty about his lack of trust and his insistence on maintaining his secret identity in all of their encounters show his inability to share who he is. He feels MJ can't be "another self" to him. Because of his superpowers and super-responsibilities, he must be content to love her at a distance. Moreover, despite being attracted to MJ and knowing she digs him, he keeps his distance because he's pursuing what's right (her safety, protecting Queens). In other words, his attraction is based on self-giving, not pleasure, but there's no room for *philia* here.

In *MJH*, MJ begins by dreaming that Spidey accepts her offer to go to homecoming with her, but she tells him that she is going with her boyfriend, Harry. The dream shows the inner conflict in MJ between the real and the fantasy, but throughout the *MJH* series, the emphasis is not on Spidey but on the relationship between Liz and MJ. Although MJ continues to see Spider-Man in the mall, among other places, the story revolves around Flash's fantasy crush on MJ and Liz's anger at the (perceived) betrayal by her closest friend. Nevertheless, it is Peter Parker, rather than Spider-Man, who seems to have the most effect on MJ in a rare dialogue between Peter and MJ, more so even than MJ's intimate one-on-one talks with Liz, Harry, and Flash.

In her frustration with the problems of her circle of friends, MJ talks to Peter, an outsider, about Spider-Man, the ultimate outsider. She asks how Spidey handles everything on his plate. Peter also seems impressed by Spider-Man, who could use his power and take out his anger on other people but does not. He says, "It's like he cares too much to see anyone else get hurt."[17] Here Parker/Spider-Man is pursuing the path of excellence, but, unfortunately, others are incapable of being "other selves" to him. Were it not so, Peter would reveal his secret identity to MJ.

What about MJ's love for Spider-Man? Spider-Man is a fantasy figure whom she loves along the lines of what Aristotle might have considered pleasure and utility. Spidey saves her life many times and is an escape outlet for her. She's not all that into Harry; Flash doesn't seem to get the hint that she's not interested in him; and Liz doesn't believe that she has no interest in her boyfriend, Flash. What's a girl to do?

Regardless of how MJ treats her friends or her own path to virtue, her attraction to Spider-Man is not a matter of excellence but of selfishness. In fact, in *SMLMJ*, Spidey and MJ go on a date in #5, Spidey offers to be her friend in #7, and he listens to her problems for the next few issues. Seeing that she is disturbed, he asks her whether she wants to talk, and she says, "That was perfect when I had stuff to work out . . . but everything's spectacular now."[18] A fleeting fellowship at best. Peter's love for her is based in virtue, but he does not seek fellowship with MJ. He often pulls away, denying himself the opportunity to have "another self." Thus, Peter's excellence is not directed toward companionship. Instead, it is composed of a healthy dose of self-sacrifice and suffering that, in our eyes, often seems unfair. Speaking of unfair . . .

Some Friend You Are! You Stole My Girl! Killed My Father!

That sounds pretty bad, but it didn't happen all at once, and it was unintentional. Still, does Harry have a right to hold a grudge? *DOGS* introduces the end of Peter Parker's first real love, as well as the gradual psychological breakdown of Harry Osborn.[19] It begins with MJ being overly flirtatious with Peter as a way to make Harry jealous, testing the friendship between Harry and Peter.

Harry had defended Peter when Flash jabbed at him for being a nerd, but now Harry feels threatened by his friend. Harry says, "Well well . . . How's the great American lover? You're a real pal . . . Playing up to Mary Jane that way."[20] This argument later escalates.

HO: I guess you're satisfied now!
PP: Huh? What do you mean, Harry?
HO: You know what I mean! Mary Jane gave me the gate—on account of you!
PP: You're way off base, mister . . . and I'm getting tired of being your whipping boy! I've got my own troubles. If you can't hold on to a girl . . . don't blame me. . . . Aw, Harry . . . I . . . I didn't mean that.
HO: Who cares what you mean? I've had it with you! So hit the road, smart guy. . . . you're movin' out.[21]

Suddenly, Peter's best friend and roommate no longer trusts him and throws him out of their apartment. Yet Peter's concern leads him to bring his erstwhile friend to the hospital, visiting him, and eventually protecting Harry from the Green Goblin, who is, of course, Harry's dad.

After the Goblin kills Gwen, an enraged Spidey almost kills the Goblin.[22] Yet he pulls back, saying, "Good Lord . . . what in the name of Heaven am I doing? In another moment I might have killed him! I would have become like him . . . a-a murderer!"[23] Peter, even while intoxicated with vengeance, refuses to cease his pursuit of excellence. Although he loses control briefly, it is momentary and he returns to his habitual relationship with others, which is based on virtue and responsibility.

In an earlier soliloquy, Peter gives us more insight into his relationship with his friends, particularly Harry. He says,

When Gwen lost her father . . . she blamed Spider-Man for his death. Gwen . . . who means the world to me. And now . . . I have to silence the father of my best and closest friend. . . . Must I always bring tragedy to those I love the most? Ever since I got my Spider Power, I've wanted to use it for good. I've tried to use it for good! But something always goes wrong. Or, maybe I'm just kidding myself! Maybe I've always been too selfish—too wrapped up in my own problems, my own hang-ups.[24]

Peter may be a whiny teenager, full of angst, but he always does the right thing eventually. Even in his frustration with the situations that surround him, he consistently sacrifices himself to protect those who, without cause, attack and/or betray him. He loves his moral inferiors more than they love him.

Was Harry ever really capable of being "another self" to Peter? Could he love Peter even as much as Peter loved him, let alone love him more? Not even close. We know he will take on his father's legacy of hatred, become the Hobgoblin and the second Green Goblin, and obsess over destroying Spider-Man. Yet before we get there, it is worth noting that in his pre-supervillain days, not only does he not show more *philia* to Peter to compensate for Peter's *agape* toward him, but his friendship has a very different motivation than Peter's.

Harry's attraction to Peter seems to be based on the ephemeral things that Aristotle associated with lower levels of friendship, such as companionship (a friend, a roommate) and pleasure and utility (as a tutor), not on his desire to share with a fellow the other's virtue. The friendship is tested on numerous occasions, and Harry fails the test, pointing to the temporary nature of Harry's feelings for Peter. Aristotle would not have been pleased.

Worse, because Harry is morally inferior to Peter, if Aristotle was right, Harry should love Peter more than Peter loves him, by either being more loyal, being a good listener, or finding ways to support him through his struggles. Instead, Harry does the opposite—such as, in *S3*, trying to kill him.

How does Peter respond? By making sure Harry receives the care he needs in the hospital.

A memory-impaired Harry tells Peter, "I always appreciated how you helped me through high school." A nice sentiment, though it confirms the idea that Peter was a useful nerd. At other points, they reminisce about playing basketball together and having fun as kids. Harry's fellowship with Peter, even at its best, is based on pleasure and use. That's not a bad thing, but such friendships, Aristotle told us, are not likely to survive—and especially not when you're hounded for revenge by your dead Goblin father.

Despite all of the malice that ensues, Peter still goes to Harry when MJ is captured by Venom and the Sandman, asking for his help for the sake of MJ, if not for the sake of their former friendship. And, true believers, Harry gives his life to save Peter! Shouldn't that count for something? Maybe Harry is not such a bad guy, after all, yet Aristotle would have argued that his love for Peter remains far from perfect, even if there is a final redeeming act. Nevertheless, when Peter tells Harry, "I should never have hurt you . . . said those things," and Harry responds that it "doesn't matter. You're my friend. My best friend," Harry is not lying. Peter is his best friend. They're just imperfect friends in a very imbalanced relationship.

Yet isn't there something morally exceptional in Harry's self-sacrifice? Aristotle believed *philia* must be built on habituated virtue—it takes a lot of time and practice—but *agape* is quite different: it's transformative and can appear to arise spontaneously. *Agape* involves not only self-sacrifice but repentance, as Harry's case makes clear. Similar to Christ forgiving all of those who persecuted Him in His passion and death, Harry forgives the injury he mistakenly thinks Peter gave him and lays down his life for those he loves. If "greater love [*agape*] hath no one than this, that one should lay down his life for his friends [*philoi*]," then Harry has overcome even the incompleteness of his fellowship (*philia*) with Peter and MJ by aiming at a higher form of love (*agape*). His *agape*, in the end, makes him Peter's equal.

Sacrificing Superheroes

Of course, in other story lines Harry is less heroic and MJ more self-sacrificing. Regardless, one constant in the various Spider-Man stories is that Peter lives a life of virtue. This makes him worthy of the highest form of *philia*, though he is often forced to web-sling it alone, searching in vain for fellows who can share his life. Occasionally it is MJ, but more often Tony Stark, Captain America, the Black Cat, or Kitty Pride with whom he tries to form true fellowship. These friendships never stick, however, and he never finds any permanent fellows with whom he can enjoy the most complete Aristotelian *philia*. His friends love him, but they do so on a level that is, from Aristotle's perspective, incomplete and without compensating for their "inferiority."

One thing we learn from Harry in *S3* is that even with their flaws, any one of those touched by Spider-Man might emulate him in remarkable ways. Until then, Spider-Man continues to love them all in the sacrificial ways of *agape*.

Our own potential for *agape* holds the key to our possible transformation into heroes. That potential is realized when we, as do Spider-Man and even Harry, sacrifice ourselves when the need of the moment requires for our friends, for those we don't know, and even for those who war against us. If those Church fathers who emphasized *agape* were right, actualizing that potential requires accepting the help of the first One who carved out this sacrificial path. Though we may rarely, if ever, show such *agape*, we recognize in it something that goes beyond anything Aristotle imagined—something that could make us, even though lacking superhero abilities, resemble our friendly neighborhood Spider-Man.[25]

NOTES

1. Many students of ancient Greek who were taught in Anglo-U.S. schools pronounce the word a-GA-pay.

2. Aristotle, *Politics*, trans. Ernest Barker (New York: Oxford University Press, 1971), 1253^{a}1–3.

3. Aristotle, *Nicomachean Ethics*, trans. F. H. Peters (New York: Barnes & Noble Books, 2004), Book VII.

4. *Nicomachean Ethics*, 1158^{b}25–29.

5. Ibid., 1158^{b}40–1159^{a}7.

6. Saint Basil, "The Long Rules," in *Saint Basil Ascetical Works*, Vol. 9, of *Fathers of the Church: A New Translation*, trans. Sr. M. Monica Wagner (Washington, DC: The Catholic University of America Press, 1950), 240.

7. I John 4:10. Translations of biblical passages are from *The Orthodox New Testament: The Holy Gospels Volume 1: Evangelistarion* and *The Orthodox New Testament: Acts, Epistles, and Revelation Volume 2: Praxapostolos* (Buena Vista: Holy Apostles Convent, 2003).

8. John 15: 12–14.

9. C. S. Lewis, *The Four Loves* (New York: A Harvest Book, 1988), 133.

10. Ibid., 128.

11. Sharon E. Sytsma, "Notes and Fragments: Agapic Friendship," *Philosophy and Literature* 27 (2003): 428–435. The Fathers of the Church would reject the idea that *agape* could be secularized or divorced from God.

12. *MJ* #1, April 2004.

13. This may be contrasted with *eros*, which is a more sensual form of love that is more intense and is more likely to lead to deviation from the logical life that appreciates and pursues the "good."

14. *MJ* #1.

15. *MJ* #1.

16. *MJ* #2, July 2004.

17. *MJH* #4, June 2005.

18. *SMLMJ* #11, October 2006.

19. It also features some of the worst Stan-Lee-Gerry-Conway wannabe-teenager-dialogue. *The Amazing Spider-Man: The Death of Gwen Stacy*, (1999 [1971]).

20. *DOGS*, chap. 2.

21. Ibid.

22. There is a controversy over how Gwen Stacy died. Physicist James Kakalios has rejected the Green Goblin's explanation that the fall killed Stacy (see http://en.wikipedia.org/wiki/Gwen_Stacy).

23. *DOGS*, chap. 5.

24. Ibid., chap. 2.

25. My thanks to Jonathan J. Sanford, Rob Delfino, Photini Spanakos, and Mark D. White for their comments.

SPIDEY'S TANGLED
WEB OF OBLIGATIONS

Fighting Friends and
Dependents Gone Bad

Christopher Robichaud

The *spectacular* Spider-Man? The *amazing* Spider-Man? If superheroes are judged by their nemeses, our friendly neighborhood wall-crawler seems to be small potatoes. His costumed adventures rarely find him facing down an A-list of supervillains: no cosmic baddies such as Galactus, no super-geniuses of the Leader's caliber, not even mutant nasties such as Magneto. His day-to-day battles are with vampires, lizard men, and, for goodness' sake, sentient costumes. He fights folks made of sand or water or molten metal. Rounding out Spidey's rogues' gallery—an egomaniac who tosses pumpkin bombs, some dude with an inferiority complex and a deadly mastery of electricity, and a bevy of lunatics wielding killer tentacles or tails. To add insult to injury, these villains often seek nothing as lofty as world domination, multiverse subjugation, or even the standard go-to goal of the enslavement of the human race. Instead, they really just want one thing—a dead Spider-Man.

Yet these bad guys aren't after Spidey just to get him out of the way; it's personal for them. *Really* personal. Just consider the second Green Goblin, Harry Osborn, and the alien symbiote that becomes Venom. These foes feel severely wronged by Spider-Man and want to make him suffer for it. Are they simply unhinged? That possibility seems too simple. Peter does, after all, play some part in making them the enemies they become. Peter is Harry's best friend, but he persistently deceives Harry about his superhero alter ego, especially about the part he played in the death of Norman Osborn. As to the alien symbiote, Spidey is the one who first, carelessly, brings about their dependent relationship while on the Beyonder's Battleworld. Nor does the living costume turn Spider-Man evil (at least in the comics). It simply makes him a little weaker—and gives him new powers—in order to live. Yet without hesitation or attempts at communicating with it, Spider-Man rejects the costume and leaves it to its own devices, giving birth to Venom.

If Spider-Man is partly responsible for the birth of Goblin and Venom, does he owe them something—morally speaking— that he doesn't owe other villains? How should Spider-Man fight friends and dependents who've gone bad?

Spinning a Web of Deceit

Withholding information sometimes amounts to deception. If a panicked Aunt May asks Peter where he's been, and he responds, "Out with Mary Jane," what he says could very well be true: he went out with Mary Jane, *and then he battled the Hobgoblin for hours on end.* Peter hasn't lied to Aunt May, but he has deceived her. Why? Because Peter's choice to withhold information is done with the intention of getting Aunt May to form a false belief—that all he's done while out was spend time with

MJ. If this counts as deceiving Aunt May, then Harry Osborn has a legitimate complaint against Peter for hiding his true identity, even though Peter never resorts to lying.

Is Peter unjust to his friend? The philosopher Immanuel Kant (1724–1804) would certainly have thought so. Kant argued that our actions should be evaluated in terms of a categorical imperative, one version of which says that we must always act in a way that treats persons as ends in themselves and not as mere means.[1] For Kant, one way that we sometimes treat persons as mere means is when we deceive them to achieve ulterior ends. In doing so, we fail to express the right attitude toward them—we fail to extend to them the respect they deserve as rational moral agents.

A blanket prohibition against deception is too strong, however. Hard and fast rules need to be balanced with common sense. Consider Spider-Man going public about his true identity as part of the *Civil War* storyline. For Kant, Peter Parker does the right thing; he stops engaging in an ongoing public deception. Yet suppose that *a lot* of bad will come from this. All of Pete's family and friends will be harassed, kidnapped, maybe even killed, because of his revelation. And suppose J. Jonah Jameson levels lawsuit after lawsuit on Peter, disabling him from fighting crime while he defends himself legally. If all of this will result from Peter going public with the news that he's Spider-Man, it seems reasonable that he isn't obligated to do so.

Kant thought that consequences were entirely irrelevant to determining what was morally permissible, and thus, no matter how much harm would occur, deception was always impermissible. Yet common sense tells us that it's morally permissible to deceive—morally permissible in the sense that it wouldn't be wrong—if *a lot* of harm would come from telling the truth. That's not the same as saying that it's permissible to deceive if *any* harm would result, and it's also not the same thing as saying that lying is sometimes the right thing to do.

In opposition to Kant, *consequentialism* holds that the right thing to do is always and only that which brings about the best overall consequences. Yet recognizing that consequences matter in moral deliberation does not necessarily make you a consequentialist. Consequentialism swings the pendulum too far in the other direction, from not caring about the consequences at all (as in the case of Kant) to caring about them too much. After all, it might bring the best consequences if Spider-Man kills some of the crazier villains he faces, rather than allow them to return to a life of crime after escaping capture and/or imprisonment. Even so, it doesn't seem right that Spider-Man ought to kill them. The consequences, in other words, aren't the only things that matter when deciding what our moral obligations are. When it comes to deception, we need moral guidance that doesn't go to extremes. We need *reflective equilibrium*, the right balance between moral principles and common-sense judgments.

With these considerations in place, here's a way to think about why Peter shouldn't keep his friends and loved ones in the dark about his true identity as Spider-Man.[2] Peter defends his ongoing deception by suggesting that a lot of bad will result if everyone knows that he is Spider-Man. That may be true, but there's a big difference between Peter letting *everyone* know that he's Spider-Man and letting those nearest and dearest to him know. Unless Peter judges his close relatives and friends to be untrustworthy people, which would raise a different issue, he is failing to satisfy the special moral obligations we all have toward those persons with whom we develop close personal bonds.

Yet might Peter have other good reasons to keep Harry in the dark? Sure. A big one is that knowledge of Peter's superhero identity will no doubt cause Harry significant psychological distress. Harry *hates* Spider-Man because he blames him for his father's death. Peter would have a lot of explaining to do, and that explanation would deliver another blow to Harry: learning the truth about his father, the first Green Goblin. Peter also feels the need to honor Norman's dying wish, which was to keep Harry from knowing about Norman's alter ego. Peter is faced with a difficult choice. On the one hand, he has a special obligation to his friend to be forthright with him about matters of great importance, and Peter surely is right to strive to be both a good friend and honest. On the other hand, Peter doesn't want to cause Harry undo psychological harm or go against the wishes of a dying man. What to do?

A just balance of these considerations leans toward Peter needing to come clean with Harry. The special obligations—such as being forthright—he has in virtue of their friendship weigh heavily. What seals the deal, though, is this: although it's true that Peter will cause Harry psychological harm by coming clean, he sets Harry up for still greater harm with his silence. Harry's hatred for Spider-Man continues to fester, and then in *Spider-Man 2*, just as he thinks revenge is within his grasp, Harry discovers the truth on his own. Harry's fragile psyche bursts asunder, leading him to become the second Green Goblin. A desire to prevent this sort of blow should also have led Peter not to honor Norman Osborn's dying wish. Whatever good intentions Norman had in his last moments, his request has put his son in line for undergoing more needless suffering than the straightforward truth—coming from a friend under the right circumstances—would have brought.

The Alien Symbiote—Not Your Typical Pile of Dirty Laundry

Has Peter also wronged Venom or, at least, the alien costume that later becomes Venom? To answer this, let's first recall the circumstances—as presented in the comics, rather than in the movie—under which Peter connects with the alien symbiote. While on the Beyonder's Battleworld during the first Secret Wars, Spider-Man finds himself in desperate need of a new costume.[3] He uses a special machine that is supposed, he thinks, to produce regular ol' new threads. Instead, it spits out the alien, which quickly covers Peter's body. The result? Black costume Spider-Man: new threads and a whole lot more. The "more" in this case involves a costume that produces webbing so that Spider-Man never has to refill his web cartridges. It also transforms to street clothes with a thought and helps enhance many of Spidey's other abilities. For these reasons, Peter keeps the costume on almost all of the time, bonding with it physically and psychologically. When Peter visits the Fantastic Four to investigate his costume, he learns that it's a sentient alien symbiote. Completely freaked out by this news, he immediately has the Fantastic Four help him detach it from his body. Utterly dejected, the symbiote takes its first step toward becoming Venom.

Of course, Peter doesn't know that the symbiote will survive being removed from his body, let alone become Venom. For all he knows, having the costume removed will destroy it. Is it morally permissible for him to put a parasitic alien's life at risk in this way, without even asking Reed Richards's opinion about its future? Common sense tells us it isn't morally permissible, on the grounds that the alien costume is in fact a sentient life form, and Peter knows this. If something possesses sentience, then it's somehow able to perceive its environment and undergo some sort of experiences of pleasure and pain. Those features are enough for many moral philosophers to conclude that creatures with sentience demand some moral consideration; the fact that a sentient creature has the capacity to suffer matters in determining what we're permitted to do to it.

That seems right, but how does it matter, exactly? Here's one way to think about it. Although we arguably need no moral justification for taking a rock, which has no sentience, and smashing it against other rocks, we do need a moral justification to do that to a sentient creature. We may, under certain very rare conditions, be morally permitted to treat some sentient creatures—a rat, say—in this way, but their having moral standing amounts to us needing to have some moral justification for our actions—we can't simply treat these creatures any way we want to without there being some good *reasons* to do so.

Now it's important to recognize that by claiming that all sentient creatures demand some moral consideration, we're not saying that all sentient creatures have the same moral standing. Cats are sentient. So are human beings. Both have some moral standing and deserve some moral consideration, but they don't have the same moral standing, nor do they deserve the same moral consideration. If Spider-Man could save either a cat or a human being from a burning building, but not both, he'd be morally obligated to save the human being, all else being equal. Admitting that an inequity exists between the cat and the person is compatible with acknowledging that the cat does still have some moral standing. If there is only the cat to save from the burning building and Spider-Man could easily save it but chooses to let it burn alive instead, then he will be doing something wrong. Yet we don't think he will be doing something wrong if he leaves, say, a chair there to burn. That's because he doesn't owe the chair any moral consideration.

These reflections suggest that in light of Peter knowing that the alien costume is sentient, he has acted wrongly in discarding it as he did—as a *mere* piece of clothing. This claim is strengthened by the following observation. Up to the point of rejecting the costume, Peter happily wears and, most important, benefits from the costume. Admittedly, he does so in legitimate ignorance of the cost of doing this. Nevertheless, at the point of rejection, Peter is, intentionally or not, casting off a being he has made dependent on him. Because of this dependency, Peter has a responsibility at least to proceed more cautiously, more responsibly, in pursuing options for removing the costume, rather than simply having it blasted off in reckless abandon the minute he finds out it is alive.

Before moving on, we should acknowledge that just because Peter acts wrongly in treating the alien symbiote as he does at the point of rejecting it, that doesn't mean removing it will be wrong, even if doing so will kill it. All we're claiming is that given what he knows at the time and the type of relationship that has developed between him and the costume, he has an obligation to at least see whether there might be a way to remove it without bringing it harm and what that course of action amounts to.

Here Come the Bad Guys!

We've seen that Peter wrongs both Harry and the alien symbiote. Does this give them warrant to become the Green Goblin and Venom? The old adage "two wrongs don't make a right" fits here. It clearly isn't morally permissible for Harry or the symbiote purposefully to transform themselves into super-villains just because Peter fails to satisfy his obligations toward them. That said, they do have a legitimate claim on Peter to atone for his wrongdoing. They're within their moral rights to confront him and seek some kind of redress, one that might require more than a mere apology. Yet they're not allowed to harass and threaten Peter or his loved ones. That much is obvious. What's not obvious is what other morally permissible options they have. What can they do, short of engaging in wrongdoing themselves?

For one thing, there's good reason to think that Harry is permitted to confront Spider-Man *as the Green Goblin*. We shouldn't take that to mean that he's permitted to confront Spider-Man as a villain. Rather, Harry is allowed to take the Goblin super-serum, wear the Goblin battle armor, and confront Spider-Man as such. Why? Spider-Man has super-powers and Harry doesn't, for starters. And for all Harry knows—building on the narrative of the films—Spider-Man did play a blameworthy role in the death of his father, Norman.

Peter never comes clean about exactly what happened. Moreover, when Harry learns that Peter is Spider-Man, he realizes that his best friend has been deceiving him for quite some time about something of utmost importance to Harry. So, reasonably, Harry may not expect Spider-Man to "play nice" when Harry confronts him about exactly what role he played in Norman's death, and why Spider-Man deceived him for so long. As a matter of self-defense, Harry has reason to become the Goblin.

Yet what if he doesn't choose to don the Goblin armor and take the Goblin serum for reasons of self-defense? What if he chooses to become the Goblin solely to seek revenge? Does this render his transformation morally impermissible? How we answer this question will reveal an important stand we can take in moral philosophy. Some philosophers, following Kant, think that the reasons we have for performing an action affect the moral status of that very action. Others, such as the consequentialists, think that the moral value of an action is independent of the reasons we perform the action. For someone in Kant's camp, whether Harry's action of "Goblinizing" himself is a morally good one or, at least, morally neutral will depend on whether he does it for reasons of self-defense or revenge. The very same action, in other words, can end up having a different moral value, depending on the reasons behind it. Intuitively, that seems right. Thus, although it may be permissible for Harry to become the Goblin, that permissibility depends on his reasons for doing so.

The same analysis goes for the alien symbiote, which goes out of its way to settle on a host who *hates* Peter Parker—Eddie Brock. This strongly suggests that the act of becoming Venom is also morally impermissible, and so we should conclude that Harry Osborn and the alien symbiote act wrongly when they become the Green Goblin and Venom, respectively, and they definitely act wrongly in their campaign to destroy Spider-Man.

Fighting Friends Gone Bad

Spider-Man now finds himself with two formidable foes, both of whom want to ruin him in a variety of ways. What moral rights and obligations does he have toward them at this point? We might be tempted to think that he has the very same ones that he has toward all of the villains he confronts. That's true, up to a point. For instance, he's morally permitted to cause them harm in the process of defending himself and others from the harm they intend to inflict. Suppose the Green Goblin is zipping around town on his glider, shadowing our friendly neighborhood wall-crawler, who's also making his rounds. Spidey is at first unaware of this, but just as the Goblin goes to lob a pumpkin bomb at him, Spidey's spider-sense alerts him to this fact. With his spiderlike reflexes, is Spider-Man allowed to spin around and thwack the Goblin with a heavy hit of webbing, knowing that it will likely cause the Goblin to crash and potentially suffer significant harm? Yes. We typically believe we're allowed to harm others in the process of defending ourselves from being harmed by them. In this case, being hit with a pumpkin bomb is not a trivial matter for Spider-Man; he stands to suffer considerable pain, possibly even death, if that bomb hits its mark. Presumably, the only way to stop that from happening is to web the Goblin.

Does it matter to our assessment of this case that the Goblin is intentionally gunning for Spider-Man? On reflection, it doesn't seem as if it does. Consider a slightly different scenario. The Goblin is again following Spider-Man, but not because he wants to attack him. He's looking to catch up with him to turn himself in and seek professional help. On his way to meet Spider-Man, though, his glider goes out of control and he hurtles toward a crowd of people. Let's suppose that if he hits them, many will die, but he will live. Spidey understands this and also realizes that the only way to stop the glider is to throw up a web, but crashing into it might very well break the Goblin's neck. In this case, it still seems that Spider-Man is permitted to web the Goblin, even if he knows the Goblin is coming to turn himself in and that he will live—though others will die—if he crashes into the crowd.

Philosophers often appeal to a line of reasoning called the doctrine of double effect to defend our verdicts in cases such as these. The doctrine of double effect says that it's sometimes morally permissible to perform an action that we know will bring about, or will likely bring about, harm to others—the kind of action that under most circumstances it is wrong to perform. The special circumstances under which the action isn't wrong are as follows: (1) The harm we will bring about has about as much moral weight to it as the good we will bring about. (2) The action we're performing is, in and of itself, morally good or neutral. (3) The harm is not the means to producing the good. And (4), we foresee the harm but don't intend it.[4]

That's a lot to put on the table! Here's an example, however, to help you understand how this kind of reasoning works. Venom is on the rampage again, and Spider-Man has lured him into another bell tower. Sound waves will likely work in tearing the symbiote away from Eddie Brock, and Spidey knows this. Yet suppose he also knows that the two have bonded so completely that their separation might cause the symbiote to be destroyed and Eddie to suffer a complete mental breakdown. Is Spider-Man nevertheless permitted to use the bell to separate the two and stop Venom's rampage? The doctrine of double effect says that he is. The good effect in this case is putting an end to Venom's reign of terror. The bad effect is the potential destruction of the symbiote and Eddie Brock's breakdown. On the assumption that Venom's rampage is significant, the good effect and the bad effect have similar moral weight. (If all that Venom was doing was annoying Spider-Man with verbal abuse, it would be a different matter altogether.) That satisfies the first condition.

The second condition is met because being in the vicinity of a ringing bell, in and of itself, is a morally neutral act.

There's nothing particularly nefarious about ringing bells. The symbiote's destruction and Eddie's psychological breakdown are not a means to stopping Venom's rampage; the means is the bell ringing, plain and simple. So the third condition is satisfied. Last, Eddie having a breakdown and the symbiote being destroyed are foreseeable but unintended consequences. Spider-Man certainly would prefer if he could keep Eddie from his fate and perhaps even the symbiote from its. Thus, by the doctrine of double effect, Spider-Man is allowed to lure Venom to a bell tower and have the bells do the rest, even though foreseeable harm will result.

Lending a Hand—Or Some Webbing

Once we acknowledge that in many cases, Spider-Man is allowed to treat the second Green Goblin and Venom as he does his other foes, should we conclude that in all cases he has the same obligations toward them that he does toward his other villains?

No. Recall that we have special obligations toward those closest to us—friends, family, and dependents. Among the duties we have to such persons are to help them *flourish*, to set them up for success as best we can, to aid them in achieving their life projects, and to support them when they suffer setbacks or other obstacles. These duties can all be derived from Kant's categorical imperative (as well as from divine command theory, virtue ethics, and other moral theories). Remember that Kant's rule says that we should never treat persons as mere means but always as ends in themselves. Admittedly, we saw that this principle can't stand simply as is; the first part of it results in a blanket prohibition against deception, among other things, which won't do. Still, many philosophers are rightly sympathetic to the categorical imperative, even if, at the end of the day, reflective equilibrium forces us to amend it.

Yet what, exactly, is it to treat persons as ends in themselves? A popular way to understand this portion of the categorical imperative is to see it as giving us duties of *beneficence*, obligations such as those I've just discussed. For Kant, each of us has general obligations to help others in these various ways. Yet Kant also recognized that if this is interpreted as meaning that we have these obligations *toward each and every person*, then this requirement would be too demanding. So there's some flexibility built into his account that allows us to choose whom to help and when. Put simply, we must help some people, but we aren't obligated to help everyone. That said, one way to interpret what it means for us to have *special* obligations toward certain persons in virtue of our relationship to them is to understand these persons as being precisely those for whom we *must* fulfill our general duties of beneficence.

What would this amount to when it comes to Harry and the symbiote? Putting aside some of the extreme cases we've looked at, Spider-Man usually doesn't have to make life-or-death decisions about the adversaries he faces. Rather, he primarily uses his skill and wits to capture villains and hand them over to the authorities, ideally causing as little harm to his foes and to everyone else—including himself!—as possible. As a superhero crime fighter, then, once Spider-Man apprehends the bad guys, his moral duties toward them are more or less complete.

Yet not so when it comes to Harry or the symbiote. His relationship to them gives him the duty to do what he can to help Harry and the symbiote abandon their villainous ways and reform their lives. He may fail at this, but he's not permitted simply to walk away from the task. This might involve Peter helping Harry get professional treatment. It might involve him trying to find a willing host for the symbiote that would result in a mutually beneficial, rather than mutually destructive, relationship. It might involve a lot of things. The main point, however, is that unlike Electro, Scorpion, or even Dr. Octopus, Spider-Man's duties toward the second Green Goblin and Venom don't end when he captures them in his web. On the contrary, in virtue of the relationship he has with them, some of his most important obligations to them kick in when he captures them.

So Spidey may not have an A-list rogues' gallery to battle, but he nevertheless faces as formidable a task as any superhero who does. Although it's obviously challenging to snag the bad guys before they do too much harm, it's all the more challenging to try to reform them. That's just what Spider-Man is required to try to do when it comes to the second Green Goblin and Venom. No doubt, our friendly neighborhood wall-crawler has his job cut out for him, but Spider-Man is certainly up to the task, and that's what really makes him amazing.

NOTES

1. Immanuel Kant, *Groundwork of the Metaphysics of Morals*, ed. and trans. Mary Gregor (Cambridge, UK: Cambridge University Press, 1998), Section II.

2. I argue along similar lines in "With Great Power Comes Great Responsibility: On the Moral Duties of the Super-Powerful and Super-Heroic," in Tom Morris and Matt Morris, eds., *Superheroes and Philosophy* (LaSalle, IL: Open Court, 2005), 177–193.

3. *Secret Wars* #8, 1984.

4. Medieval philosopher Thomas Aquinas is considered to be the first person to introduce formally the doctrine of double effect reasoning. Contemporary philosophers who have examined this idea include G. E. M. Anscombe, Frances Kamm, Warren Quinn, and Philippa Foot.

PART SIX

THE AMAZING SPEAKING SPIDER: JOKES, STORIES, AND THE CHOICES WE MAKE

THE QUIPSLINGER
The Morality of Spider-Man's Jokes

Daniel P. Malloy

Please—no jokes!

> —Vulture, *Amazing Spider-Man* #7 (1963)

How *about* that! I've got a new weapon I didn't even *know* about! My *spider speech*!

> —Spider-Man, *Amazing Spider-Man* #23 (1965)

Imagine being a criminal in Marvel's New York City. Imagine getting caught. Who caught you? Well, because you're reading a book about Spider-Man, I'm guessing it was the web-slinger. Yet think about the other possibilities: the Punisher, Daredevil, Dr. Strange, Thor, Captain America, Iron Man, just about any member of the X-Men or the Avengers, or simply the plain old NYPD. I don't know about you, but I'd rather be taken down by any of these guys (except the Punisher, for obvious reasons) than by Spider-Man, and I'll tell you why. See, any of Marvel's masked heroes is going to beat me up and take me in (again, except the Punisher), but Spidey's going to beat me up and take me in *and* crack jokes about it *the whole time*. That is quite literally adding insult to injury. Anyone else may hurt me (a lot), but they're also going to treat the situation with the gravity it deserves: I've broken the law and now have to be punished. (Please! Dear God! *Not* the Punisher!) Spidey'll treat the whole encounter as if it's open mic night at the Improv.

Webhead's habit of cracking jokes is quite frustrating for his enemies, and no less so for his allies—being on the right side of the law doesn't grant immunity from the wall-crawler's rapier wit. So, why does he do it? It seems unwise, at best, to spend time cracking jokes when people are trying to kill you or doing it to insult your allies. The fact that Spidey does make jokes about his allies seems to speak against the idea that his jokes are a form of "trash talking," intended to psyche out or distract his opponents. So, what's the purpose of Spider-Man's jokes? Why doesn't he just shut up?

What's So Funny, Webhead?

Some people are born joke tellers. Others simply can't seem to get the timing right, or they always flub the punch lines. Aside from differences in ability at telling jokes, we also have different ways of receiving jokes. Some people seem to have no sense of humor whatsoever. Leaving them aside (because I can't imagine one of them being interested in this chapter), we still have vast differences in what makes us laugh. Some people have dark or warped senses of humor; others laugh at puns and knock-knock jokes; some love a joke but have no sense of humor about themselves. Yet we all speak the same language: jokes, laughter, humor. Given our vast and varied opinions on what's funny, it shouldn't come as a surprise that philosophers have been arguing about the nature and purpose of humor since Plato. They may not always refer to jokes, but the basic question of what makes us laugh has been one of those delightfully contentious minor background skirmishes throughout the history of philosophy.

The oldest theory of humor is the superiority theory, first formulated by Plato (ca. 428–348 BCE) in *Philebus*. Put simply, the superiority theory claims that what makes a joke funny, what makes us laugh, is the feeling that we are somehow better than some other poor schmo, the butt. The theory was given its most famous and succinct formulation by Thomas Hobbes (1588–1679), who wrote, "Sudden glory, is the passion which makes those grimaces called laughter; and is caused either by some sudden act of their own, that pleases them; or by the apprehension of some deformed thing in another, by comparison whereof they suddenly applaud themselves."[1] There are a number of ways we can feel superior to others, each of which can explain some type of humor. For instance, the humor of slapstick comedy is often based on a viewer's feeling of superiority to the clumsy fool.

So, when Spidey makes one of his self-deprecating remarks—such as, "Yeah *some* career! No vacations! No pension plan! Not even a salary!"—what makes us laugh is not any kind of identification with or sympathy for our friendly neighborhood Spider-Man.[2] Rather, we laugh at the comment because it reminds us how much better off we are than the wall-crawler. In this case, our superiority has the form of simply being better off. The superiority theory could also go a long way toward explaining Spidey's overall appeal—ever since he first appeared, the webslinger has been a classic lovable loser. It's particularly nice to be able to feel superior to a guy with superpowers.

A more recent theory, first proposed by Francis Hutcheson (1694–1746), partly as a rejection of Hobbes's version of the superiority theory, is the incongruity theory. In its classic formulation, the incongruity theory claims that humor is based on disappointed expectations—sounds hilarious, doesn't it? As Immanuel Kant (1724–1804) explained it, "Laughter is an affect resulting from the sudden transformation of a heightened expectation into nothing."[3] A joke's setup creates a certain expectation—it establishes a logical sequence. The punch line creates amusement by upsetting that logical sequence and frustrating our expectations. Yet that's only one version of the incongruity theory. In broadest terms, the theory holds simply that humor is based on some sort of incongruity between expectation and fulfillment or between conception and experience.

In a sense, this could also explain Spidey's appeal. There are certainly incongruities involved in many of the wall-crawler's defining characteristics: his habit of joking when his life is in jeopardy, for starters. There's also the incongruity of a guy with superpowers, a young man who can do just about anything he wants, who has a life as bad as poor Peter Parker's.

At least some of Spidey's jokes can be explained this way, as well, like when the wall-crawler responds to a warning from Jolly Jonah Jameson by saying, "Mister, I *thrive* on warnings! In fact, some day I'm going to write an article for the *Readers' Digest* titled: 'The Most Unforgettable Warning I've Ever Known!'"[4] The same explanation applies when he responds to another warning, this one from the Schemer, by saying, "People are *always* warning me! It's nice to know they *care*!"[5] In both cases, what makes us laugh is the clash between the warning, the danger it represents, and Spidey's attitude toward it. The words in Spidey's quip aren't really important—what matters is the attitude. Spidey's being warned. He should be afraid. Instead, he quips. Hence the incongruity.

A third theory of humor is the relief theory. Most famously, this theory was put forward by Sigmund Freud (1856–1939) in his *Jokes and Their Relation to the Unconscious*. Essentially, the relief theory holds that laughter arises from the release of some sort of pressure. In Freud's theory, the pressure is unconscious, caused by our internalization of societal norms and their conflict with our natural urges. We are relieved when this tension is released—as through a bawdy joke that gives us permission to ignore these norms. Other relief theories focus on various sources of pressure or tension.

Again, it's not hard to see how we could apply the relief theory to Webhead's jokes. After all, fighting criminals, mad men, and monsters has to make a guy tense, and in a tense situation, there's nothing quite like a joke to provide a release. There's a reason they call it "comic relief." When the Red Skull—not one of Spidey's usual nemeses, but deadly nonetheless—expresses surprise at the wall-crawler's return, Spidey responds, "What do you mean *again*! I've *always* been *me*!"[6] Clearly, he's trying to distract someone, most likely himself, from the dire situation.

Each of these theories has a number of variations and a number of flaws. The superiority theory makes laughter and jokes seem inherently cruel and arrogant. The various versions of the incongruity theory all manage to include incongruities that are strange and weird, sometimes even frightening, but not funny. As for the relief theory, it also has a few counterexamples. Perhaps unsurprisingly, Freud's version of the relief theory is great at explaining the humor of off-color or smutty jokes but has difficulty dealing with puns and knock-knock jokes—at least, the clean ones.

Each of these theories can explain what makes some of Spidey's jokes funny, but not all of them can explain why he tells them. Incongruity may explain why people laugh at puns, but it can't tell us why people tell puns. The superiority and relief theories both give us some idea of why we tell jokes. As we'll see, one version of the superiority theory is particularly apt for our purposes, holding the point of all jokes, Spidey's included, to be moral.

Joke's on You, Bad Guy!

There's sometimes a tense relationship between humor and morality. In fact, there are times when the two conflict. We've all laughed at a joke only to realize later that we really shouldn't have—we feel guilt for our amusement at some off-color remark. Likewise, we've all made jokes only to realize that we went too far—perhaps by telling the joke too soon after a particular tragedy. We all know that uncomfortable feeling. Our moral sense tells us that there's something wrong with laughing about certain things—but we laugh anyway. Yet although humor sometimes conflicts with morality, it also often helps enforce morality. Satirists such as Juvenal, Jonathan Swift, and Molière have used humor to encourage people to behave morally. In our own lives, we can see this function as well. Among friends, we often tease one another for our little infelicities and moral failings.

Some superiority theories have argued that this function of humor is more than merely a function—it's actually what makes funny things funny. Henri Bergson's (1859–1941) essay *Laughter* is one of the more influential versions of this theory. Bergson's theory is that we laugh at people primarily for a lack of grace and social polish. Recently, F. H. Buckley has proposed a more developed version of this theory in his book *The Morality of Laughter*.[7] Buckley's superiority theory consists of two linked theses, the positive thesis and the normative thesis. The positive thesis holds that joke tellers believe that they are morally superior in some way to the butts of their jokes. So, in the case of Spidey, Buckley's first thesis holds that the webslinger thinks he's a better person than the people he insults and teases, both the villains and the heroes. The normative thesis, on the other hand, is a bit stronger. It holds that the joke teller doesn't only *believe* he's better than the butt of his joke, he really *is* better in the relevant way. That is, when Spidey teases Jolly Jonah for being a sourpuss, part of what makes the joke funny is that Spidey has the right to make the joke because he is, in this way, a better person than Jameson. Although it's a stronger thesis, it can be easier to swallow than the positive thesis—at least, in Spidey's case. The positive thesis could mean that Spidey's simply an arrogant jerk; the normative thesis means that he really is a hero.

Although Buckley's arguments are based only on his own observations and interpretations of various jokes, there is also some sociological and anthropological evidence to support them. Studies of humor in these fields are generally not conducted from the joke teller's perspective, but from those who hear the joke. These studies show that many jokes have a social function.[8] In particular, jokes made at the expense of a butt serve to bolster social cohesion. The audience gains a sense of solidarity from the joker's pointing out the differences between them and the butt, the butt's failing or failings. So when we laugh along with Spidey, part of what we're doing is reaffirming our own identities as law-abiding citizens. When we laugh at the way Webhead ribs one of his enemies—or one of his allies—we're experiencing Hobbes's "sudden glory" based on our common feeling of superiority.

Although Buckley's theory is appealing and does have some empirical evidence to support it, there are some problems with it as well. For instance, Buckley has to dismiss a wide variety of jokes in order to make his theory work—any joke without a moral agent for a butt simply isn't a joke, according to Buckley. So puns, jokes about animals, or humorous nonsense, no matter how funny, are not jokes. Buckley says, "We do not laugh at animals unless they remind us of humans."[9] That might be acceptable if Buckley were proposing a new definition of the joke, but he's not. Instead, he is making the stronger claim that we only really laugh at jokes with butts. Now, I will not deny that I tend to laugh hardest at jokes with butts, but I also laugh at jokes about animals and even at the occasional pun.

In light of these weaknesses, we face two choices: either abandon Buckley's superiority theory in its entirety or alter it to accommodate the criticisms. Taking account of the criticisms means weakening the theses somewhat, but that's the course I choose. So, to explain the purpose of Spidey's jokes, I have to change Buckley's theory in one important way. Namely, I deny the scope of Buckley's theory: not all humor is based on superiority over someone; in other words, not all jokes require a butt. I make the more limited claim that all jokes with butts are based on some moral superiority. And let's add to it this corollary: jokes at a butt's expense are attempts to get the butt to reform particular habits.

Professor Spidey and the Bad Guys

There are three basic types of butts for Spidey's jokes: villains, fellow heroes, and Jolly Jonah Jameson. Yes, ol' J.J. is a type of butt all to himself. The editor of the *Bugle* isn't bad enough to be considered a villain (despite a few forays in that direction, such as his role in creating the Scorpion) and he certainly isn't a hero (despite what he thinks). The most common butts of the Webhead's jokes are villains. Spidey makes quite the effort to put down his more dangerous villains—not to mention the anonymous street thugs he tangles with on a regular basis. Sometimes he mocks their moral failings explicitly, sometimes he remarks on their incompetence, and at other times he simply insults them. In his dealings with the Kingpin, for instance, Webhead often resorts to making fun of the villain's apparent obesity. Normally, fat jokes are cruel, but we make an exception in the Kingpin's case, because he's a bad person.

The standard version of the superiority theory entails that there is some element of cruelty in much humor. We laugh at someone because she is in some way inferior to us—the butt of the joke fails or is somehow defective. Our glee is based on that failure. This is why most proponents of superiority theories, from Plato to Hobbes, have discouraged excessive laughter. They probably would have disapproved of Spidey's wise-cracking ways. My version of Buckley's theory, however, frees us from this problem because of who we are laughing at—bad people. Spidey's jokes about Kingpin's weight or the Vulture's ridiculous look or the stupid bowl Mysterio wears on his head may seem cruel. Some of the jokes may even be irrelevant, unless we count them as attempts to get these guys to take themselves less seriously. Yet they are morally acceptable because they are not truly cruel. Their targets are morally bad, and Spidey's goal is to see these villains reform.

We can analyze some of Spidey's jokes and find clear moral messages. Often, Spidey is plainly encouraging his enemies to change their ways, albeit in a less than serious manner. For instance, in his second encounter with the Vulture, Webhead makes constant references to moral virtues that Adrian Toomes clearly lacks. "I think your *modesty* is what I like best about you" is delivered after a typically grandiose boast from the winged criminal. Or, as the two are falling from quite a height, with the Vulture begging Spidey to save him, Webhead explains that he can't save either of them because "I'm too busy admiring your tight-lipped *courage!*"[10] Or, again, when Dr. Octopus says he's not going to show the wall-crawler any mercy this time, Spidey replies, "What do you mean *this time*? A Florence Nightingale you've *never* been!"[11] Clearly, Spidey is encouraging Doc Ock to mend his ways and become a bit less ruthless. In these and many other cases, Webhead's jokes have an obvious moral message. It's never as clear as "Stop committing crimes!"—let's face it, that's not funny and probably won't lead to any reforms. Rather, the moral message in Spidey's jokes encourages his foes to adopt lives of virtue. In each case, Spidey is encouraging his foes to adopt specific virtues that they lack: modesty, courage, compassion. Who knows, maybe the shock of a bit of humor can wake them from their vices.

On other occasions, there isn't a clear moral message in Spidey's jokes. Sometimes they seem like pointless insults—particularly when the object of Webhead's derision is unconscious. Nonetheless, most of these jokes carry an encouragement of *social* virtues. A social virtue is slightly different from a moral virtue. Moral virtues are how we ought to behave as human beings. Social virtues are how we ought to behave in order to get along with one another. Courage is a moral virtue, but courageous people—at least, if we aren't being too picky about what we mean by "courage"—can be antisocial and downright mean at times. Think about it: some of Spidey's foes are quite courageous but are simply not very nice—some of them can even be downright rude. That's what many of Spidey's jokes aim to correct: rude behavior. When Webhead asks Beetle, "Tsk tsk! Don't you *ever* knock before entering?" it's more than just a witty way of observing that Beetle came in through the wall,[12] it's Spidey's way of encouraging socially acceptable behavior. These jokes aren't limited to discouraging rudeness, though. They also discourage annoying behaviors. Spidey often takes his enemies to task for such irritating behaviors as repeating themselves, as when he asks the Vulture, "Are you sure you were never vaccinated with a *phonograph needle*?"[13]

Okay, you say, so Spidey makes jokes about villains as part of some bizarre reform program. I'll give you that. Yet Webhead's rapier wit isn't aimed only at villains. J. Jonah Jameson may be a pain in the neck, but he's hardly a villain—yet Spidey has subjected J.J. to as many jokes as he has any of his foes, if not more. Of course, Jolly Jonah is still quite rude, not to mention delusional. He doesn't pose much of a problem for the superiority theory, but the wall-crawler doesn't limit his jokes to those with obvious moral and social failings. He also cracks jokes about people who put their lives on the line to help others—about heroes! He's even taken a few pokes at Captain America! It seems we have a problem here. Spidey isn't superior to all of the heroes in the Marvel Universe he makes fun of—he doesn't think he is, either. For example, following a particularly stirring speech from Captain America, Spidey asks whether he can carry the star-spangled Avenger's books.[14] So, there's an apparent oversight in the superiority theory.

Spidey Corrects Heroes

Maybe we can accept the superiority theory when thinking about Spidey's jokes on villains and Jolly Jonah. Spidey's got a right to think he's superior to them: he's our *friendly* neighborhood Spider-Man, and they're generally jerks. Fine and good, when the butts of Spidey's jokes *are* jerks—but they aren't always. Spidey's jokes are just as likely to be directed at his friends and allies, when they're around, as they are at villains. Sometimes, this may be because Webhead and his friends are on opposite sides of a fight. We don't have to think about a situation as dramatic as Marvel's Civil War story line for an example of this. Sometimes it seems that if you get two or more superheroes within a single square mile of each other, they're going to fight. After the fight, though, they usually team up to go after some menace or another—and Spidey will keep cracking jokes! It seems he just can't help himself.

At least, that's what one important philosopher would have said. Aristotle (384–322 BCE) warned those who were fond of joking against the danger of becoming a buffoon. Aristotle ascribed to a superiority theory, but he wasn't down on joking as such. He saw the virtues of joking and even the need for it, *but* Aristotle warned us that there is an appropriate time and place for joking. A wit knows that—a buffoon doesn't. As Aristotle described him, "The buffoon cannot resist raising a laugh, and spares neither himself nor anyone else if he can cause laughter, even by making remarks that the sophisticated person would never make, and some that the sophisticated person would not even be willing to hear."[15]

A case could be made that Webhead is a buffoon in Aristotle's sense, but I don't think that's fair to the webslinger. Yes, he jokes a lot. He jokes when others wouldn't. He jokes about things and people—such as Cap and Thor—whom others wouldn't. Yet unlike a true buffoon, Spidey is capable of restraining himself when the situation requires. After the death of Gwen Stacy, for instance, or in the face of truly overwhelming odds, Spidey can be serious.

Of course, he often isn't serious when we expect him to be—such as in the heat of battle. Certainly, any time someone is trying to kill you, a serious response and a solemn attitude are expected. We've seen some of the reasons that Spidey isn't always serious in these situations—he's trying to correct the villains' behavior. Yet the problem is that Spidey also jokes with and about his allies. One possible explanation for this is that Spidey's jokes break tension. It's possible that because the wall-crawler is generally a loner, he needs to crack jokes when he teams up with other heroes in order to make himself feel comfortable—and not only himself. His teammates (depending on who they are) generally respond well to his jokes—it's a nice way to forge instant team unity and to keep people loose. The last thing you want in a life-or-death struggle is for everyone to treat it as if it's a matter of life or death—someone's bound to crack up. Spidey's little jokes on his fellow heroes—at least, some of them—could be a survival strategy of sorts.

Although there may be some truth to that, if we analyze the insults Spidey tosses at his fellow heroes, we find that he's still delivering moral messages. Now, clearly, he doesn't have to instruct his fellow heroes (for the most part) on how to live their lives on the straight and narrow. With a few notable exceptions, they already know that. Yet what Spidey can school many of them on is the social virtues. He's not far off when he says, "I always thought of myself as the most *lovable* little hero in town."[16] Compared to many of his compatriots in the spandex business, Spidey is generally quite personable. So, he's got a right to give these little etiquette lessons. For example, while battling alongside the ever lovin', blue-eyed Thing, Spidey tries to encourage Mr. Grimm to show just a little originality, rather than repeat his notorious catch phrase for the millionth time. "Don't *say it*, Benjamin!" says Spidey. "Please! Try something *else* for once! *Anything!*"[17] This is typical of Spidey's jokes on his fellow heroes. They most often focus on their attitudes or speech patterns, rather than on their actions. Following a particularly cryptic comment, he tells Iron Fist, "Great. You're a walking *fortune cookie*."[18] Or commenting on Dr. Strange's rather grandiose way of bidding farewell, Spidey says, "And may your amulet never tickle."[19] Dr. Strange and Thor are favorite targets of this type of correction.

Whether for good or ill, Spidey's jibes aren't always appreciated by his peers. Granted, the Thing did try to restrain himself from declaring "clobberin' time" but failed. For the most part, though, Spidey's fellow heroes brush aside his advice. They're usually too busy fighting for their lives to enjoy a good laugh. So, his advice goes unheeded, and his jokes go unappreciated. Sounds about right for Spidey—he's lived a thankless life. The central problem of his joking is, in a way, the same as the central problem of his entire crime-fighting career: why does he bother?

The Punch Line

We could offer a variety of other reasons for Webhead's jokes. Perhaps I was wrong earlier, and Spidey really is a buffoon, in Aristotle's sense. Or maybe his jokes are simply his way of enjoying the freedom and anonymity that his mask brings. Perhaps it's just about easing tension, reassuring bystanders and allies, and distracting his enemies. All of these are good psychological reasons for Spidey's motor mouth, but they don't explain the jokes—only the talking. The true purpose of the jokes is the moral message—encouraging the butts to reform their ways by adopting some moral or social virtue.

Now the only question left is how effective jokes are at influencing behavior. In Spidey's case, it seems that the answer is: not very. No matter how many times he "encourages" Doc Ock or Electro to change their ways, they always come back for more. The same goes for the heroes who serve as butts for Spidey's jokes. Thor still talks as if he thinks he's a god or something. Yet Spidey keeps trying.

As with many other things, jokes tend to work better in our everyday, mundane lives than they do for the wall-crawler. Consider your own experience: none of us likes to be ridiculed. We want to be laughed with, not laughed at. So, when some habit of ours becomes the subject of jokes, we tend to change our ways. Thus, not only do we have the right to enjoy the occasional joke, we have a positive duty to joke! It's the best way to make one another better. And the most fun. So go out and annoy someone today. It's for their own good!

NOTES

1. Thomas Hobbes, *Leviathan* (New York: Cambridge University Press, 1996), 43.

2. *Amazing Spider-Man* #11 (1964).

3. Immanuel Kant, *Critique of the Power of Judgement*, trans. Paul Guyer and Eric Matthews (New York: Cambridge University Press, 2001), 209.

4. *Amazing Spider-Man* #7 (1963).

5. *Amazing Spider-Man* #85 (1975).

6. *Amazing Spider-Man* Annual #5 (1963).

7. F. H. Buckley, *The Morality of Laughter* (Ann Arbor: University of Michigan Press, 2003).

8. See, for example, Richard M. Stephenson, "Conflict and Control Functions of Humor," *American Journal of Sociology* 56, no. 6 (1951): 569–574.

9. Buckley, *The Morality of Laughter*, 17–18.

10. *Amazing Spider-Man* #7 (1963).

11. *Amazing Spider-Man* #12 (1964).

12. *Amazing Spider-Man* #21 (1965).

13. *Amazing Spider-Man* #7 (1963).

14. *Amazing Spider-Man* #537 (2006).

15. Aristotle, *Nicomachean Ethics*, trans. Terence Irwin (Indianapolis: Hackett, 1999), 66, 1128^a35-1128^b1.

16. *Amazing Spider-Man* #43 (1966).

17. *Marvel Team-Up* #47 (1967).

18. *Marvel Team-Up* #31 (1965).

19. *Amazing Spider-Man* Annual #2 (1963).

THE SOUND AND THE FURY BEHIND "ONE MORE DAY"

Mark D. White

It's safe to say that quite a few Spider-Man fans dropped Marvel editor in chief Joe Quesada from their Christmas card lists after "One More Day" was published in 2007.[1] Coming hot on the heels of Aunt May's being shot after Peter Parker unmasks on national television during "Civil War," and Peter's adopting the black costume to hunt down those responsible in "Back in Black," the four-part "One More Day" story finds Peter desperate to save his aunt's life. He begs Tony Stark (one-time mentor and now head of superhero registration charged with bringing Peter in) for help, only to be rebuffed. He approaches a number of his superpowered and magical friends for help, including Dr. Strange, with whom he has an eventful visit, during which Peter revisits the scene of May's shooting, but no one can help. Due to her advanced age and the damage done by the bullet, May is doomed, and Peter will likely never get over the guilt and responsibility he feels for putting her in mortal danger by revealing his identity to the world.[2]

Just when all seems lost, and Peter and MJ are ready to reconcile themselves to the inevitability of Aunt May's death, opportunity knocks—and his name is Mephisto, the personification of Satan in the Marvel Universe. Mephisto makes Peter and MJ an offer: he will save May's life in exchange for Peter and MJ's marriage. He will change history so that the two will never be married, and he will also erase everyone's memory of Peter's unmasking, so that May's life will no longer be in constant danger. MJ agrees first, and then, after much deliberation and discussion, Peter agrees as well.

Yet the fans definitely did *not* agree. Reaction on Internet discussion boards was almost unanimously negative, and that's putting it mildly. Many lifelong fans of Spidey dropped the title. Many fans who didn't drop the title were nevertheless dissatisfied with the new direction taken in the "Brand New Day" era, which seemed to ignore or trample on years of established continuity by erasing the marriage and the unmasking (which everyone remembers seeing, but no one remembers who they saw doing it—*huh*?).[3] Years later, feelings still run hot about this radical change in the story line, but *why* did fans feel so intensely about Peter and MJ's marriage? *Why* were so many fans upset that Peter did something that seemed so out of character?

Do We Lack Character?

Often, when we say someone has "character," we mean that the person is strong-willed or honest or reliable. Obviously, this use of the word is a compliment, but a person can certainly be of bad character as well—weak-willed, dishonest, unreliable. We can draw something from these opposite uses of the word *character*: they both assume fairly stable features of personality, or *character traits*. For instance, if character implies honesty, we're not going to say that Aunt May has character if she tells the truth only some of the time or just when it serves her interests. She has to tell the truth all, or at least most, of the time, *even* when it would be in her interest to lie. Only then do we feel comfortable calling her a genuinely honest person or saying she has an honest character. Likewise, if we saw her being brazenly dishonest, we would likely view her actions as being "out of character," because it would conflict with our well-evidenced belief about her character.

It seems natural to assume that people have such character traits and to "characterize" them by their good (or bad) qualities. Aunt May is honest, MJ is sweet, Harry Osborn is funny, J. Jonah Jameson is a—well, you get the idea. It's not just an everyday thing—philosophers do it in their work, too. A prominent school of moral philosophy, *virtue ethics*, evaluates the moral quality of a person by judging her character: does she have the virtues of honesty, courage, kindness, and so on? Virtue ethics is less about what someone does, or the effects of her actions, than about what kind of person she is.[4]

Yet there's a great deal of evidence that character traits are less stable than we'd like to think. A person's behavior in a given situation may in fact be quite unrelated to any general traits we may associate with him or her (such as kindness or honesty). So perhaps we aren't justified in drawing a clear picture of the person's "character" at all. Psychologists have conducted experiments that show significant changes in people's ethical behavior resulting from seemingly insignificant changes in their environment. For instance, one experiment conducted near a pay phone revealed that when people found change in the phone, they were much more likely to help a stranger immediately afterward. If character traits were as stable as we (and virtue ethicists) like to think, then a person's willingness to help a stranger shouldn't depend on whether he or she found some coins in a pay phone. *Situationists* claim that decisions and actions are much more responsive to particular details of the current situation than to persistent, stable character traits, and this poses a problem for our common understanding of character, as well as for the basis of virtue ethics.[5]

Well, let's just say that the members of the League of Virtue Ethicists (L.O.V.E.) are not taking the critiques of the Situationists Hard Against Fixed Traits (S.H.A.F.T.) lying down. (Take *that*, S.H.I.E.L.D.) L.O.V.E. members argue that the situationists' experiments don't track a person over time but simply pick out differences among persons reacting to one situation. Character isn't seen in one isolated action, but rather in a lifetime of behavior that reveals consistent, principled decisions, including more significant, life-altering ones that aren't easily simulated in experiments. Furthermore, that pattern of behavior doesn't have to be perfectly consistent—no one is perfectly honest or perfectly courageous, so we shouldn't be surprised when people occasionally deviate from their traits. Finally, virtue ethicists have subtle and elaborate concepts of traits such as honesty and courage. Honesty doesn't simply mean telling the truth in every situation, no matter what, and courage doesn't mean only fearlessness—there's far more to these traits than that. So, simple experiments cast little light on these multifaceted character traits.[6]

Enough about Normal People—What about Superheroes?

Let's give S.H.A.F.T. some love (and, in turn, give the shaft to L.O.V.E.) and grant that recognizing stable character traits in real people is, at the least, problematic. Yet what about fictional characters, such as those in comic books? After all, Peter Parker, MJ, Aunt May, and even Mephisto aren't real people. (I know you *think* you saw them in San Diego last July, but it wasn't really them.) How does our previous discussion of character traits translate to fictional characters?

In many ways, we expect *more* consistency of character from our comic book characters than from people we know.

Why? One reason is that real people are complex (yes, even men), normally displaying a multitude of different character traits, some strong and others weak, some admirable and others not, and always conflicting with one another. Yet fictional characters, even comic book characters who've been around for decades, are much simpler and are often defined by a few central characteristics. Captain America is honorable, brave, and honest; Iron Man is pragmatic, smart, and sometimes weak-willed; and Mr. Fantastic is scientifically brilliant but clueless about human relationships (especially where his wife is concerned). If the broad outlines of a superhero are clearly drawn and well-established, that character becomes known for those traits, and any deviation from them is seen as bad writing or as portraying the hero "out of character." If Captain America stole candy from a baby, Iron Man lost a game of chess to the Hulk, or Mr. Fantastic became the new Dr. Phil, fans would rightly wonder what the heck the writers were smoking.[7]

Consistency of character lets the reader know what to expect from the hero or the villain in a story. We may not be sure what behavior to expect from many of our friends in any given situation, but superheroes are different. You read *Captain America* to see how an honorable, noble hero is tested in extreme circumstances; you read *Iron Man* to see how brain wins out over brawn; and you read *Fantastic Four* to see how long Sue Richards will stay with her husband.[8] Fans of comic books, TV shows (especially soap operas), or long-running book series often feel that they know the characters in these stories better than they know their own friends and family. In a very real sense they do, if only because the characters' personality traits are better defined than those of real people, and the writers mostly stay within these hard boundaries when writing new dialogue and action for their characters. So the character becomes "reliable" to the fan: he knows Captain America will do the right thing, Iron Man will figure out how to save the day, and Mr. Fantastic will ignore his loving wife (just not enough to drive her away—usually).

This partly explains why fans were so upset at Peter's deal with Mephisto: Peter Parker has been written, fairly consistently from his inception, as a good, responsible, stand-up kind of guy. Like Captain America, whom he looks up to, Peter has always tried to do the right thing, never taking the easy way out or following the path of least resistance, no matter what life throws at him. As his Uncle Ben famously taught him, "with great power comes great responsibility," when Peter is held responsible, he wants to be sure, in his heart, that he has done the right thing.[9] Therein lies the problem: in what topsy-turvy, cats-lie-with-dogs, Norman-Osborn-gets-a-real-haircut kind of world is making a deal *with the devil* ever the right thing to do? Forget the right thing to do, it's never even the smart thing to do—if you think it is, I've got a nice monkey's paw to sell you.[10]

Does this mean that characters can never change, grow, evolve, or adapt? Of course not, but these processes are gradual (we don't expect Reed Richards to become the perfect husband overnight). Also, they usually start in a way that is consistent with someone's character (Reed finally decides to dedicate a little bit of his big brain to understanding his wife's feelings). Absent a life-altering event or a mind-blowing epiphany, we don't expect fictional characters—or real people—to alter their deep-seated behavior abruptly and for no reason. Given the fantastical circumstances Peter Parker has faced throughout his career as Spider-Man, even the impending death of his aunt and a surprise offer from Mephisto don't seem enough to trigger and justify such an about-face.

So, Who's Responsible for This Outrage?

If you do something out of character, chances are that someone will hold you responsible for it. Yet if we take Peter's actions in "One More Day" to be out of character, we obviously can't hold him responsible (though someone in the Marvel Universe certainly could, if anyone could remember what happened). The people who actually "did" this, who pulled Peter's puppet strings, so to speak, are the creators: the writers and the editors of "One More Day."[11] For the sake of simplicity and also because he was the public voice of the controversial story line and Marvel's head honcho, I'll treat Joe Quesada as the man behind it all.[12]

Fairly or not, fans hold Quesada responsible if they don't like a story or anything else about Marvel Comics (including things he has no control over, such as comics pricing and movie casting—I got your back, Joe). But greenlighting "One More Day" wasn't your average editorial decision, not in the same category as letting Brian Michael Bendis launch a *Happy Avengers* book or making Deadpool the director of S.H.I.E.L.D. Nor was this a minor lapse in character consistency, similar to having Emma Frost kiss a puppy or letting Matt Murdock have a successful relationship.[13] Peter Parker made a deal with Mephisto to mind-wipe the entire world and change history; this isn't the Peter we know.

Fans weren't happy with "One More Day," but did Quesada do anything *wrong* by publishing it? Can we say he had a responsibility to the fans to be true to the character of Peter Parker? Does it matter *why* he did it? To be sure, Quesada and the editors and the writers working under him have the legal right to do anything they want with the Marvel characters— Marvel owns the characters, at least in a legal sense. Yet moral rights are different from legal rights; Chad has a legal right to lie to his friend about why he left her stranded at New York Comic-Con, but he doesn't have a moral right to do so. (Bad Chad.) Another way to put the question is: did Quesada betray any moral obligation he had to the fans when he had Peter act so drastically out of character?

We can answer this question based on our discussion of why readers value consistency of character. Casual fans might simply want to read stories about a guy in red-and-blue tights swinging around the city on webs and cracking wise, but if this was all there was to Spider-Man, that would get old very quickly. After a while, we want to know about the man beneath the tights, and as we get to know him, we expect him to behave in a similar way in whatever circumstances he finds himself. As a result, we as fans feel cheated if we hand over our hard-earned money to buy a comic starring someone else—same name, same costume, same secret identity but who acts like a completely different person.

This sudden change on Peter's part was not a natural evolution of his character, and it was seen as a desire on the creators' part to revert to an earlier status quo, a simpler version of Spidey that would be more accessible and would bring in new fans. Quesada gave credence to this view when in many interviews he stated that there were stories that could be told with a single Spidey that couldn't be told with a married one. Whatever the behind-the-scenes motivation, the general impression is that it was not handled well in the story line itself. If the powers-that-be wanted Peter to split from MJ, they should have found a way to do it that was consistent with their established characters. Instead, they had them make a deal with devil—definitely not what Uncle Ben meant by responsibility!

You may ask (as many fans did): why not simply have them get a divorce? Quesada's explanation was that they didn't want to introduce the stigma of divorce into Peter's backstory. If we're being nice, we could interpret this as a character-based concern. Perhaps Quesada didn't think Peter was the type of guy who could live with being divorced. Without getting into the ethical issues surrounding divorce or its prevalence these days, it's safe to say that there isn't much stigma attached to divorce among Peter's generation, especially if there are no children involved. Yet even more to the point, if Peter did have a personal issue with divorce, don't you think he would have more of an issue with *making a deal with Mephisto*? "Sorry, divorce is out, but Faustian bargains are cool!"

Secret Interpretation

It's possible that Quesada and his Amazing Friends simply have a different opinion regarding the true character of Peter Parker than we do. After all, character isn't like height or eye color; reasonable people can disagree about whether an action was in or out of character for a particular person.[14] Judging someone's character is an act of interpretation: you take all of the person's actions and try to generalize characters traits from them. The unique challenge of writing serial fiction—such as comic books, TV shows, or franchise novels (set in the world of *Star Trek* or *Buffy the Vampire Slayer*, for instance)—is writing original stories about established characters that are consistent with the creator's interpretation of how people wrote them up to that point.[15] A new writer on *Captain America*, who has read all of the earlier Cap stories, should not—if he's going to be consistent to the character—write him like Deadpool, Johnny Storm, or Electro. Rather, he should write Cap so that the loyal reader recognizes him as the same hero she's read for years, though the problems Cap faces may be new.

Of course, different people disagree about how a character should be interpreted, but that doesn't make all interpretations equal. A person might interpret Norman Osborn as a cute, cuddly guy who likes big hugs and bunny rabbits, but we all know that would be a poor interpretation because it's inconsistent with every word Osborn has ever uttered and everything he has ever done. We can evaluate interpretations if we can come up with some independent standard of judgment. In the case of ol' Normie, the comics themselves are the best evidence, and they show he's not a nice man at all—don't call him cute, don't hug him, and don't leave him alone with your pet bunny. Of course, the comics themselves are open to interpretation ("He didn't *mean* to kill Gwen, really!"), but if they're clearly written, they provide strong support for judging interpretations of character.

So, if we give Quesada the benefit of the doubt and assume he thought that making a deal with Mephisto was consistent with Peter Parker's character (based on his interpretation), does that mean we have to accept his reading? Is the Black Cat shy? Of course not—Felicia's definitely a people person, and we can certainly disagree with anyone's reading of any character—even with the editor in chief of Marvel Comics. Longtime fans know, based on the most obvious interpretation, that Spidey always tries to do the right thing and never takes the easy way out, and that cutting deals with the supreme ruler of the netherworld doesn't fit that bill. This interpretation of Peter's character seems more consistent with the decades of stories than Quesada's does, so even if we ascribe the best intentions to Quesada, we still find room to criticize.[16]

What If You Had One More Day?

Earlier, I said that consistency of character is easier to achieve with fictional characters such as those in comic books, because they're less complex and their actions are under the direct control of writers. Real people are more complicated, and that includes you and me (and that creepy guy reading over your shoulder—oh, sorry, Mr. Quesada). Yet even if S.H.A.F.T. ultimately wins the battle, L.O.V.E. nonetheless seems worth aspiring to.[17] In other words, even if we're not guaranteed to have stable character traits, shouldn't we at least *try* to behave consistently? If we accept this goal, and if we consider ourselves to be the narrators of our own lives, do we have a similar responsibility to our "fans" to maintain a consistent character—especially if we count ourselves among our fans?

Consistent behavior is a worthy goal. Another term for consistency of character is *integrity*, and integrity has long been considered by philosophers to be one of the primary virtues.[18] In this context, integrity means being the same person in different situations or displaying the same character traits regardless of the specific circumstances we face. If Jim lies when he's generally believed to be honest, or if he treats somebody rudely when he's generally held to be kind, he lets down people who count on him to be *him*, to be true to who he is (or who they believe him to be, based on his past behavior). Generally, if someone acts against the character traits people expect from him, these people lose faith in him as being the person they thought he was: they'll either change their estimation of his character or they'll simply give up trying to understand him at all—both of which spell disaster for building friendships.

Even more important, we owe it to ourselves to preserve our integrity. We all have conceptions of who we are (our identities), what we stand for, and what we value in ourselves. How many times have you felt disappointed in yourself because you let yourself down by not living up to your personal standards? If I believe I'm an honest person, then I'll be disappointed if I lie, even if no one else ever finds out. Often, other people are quicker to forgive us for failures of character than we ourselves are, perhaps because we know better than they do what we expect from ourselves. As Shakespeare wrote, "To thine own self be true," at least according to what kind of person you believe yourself to be. And if we *do* aspire to personal standards—or consistent character traits—that's something we all can L.O.V.E.

NOTES

1. "One More Day" was published in four parts: in *Amazing Spider-Man* #544 (November 2007), *Friendly Neighborhood Spider-Man* #24 (November 2007), *Sensational Spider-Man* #41 (December 2007), and *Amazing Spider-Man* #545 (January 2008), and was collected in trade paperback in 2008. (After this storyline, *Friendly* and *Sensational* were canceled, and *Amazing* was published thrice monthly under the "Brand New Day" banner until November 2010.)

2. For more on Peter's unmasking and the ethical questions behind it, see my explanation in Chapter 1, "'My Name Is Peter Parker': Unmasking the Right and the Good," in this book.

3. This was later explained—probably as well as possible—in the "One Moment in Time" storyline in *Amazing Spider-Man* #638–641 (September–October 2010).

4. For a great introduction to virtue ethics, see Rosalind Hursthouse, "Virtue Ethics," *Stanford Encyclopedia of Philosophy*, at http://plato.stanford.edu/entries/ethics-virtue/.

5. For the most exhaustive treatment of situationism from one of its leading figures, see John Doris, *Lack of Character* (Cambridge, UK: Cambridge University Press, 2002).

6. For a very readable and critical perspective on the situationist argument, see Kwame Anthony Appiah, *Experiments in Ethics* (Cambridge, MA: Harvard University Press, 2008), particularly Chapter 2.

7. Things become more complicated when multiple writers and editors handle one character in different books (I'm looking at you, Wolverine). To cite a recent case, fans were puzzled and infuriated when Green Lantern (Hal Jordan) was written as expressing two rather contradictory feelings regarding the recent death of Batman (Bruce Wayne) in two comics supposedly taking place at roughly the same time. (See the very revealing discussion of this on the "Comics Should Be Good!" blog at http://goodcomics.comicbookresources .com/2009/09/05/character-personality-consistency-in-team-books-do-you-care/.)

8. Okay—*and* to read "it's clobberin' time!" (A catch phrase is a simple way to establish consistency of character, though it tends not to run very deep.)

9. I explore this theme further in Chapter 1, "'My Name Is Peter Parker': Unmasking the Right and the Good," in this book.

10. Hey, kids—literary allusion!

11. The writers were longtime Spidey (and *Babylon 5*) scribe J. Michael Straczynski (commonly referred to as JMS) and Marvel editor in chief Joe Quesada, with JMS writing the first three parts and Quesada taking over for the last issue (due to disagreements with JMS over how the story should end). See the Wikipedia entry for "One More Day" (and references therein) at http://en.wikipedia.org/wiki/Spider-Man:_One_More_Day.

12. He penciled the story and the covers, too, but his work in that respect was stunning as far as I'm concerned, so no points off there!

13. Foggy doesn't count.

14. For example, fans disagreed widely over whether Iron Man's actions during the Civil War event were out of character. (I implicitly argue that they were very much *in* character in my chapter "Did Iron Man Kill Captain America?" in Mark D. White, ed., *Iron Man and Philosophy: Facing the Stark Reality* (Hoboken, NJ: John Wiley & Sons, 2010), 64–79.

15. This idea comes from contemporary legal and political philosopher Ronald Dworkin, who actually compares judicial decision making to this literary process; see his essay "How Law Is Like Literature," in *A Matter of Principle* (Cambridge, MA: Harvard University Press, 1985), 146–166.

16. But I *did* love the art!

17. After all, who's the cat that won't cop out when there's danger about? Even S.H.A.F.T. can be about the L.O.V.E. sometimes. (Right on.)

18. In philosophy, integrity actually has many different meanings, but all of them are related in some way to character and virtue; see the entry on "integrity" by Damian Cox, Marguerite La Caze, and Michael Levine in the *Stanford Encyclopedia of Philosophy*, http:// plato.stanford.edu/entries/integrity/.

SPIDER-MAN AND THE IMPORTANCE OF GETTING YOUR STORY STRAIGHT

Jonathan J. Sanford

"Who am I? You sure you want to know? The story of my life is not for the faint of heart." Thus begins Sam Raimi's *Spider-Man* trilogy, and yes, we're sure we want to know. From his first appearance in *Amazing Fantasy* #15 in 1962 through his spectacularly successful film career, Spider-Man has been trying to make sense of Spider-Man. No doubt, his efforts at self-examination have their narcissistic moments, but those don't suggest that attempts to make sense of your life are generally doomed to the proverbial pile of megalomaniacal manure. It's just the opposite, for *failing* to make sense of your life dooms you to live a miserable one.

One way to approach what it means to be self-reflective and to make sense of your life is to focus on how you tell your life's story. Telling your life's story is as natural as laughing at a joke. Yet just as there are bad jokes, there are also poorly told life stories, so merely telling your life's story is not enough to make you happy.[1] By reflecting on Spider-Man's story, we can see some of the ways in which human beings in general are storytelling animals and come to understand how it is that beings of our sort can become good only by learning to get our own stories straight.

Do We Always Have a Choice?

Speaking of Spider-Man and stories, we have a lot to choose from. In this chapter, we'll focus on the arc made up of the Raimi films because of their familiarity to Spidey fans of all sorts, because of their continuity and character development, and because we find in them Peter growing in virtue—despite some obvious failures. Spider-Man's ethical development is possible because of the progress he makes as narrator of his own life; that is, he comes to understand himself better—what motivates him, what tempts him, what scares him, what his obligations are, and what he really wants out of life—and in understanding himself better, he becomes a better (spider) man.

The twists and turns of any life are evident in the choices we make. Most of our choices keep us on the same path we've traveled for some time, but some choices signal new chapters in our lives. Norman Osborn makes his choice to pursue the path of unbridled power and vengeance and presents Spider-Man with the choice to join forces with him. Mary Jane first makes a choice to build a life without Peter Parker, then makes another choice to embrace the challenges of loving the Peter Parker who's also Spider-Man. Dr. Otto Octavius makes a choice to ignore the warning signs that his fusion reactor is too unstable to control and later chooses to destroy it so that he "will not die a monster!" Harry makes a choice to follow the path paved by his father and later chooses to die for the sake of his friend and erstwhile foe. Flint Marko makes a choice not to put away his gun and just go home, as Uncle Ben suggests, but then chooses to come clean to Peter Parker and accept his forgiveness.

Peter's story is a page-turner with one skyscraper-hanging choice after another: he embraces his new powers for good, lays them aside, picks them up again; seeks vengeance on Flint Marko, Harry Osborn, Mary Jane, and Edward T. Brock Jr., then forgives them; forgives himself; and pursues again the greater good. No doubt, the choice to embrace Uncle Ben's exhortation that "With great power comes great responsibility" provides the cornerstone for his moral character, and, despite attempts to reject that moral character, it abides.[2]

At the end of Raimi's *Spider-Man* trilogy, Peter sums up the wisdom he has garnered through telling his tale: "Whatever comes our way, whatever battles we have raging inside us, we always have a choice. My friend Harry taught me that. He chose to be the best of himself. It's the choices that make us who we are. And we can always choose to do what's right." We can always choose to do what's right, even if that means giving up the things we love the most, as Aunt May tells Peter in *Spider-Man 2*. (I think Aunt May really means we ought to love what's right most of all.) Spider-Man's wisdom stands, I think, but philosophers have the irritating habit of analyzing claims, and it's time for some logical dissection now.

Do we *always* have a choice? Well, it seems we always have a choice about things we can intentionally do or intentionally refuse to do. Peter intentionally chooses to refuse to come to the aid of a mugging victim in *Spider-Man 2*, but then later chooses to rush into a burning apartment to save a young girl, even though his superhero powers are inoperative. Those and so many others are choices that are his to make. Yet think of all of the significant parts of his life over which he does not exercise any choice. He does not choose to be born to his parents or orphaned by them. He does not choose to be raised by Uncle Ben and Aunt May, he does not choose to feel great affection for the lovely girl next door, he does not choose to have his great natural intelligence, and he does not choose to be bitten by the spider that gives him his superpowers. Yet each of these events has a profound effect on the man and the superhero he becomes.

These unintentional, involuntary, yet profoundly formative events of Peter's particular life also come with an enormous price tag: they each give Peter some of the most important obligations of his life. He's obliged to love Uncle Ben and Aunt May for the love and care they shower on him; he's obliged to care for the woman he secretly loves; he's obliged, as Dr. Octavius reminds him, to use his great intelligence for the good of mankind; and he's obliged to bear the mantle, his gift and curse, that his great superpowers confer on him.

These involuntary obligations are definitive of the man Peter Parker *should* become, long before he makes the choices that define that man. He is who he is, first, because of factors beyond his control: his life, his upbringing, and his natural and supernatural powers. These sorts of nonchosen features of someone's life have just as much claim to "make us who we are" as do our choices, and both together make Spider-Man the one-of-a-kind individual he is. Like Peter, we, too, are unique individuals. Yet we shouldn't be surprised that we grow into those individuals only by imitating others, as Peter models himself on Uncle Ben, as you model yourself on Spider-Man. Our individuality is ever forged in the fires of dependency on others, and the stories we tell about ourselves always take their cues from and include the stories of others.

You may delude yourself into thinking you are obligated to do only what you've promised to do, as though you are a completely independent individual, creating your own identity through an act of will. Yet then you realize that you forgot to call your mother yesterday, you need to buy a card to send your sister on her birthday, and you have to shovel and salt the front steps so that the elderly man in the next apartment doesn't slip on them. You really don't choose to be obligated to take care of yourself, your parents, and your neighbors and to pursue what is true and right in your various activities—yet these obligations are definitive of the sort of being you are. Pretending those sorts of obligations don't exist doesn't make you strong and independent but, rather, callous and stupid. It's only where the involuntarily incurred obligations meet the moments of free choice, when you decide how in particular you are going to respond to your basic obligations, that you contribute in an active way to the person you become. So it is for Peter Parker, who has enough wisdom to recognize that his successes and failures as a man come down to the ways in which he fulfills his obligations.

There is, of course, another class of obligations that we incur through a mixture of involuntary obligations and free choices, that is, through the ways in which we decide to live out our basic obligations. Spider-Man, for example, chooses to reciprocate Mary Jane's love at the end of *Spider-Man 2* and by that choice incurs a whole host of other obligations toward her—many of which he does not live up to at the beginning of *Spider-Man 3*, such as failing to listen to her attempts to share with him her professional disappointments and making her unnecessarily jealous by bestowing his patented upside-down kiss on Gwen Stacy. Similarly, Aunt May, having chosen to accept the young Peter in her and Ben's home, becomes obligated to love Peter Parker as if he were a son, and she chooses to forgive Peter for his role in her husband's death. We often tend to focus on these sorts of voluntary obligations to the exclusion of the involuntary ones. We rationalize that if we did not voluntarily obligate ourselves to another, then no such obligation can exist, but we know in our hearts that involuntary obligations lay the ground for our voluntary obligations.

There are other types of events that touch us profoundly and that we wish we had a choice over but don't. Aunt May wishes Uncle Ben were still alive, Mary Jane wishes she had a more nurturing father, and J. Jonah Jameson wishes he had Mary Jane as a daughter-in-law—or at least that his son wasn't embarrassed by her at the altar. When this sort of wishing springs from events we played a negative role in, we have regret.[3] Peter regrets his part in Uncle Ben's death, Harry regrets the wrong he does to Peter and Mary Jane, and Flint Marko regrets killing Uncle Ben and wreaking havoc as Sandman. Yet these events, once done, can't be undone. Such is life. Here again we come to Peter's great moral truth: we do have a choice about how we will act *now*. Peter can dedicate himself to living out faithfully the wisdom Uncle Ben imparts to him, Harry can decide to come to the aid of his friends, and Marko can choose to come clean to Peter and, literally, drift off into the sunset.

So, we don't *always* have a choice if that means getting to determine our basic obligations or the consequences of our actions, but we do *always* have a choice over how we'll respond to our basic obligations and our past wrongs. We can choose, as Harry did, to be "the best of ourselves" (and hopefully we'll get started a little earlier than he did!). To do that, we need to know enough about ourselves to be able to determine just what that "best of our ourselves" is, and this—you were wondering when the heck I was going to get to it, weren't you!—is where storytelling comes in.

What Storytelling Is All About

A story, as Aristotle (384–322 BCE) told us in what may be the clearest line in all of his works, is something whole or complete and so has "a beginning, middle, and end."[4] Art, including the art or skill of storytelling, imitates life.[5] A story, whether it's a dramatic performance, a novel, a comic book, or a movie, is good to the extent that it imitates life in a compelling and believable way and teaches us something about our own lives. There is great joy and value, Aristotle explained, in witnessing a compelling story, not only because of the emotional affects of the performance but because we learn from what's imitated about human action and character in the performance. It's our emotional involvement with the story that makes such learning possible.[6] Even the painful events we witness onscreen, such as Peter turning his back on those in need after deciding to be Spider-Man no more, are valuable insofar as they teach us about human nature—about the limits, possibilities, pitfalls, and glories of actions we ourselves might perform.

Just as we learn much about human nature in general, and ourselves in particular, through our attention to dramatic stories, so, too, do we learn to begin to understand ourselves through telling the stories of our own lives. Just as art imitates life, so, too, do our reflective lives imitate art. That is, we learn to apply the technique of telling a story to the soon-to-be-told story or network of stories of our own lives. The *Spider-Man* movies depict the story of Peter's life, but it's Peter who tells that story through his voiceover introduction and occasional commentary. It's Peter's story that's being told and Peter who tells it. He can tell it to us because he has practiced long and hard at telling it to himself. Through that practice, he has learned to pick out the salient episodes of his life, those moments that are especially formative of the person he's becoming, so that bringing his beginnings through their middle stages, he can orient himself toward the end of his life's story.

A story has a beginning, a middle, and an end, just as your life does. We don't begin nowhere, for we have parents and other early nurturers. We have the individual set of talents, hopes, and disappointments peculiar to ourselves. We face the moments of significant challenge in our lives. And we make sense of it all by anticipating what it's all about—by having, in other words, some inkling about the grand purpose of our lives so that we might strive to fulfill it. In epic stories and legends, that anticipation of purpose is one of the essential ingredients of a quest, and we ought to learn from those stories that we can make sense of the adventure of our own lives only by figuring out what sort of quest we're on.

The contemporary philosopher Alasdair MacIntyre has done more than anyone to bring the insights of Aristotle to bear on a narrative view of life. MacIntyre's influential work *After Virtue* is a polemic against what he argues are the dominant and destructive features of modern moral philosophy and at the same time a creative retrieval of an Aristotelian approach to morality.[7] One of the most significant cultural problems MacIntyre tries to repair through his work is the misconception that we are independent individuals who are justified in promoting an ethic of personal preference. MacIntyre calls this misguided theory *emotivism*. The emotivist contends that there are no discernible and defensible moral standards by which to guide our lives, so we ought just to do whatever we want. MacIntyre argues that emotivism is a false theory about human life, yet it's the dominant moral view of our culture because of the appeal of its half-truths. Seeking to pull the truth from the lie in the emotivist mixture, MacIntyre argues that we aren't truly independent individuals and that pursuing an ethic of unbridled preference can only frustrate our best efforts at achieving our true goods.

In order to see beyond the facade of individualism and emotivism, in order, that is, to get the story about ourselves right, we need to recover the notion that each of our own stories interlocks with the life stories of many others, and that such an interlocking network of stories is connected as well with a historically extended past. Peter, for example, tells us that his story, "like any story worth telling, is all about a girl" (*Spider-Man*). That girl is Mary Jane, and Peter can't tell his story without telling how it intertwines with hers. Yet it's also a story about his aunt, his uncle, his friends, and his enemies, all of whom have their own stories, parts of which are introduced to us in the movies and the comic books. In turn, each of their stories is interconnected with other stories, and so on. Of course, these are fictional stories, but remember Aristotle's lesson—art imitates life (with a few embellishments!).

MacIntyre wrote, "Man is in his actions and practice, as well as in his fictions, essentially a story-telling animal. . . . I can only answer the question, 'What am I to do?' if I can answer the prior question, 'Of what story or stories do I find myself a part?'"[8] The roles we have to play in our interconnected life stories have already been in large part scripted for us, but *how* we play them is up to us. Measuring ourselves up to the goods intrinsic to those roles we play—that of daughter, student, mother, friend, citizen, carpenter, businessman, and so on—serves as the standard for determining true success. We can also see each of the roles we've played and continue to play in our stories as part of our entire unified lives, a whole with a beginning, a middle, and an end. By "end," I don't mean the terminus of your life. I mean its goal or purpose, its completion. Aristotle told us that when we reason about action, the end is the starting point of our reasoning.[9]

We can't direct ourselves to what we should do unless we have some end or goal or good (the words are synonymous in this context) in view. This same sort of structure of practical reasoning is at work when we reflect on that basic ethical question whose scope is our life as a whole, "How ought I to live?"[10] We press this sort of question by asking about what the end or good is for a human being in general and more specifically what my particular good is. We answer it both in word and in deed and, in doing so, form the narrative of our lives. MacIntyre wrote of the overarching good of our lives in terms of our quests: "The unity of a human life is the unity of a narrative quest. Quests sometimes fail, are frustrated, abandoned or dissipated into distraction; and human lives may in all these ways also fail. But the only criteria for success or failure in a human life as a whole are the criteria of success or failure in a narrated or to-be-narrated quest."[11]

Peter is on a quest to live out a life dedicated to using his great powers responsibly. He meets challenges and sometimes nearly fails in that quest, but he rights himself again by refocusing on his goal. In those moments of near failure, Peter loses sight of who he is—such as during his performance at the jazz club in *Spider-Man 3*. In such moments, the importance of the interconnection of other narratives to his own becomes evident—whether the timely wisdom of Aunt May or the clanging of a church bell beckoning him to be cleansed of his hatred—for these help recall Spider-Man to his quest. In remembering his quest, he remembers again himself. Peter didn't sign up to become Spider-Man, but his life would end in dissipation, a dissolving of self, if he didn't play out that role. He can be happy only if he plays it well.

But wait a second! Is it fair that Peter Parker has to face so many challenges because of the superpowers given him? Is it fair that some people are obligated to care for their ailing mothers instead of going away to college? Is it fair that some are obligated to take burdensome leadership positions in their communities, universities, churches, or businesses? No, it isn't. So what? There's no use complaining about the tasks foisted on us in our various roles. We each have our own unique set of roles to play, obligations to fulfill, and tasks to perform. Success or failure in our lives will be measured by how well we respond to them, which is to say, how *virtuously* we act.[12]

Not Every Action That Glitters Is Virtuous

Just as we can and should discriminate between good and bad works of fiction, so, too, we can and should discriminate between different ways a life can be lived—and we should be especially concerned to discriminate between the good, the bad, and the ugly in our own lives.

For example, if one of our roles is that of a student, then the sorts of actions we are engaged in include reading, note taking, and reflecting. The *practice* of which those actions are a part is studying. We are good students if we pursue and achieve the goods of studying, which would be learning the material we study for its own sake and to such an extent as to be able to teach it to others. Learning is its own good or end here, and if you are a student who wants to learn only enough to, say, pass a course, then you aren't a good student, even if you learn enough to get an A. You might, as the bad student, do the same sorts of things that the good student does, but the fact that you do them for the wrong reasons is significant from the perspective of determining whether you're a good student. The correct standard here is that of the *intrinsic* good of being a student, not various ulterior and external goods. There's nothing wrong (of course!) with wanting to pass a course, and both the bad and the good student want this good; the difference is that the good student is not *motivated* primarily by the extrinsic good.

It's not enough to do what's right for the right reasons, but we ought also to do that right thing for the right reason *because* we are the sort of person who does the right thing for the right reason. Yet to do what's right for the wrong reason is in fact— as seen from the perspective of the moral value of the whole action, which includes the agent from whom it proceeds—to be engaged in some sort of deception, and often this is a self-deception.[13] We ought to strive to be people of consistently good character, people others can count on, people whose characters deepen and grow stronger throughout the narratives that are our lives.

How does Spider-Man measure up to the standards of doing what's right for the right reason and doing what's right because he has a good character? We never see him acting *viciously*, striving to do what's wrong as though it's right—that's left to the villains. Yet we do see him acting *incontinently* (that is, without self-control) on occasion, letting his desire for revenge blind his right reason.[14] We often find Spider-Man acting *continently* (that is, with self-control), doing what's right for the right reasons, but struggling against his passions in the process. This is most evident in the way he struggles to accept fully his life's quest of bearing his burden to use his superpowers for the greater good when that entails forgoing other goods he desires. Overall, however, and this is what really intrigues us about our favorite man-in-tights, we see Spider-Man grow in genuine *virtue* during the course of the three movies.[15] His character deepens, and he becomes more honest, wise, just, generous, compassionate, and courageous.

The Virtue of Spider-Man's Story

Playing our roles, fulfilling our obligations, and performing our tasks well require virtue. Indeed, the virtues Peter already has and the virtues that he's developing enable him to pursue truly lasting goods, those goods that are intrinsic to the important features of his life's story. MacIntyre described how virtues make this possible:

> The virtues therefore are to be understood as those dispositions which will not only sustain practices and enable us to achieve the goods internal to practices, but which will also sustain us in the relevant kind of quest for the good, by enabling us to overcome the harms, dangers, temptations and distractions which we encounter, and which will furnish us with increasing self-knowledge and knowledge of the good.[16]

We certainly find Peter struggling with more than his share of harms, dangers, temptations, and distractions. Yet we also see his reliance on the virtues, both those he already possesses and those he's striving to possess, as sustaining him in his quest to live out faithfully his obligations as Spider-Man.

To be sure, we love to imagine ourselves climbing walls, swinging down boulevards, and shooting web bullets at bad guys. What we really admire Peter for, however, is the moral development he has already achieved and his continuing efforts on the path of moral progress. That progress is facilitated by narrating his life's quest, by making sense of his life through telling its story. To live his life well, he learns to achieve those goods intrinsic to his life's quest of being the best Spider-Man he can be. The virtues that he has and those others he's acquiring enable him to make the choices that sustain him on his quest, that bring him closer to living his entire life well. In the end, spending time with Spider-Man is not just entertainment. Through the moral growth Spider-Man achieves by telling his own story well, he teaches us how and why we ought to get our own stories straight.

NOTES

1. For a philosophical discussion of different senses of happiness, see chapter 1 by Neil Mussett in this volume, "Does Peter Parker Have a Good Life?"

2. See Chapter 6 by Philip Tallon in this volume, "With Great Power Comes Great Culpability," for a consideration of some of the implications of this moral dictum.

3. Consider Taneli Kukkonen's reflections on regret and guilt in Chapter 2 in this book, "What Price Atonement?"

4. Aristotle, *Poetics*, trans. I. Bywater, in Jonathan Barnes, ed., *The Complete Works of Aristotle*, vol. 2 (Princeton, NJ: Princeton University Press, 1984): 7, $1450^{b}26$.

5. This is implied by Aristotle's dictum that "art imitates nature," because everything living is natural (*Physics*, II, 2 $194^{a}21$; $199^{a}15$–19).

6. *Poetics*, 4, 1448b5–1448b24.

7. Alasdair MacIntyre, *After Virtue*, 2nd ed. (Notre Dame, IN: University of Notre Dame Press, 1984 [1st ed., 1981]).

8. MacIntyre, *After Virtue*, 216.

9. Aristotle, *Nicomachean Ethics*, VI, 12 $1144^{a}30$–32.

10. This is the question Plato's Socrates teaches us to ask. See, especially, his exchanges with Thrasymachus in *Republic* I and with Gorgias and Polus in *Gorgias*.

11. MacIntyre, *After Virtue*, 2nd ed., 219.

12. Both Spencer and White (in his Chapter 16, "The Sound and the Fury behind 'One More Day'") consider aspects of virtue theory in this volume.

13. Plato spoke of such self-deception in terms of trading on false coins; see *Phaedo*, 69a–69b. The result is that of the illusion of virtue, not the real thing.

14. Aristotle was the first to categorize different sorts of moral actions by vice, incontinence, continence, and virtue. See *Nicomachean Ethics* VII, 7, $1150^{a}9$–33.

15. See Aristotle, *Nicomachean Ethics* VII, 2, $1146^{a}10$–21, on the difference between continence and virtue.

16. MacIntyre, *After Virtue*, 219.

CONTRIBUTORS

Adam Barkman received his Ph.D. from the Free University of Amsterdam and is an associate professor of philosophy at Redeemer University College. He is the author of *C. S. Lewis and Philosophy as a Way of Life*, *Through Common Things*, and *Above All Things* and is the coeditor of *Manga and Philosophy* and *The Philosophy of Ang Lee*. Despite having read a web-load of books about God, Barkman now lists *The Sensational Spider-Man* #40 as one of the top ones.

Meaghan P. Godwin is a Ph.D. student in the Human Development program at Marywood University. Since 2004, she has taught in several philosophy and religious studies departments and has pondered what it is like to hang upside-down from a skyscraper wearing nothing but latex. She is currently studying education, attitude, and habit, hoping to build on the idea that if Harry and Peter can ultimately make it work, there is hope for the rest of us.

J. Keeping was bitten by a radioactive philosophy bug at an early age and grew up (sorta) to become an assistant professor in the Department of Humanities at York University in Toronto, Canada. He has published scholarly articles too numerous to count (assuming you get bored and give up at around six) on topics ranging from Nietzsche's will to power to the phenomenology of cats. He also contributed a chapter to *Watchmen and Philosophy*, in which he invited the reader to deduce which of the superheroes in *Watchmen* qualified as a Nietzschean superman. In his secret identity as "J.F. Keeping," he writes science fiction and has been published in magazines such as the *Grantville Gazette* and *Andromeda Spaceways Inflight Magazine*.

Taneli Kukkonen recently became a senior lecturer in religious studies at the University of Otago, after first sampling a Canada Research Chair in Philosophy at the University of Victoria and then professing history at the University of Jyväskylä, Finland. Next stop: chemistry in Chile! Taneli has written extensively on topics in Arabic philosophy and is busy at work on a book on al-Ghazālī, but when he tries to picture the good life, it all comes out in John Romita Sr. illustrations.

Tricia Little, a Midwestern land-locked writer and professional photographer, has assisted in editing and managing a host of philosophy-inspired books and articles. She enjoys long walks on the beach and world travel and is currently working on perfecting her web-slinging technique.

Daniel P. Malloy is a lecturer in philosophy at Appalachian State University. His research focuses on issues in ethics. He has published numerous chapters on the intersection of popular culture and philosophy, particularly dealing with the illustration of moral questions in movies, comic books, and television shows. Before turning to philosophy, Daniel spent a brief period writing a humor column for the *Daily Bugle*. He was fired due to his vocal support of Spider-Man. He may have also had a habit of calling J. Jonah Jameson "the old Buzz Head."

Neil Mussett hasn't quite gotten around to finishing his Ph.D. in philosophy from the State University of New York at Buffalo. He will not stop until he becomes Spider-Man's arch-nemesis, using his skills as a programmer, a graphic designer, a forensic accountant, a Krav Maga green belt, and, of course, an amateur philosopher.

Ron Novy is a lecturer in philosophy and the humanities in the University College at the University of Central Arkansas. He has contributed to volumes on Dr. Seuss, Batman, Iron Man, Green Lantern, and supervillains. Ron has recently taught courses in metaphysics, Marx, and moral problems; he's quite pleased to be using graphic novels in his introduction to philosophy classes. Purportedly, Dr. Novy is in possession of the original Mysterio costume and spends every other weekend in his makeshift lair trying to reassemble the Sinister Six.

Christopher Robichaud is a lecturer in ethics and public policy at the Harvard Kennedy School of Government. His earliest memories of Spider-Man include watching his rope-flinging exploits in the 1970s live-action TV show, having a chance photo-op with our friendly neighborhood wall-crawler at the local mall, and learning how to read by pouring over *The Amazing Spider-Man* and *Peter Parker, the Spectacular Spider-Man*. To this day, whenever he visits New York, he keeps his eyes peeled on the buildings in the hopes of catching a glimpse of his favorite superhero.

Jonathan J. Sanford is a professor and the chair of the Philosophy Department at the Franciscan University of Steubenville. He writes and teaches on issues in metaphysics and moral philosophy and on classical and medieval philosophers. He's lately had to give up on climbing buildings and slinging webs, but you can find him tossing balls with his kids most evenings.

Tony Spanakos, since discovering that with "great power comes great responsibility," has pursued political science and philosophy to discover what justifies his great irresponsibility. Following many years of chasing all varieties of insects and arachnids, hoping to be bitten, he has accepted the mediocre role of university professor to which Peter Parker would likely have been fated. He is currently an associate professor at Montclair State University and an adjunct professor at New York University. He has published articles on political economy and democratization in Latin America, as well as writing essays for *Batman and Philosophy*, *Watchmen and Philosophy*, *Iron Man and Philosophy*, and *Avengers and Philosophy*.

Mark K. Spencer does whatever a philosopher can as a doctoral candidate at the University at Buffalo and an adjunct professor at Canisius College. He specializes in medieval philosophy, metaphysics, and phenomenology and has published papers on these and other topics. When a bit younger, he considered becoming a mad physicist like Dr. Octopus, but he's lately scrapped that idea for the glories of a mild-mannered academic.

Jason Southworth is an adjunct professor of philosophy at Fort Hays State University, Hays, Kansas. He has written chapters for many pop culture and philosophy volumes, including *Inception*, *X-Men*, and *Batman*. He's ready for Aunt May to die. She's been at death's door in the hospital a half-dozen times, only to recover miraculously. It's getting old, so let's hope for death or a story about how she was bitten by a radioactive highlander.

Charles Taliaferro, a professor of philosophy at St. Olaf College, is the author, the coauthor, or the editor of seventeen books, including *The Image in Mind* with Jil Evans. Like Peter Parker, Charles has a wonderfully supportive aunt, but he is otherwise quite different from Peter, and he admits that most of the time he lacks some of the agility of Spider-Man.

Philip Tallon received his Ph.D. from the University of Saint Andrews and is an affiliate professor of philosophy and religion at Asbury Theological Seminary. He's the author of *The Poetics of Evil* (forthcoming from Oxford University Press) and the coeditor (with David Baggett) of *The Philosophy of Sherlock Holmes*. Like Peter Parker, he married a fashion model. Unlike Peter Parker, he has no spider sense to let him know when he's gotten into trouble with his wife.

Andrew Terjesen has a Ph.D. in philosophy from Duke University and is currently pursuing a J.D. at the University of Virginia School of Law. He has been a visiting assistant professor of philosophy at Austin College, Washington and Lee University, and Rhodes College. Andrew's philosophical interests include moral psychology, early modern philosophy, Chinese philosophy, and business ethics. He has published several articles on these topics in scholarly venues, as well as in the Philosophy and Pop Culture series, including essays on *Watchmen*, *X-Men*, *Iron Man*, *Green Lantern*, and the forthcoming *Avengers* volume. He likes his Spider-Man with a fantastical spidey sense, not slo-mo reflexes or kung fu training.

John Timm is a biologist at the University of Michigan, Ann Arbor, Michigan. He finds it amusing that while Sam Raimi and company thought it was unbelievable that a teenage boy could invent a super-strong sticky adhesive and a device to fire it, they thought it was entirely reasonable that overnight the boy's body could develop glands in his forearm that produce the adhesive and that he would be able to shoot it from an invisible hole in his wrist.

Mark D. White is a professor and the chair of the Department of Political Science, Economics, and Philosophy at the College of Staten Island/CUNY, where he teaches courses that combine economics, philosophy, and law. He is the author of *Kantian*

Ethics and Economics: Autonomy, Dignity, and Character and has edited (or coedited) books for the present series on Batman, *Watchmen*, Iron Man, Green Lantern, and the Avengers. He thinks that Carlie Cooper is much better for Peter than MJ was; anyway, what MJ really needs is a college professor, perhaps one who teaches courses that combine . . .

INDEX